TRIALS and TRIUMPHS

Volume II of the A.M. PATE, JR., Series
on the American Presidency

TRIALS *and* TRIUMPHS

George Washington's Foreign Policy

by FRANK T. REUTER

TEXAS CHRISTIAN UNIVERSITY PRESS / FORT WORTH

Library of Congress Cataloging in Publication Data

Reuter, Frank T. (Frank Theodore), 1926–
   Trials and triumphs.
   (A.M. Pate series on the American presidency ; 2)
   Bibliography: p.
   1. United States—Foreign relations—1789–1797.
2. Washington, George, 1732–1799. I. Title. II. Series.
E311.R385   1983   327.73'0092'4   83-675
ISBN 0-912646-70-5
ISBN 0-87565-243-3 (pbk.)

Cover portrait courtesy New York
Historical Society.

Contents

to my son
CHRIS
whose quest for languages and learning
was never fulfilled

Preface

EVER SINCE FRANKLIN ROOSEVELT'S New Deal we Americans have been increasingly fascinated by the expanding role and responsibilities of the President of the United States. We have watched as the president assumed more and more authority and power and became our nation's principal problem solver: we have expected him to guarantee our employment, assure our business profits, and defend our shores. In the years following the Second World War we learned to expect our chief executive to stride across the world's stage as the major arbiter of international affairs, capably defending American national interests wherever and however they might be challenged. By the 1970s the office had become what Arthur Schlesinger, Jr. called the "Imperial Presidency," a term that whetted further the national appetite for president-watching. In the past decade, as a result, the Presidency of the United States has become history's most scrutinized public office, with a vast multi-national White House press corps, hundreds of books and thousands of articles on the office or its incumbents, several professional societies devoted exclusively to presidential research, and scholarly journals to publish that research.

This proliferation of words unfortunately does not always enable the curious to understand how the elected leader of a simple agrarian society, the modern world's first democratic republican society, became in less than 200 years as powerful as any Caesar. The presidency is, of course, an organic office that has assumed added authority in response to the ever-changing needs of a rapidly-expanding America in a too-frequently hostile world. From the very beginning each president added to this organic growth to meet new conditions, leaving to his successors a collection of new as well as old precedents, practices and working policies. Regardless of campaign rhetoric, no new president began his administration with a clean slate. Instead, each was trapped in the heritage from his predecessors which circumscribed his options or predetermined his programs. There can be no doubt that the accumulating legacy of the American presidencies is and has been an unavoidable but consistent factor in determining the policies of each successive president. If we Americans are to understand—and perhaps judge—our recent presidents fairly, we must consider the extensive influence of this heritage.

In no part of the presidential legacy is this more true than in the foreign policy tradition. Because of its complexities perhaps the least understood of presidential responsibilities, foreign policy nonetheless has drawn increased public attention over the past 40 years as the United States assumed a new role as leader of the "free world." Concern over decisions involving war or the threat of war is obvious. But the public has also been influenced by presidential actions on less dramatic issues. Such mundane matters as tariff policy, trade agreements, foreign loans, and international banking laws have a direct impact on the price of corn in Chicago or cotton in New Orleans as well as employment levels in Detroit or Pittsburgh. International policy questions are now so closely intertwined with internal issues that modern presidents must be equally adept in foreign affairs as they are with domestic programs. But this requirement could have applied in some degree to each of the preceding presidents, because the foreign policy tradition that began with President Washington was an inescapable part of the adminsitrations of his successors.

As fascinated by the presidency as any American, I was

delighted when the TCU Press asked me to write a monograph on George Washington's foreign policy. Intended for a contemplated series on the American presidents written for the general reader, my project would give me the opportunity to delve deeply into the origins of the foreign policy tradition. For over 20 years I have taught courses on the diplomatic history of the United States. More recently, to satisfy my own as much as my students' curiosity, I have developed a course on the history of the presidency. Teaching that class confirmed my conviction that continuous themes in American foreign relations have influenced the policies and practices of every presidential administration. Serious foreign policy questions caused by these themes were intimately involved in the monumental domestic crises confronted by Abraham Lincoln and Franklin Roosevelt. Certainly Washington found them inescapable as he established the structure of our government.

But Washington did not start with a clean slate either. The Constitution which created his office was, when it was written in 1787, the culmination of generations of the Anglo-American political experience. Precedents and attitudes concerning executive leadership had already been established. Also apparent were some widely held concepts of how the United States should conduct its affairs with other nations, while at the same time the pattern of past relationships with those nations was clearly discernable. Indeed, the last third of the eighteenth century, with its super-powers, bi-polarized alliance structure, and revolutionary philosophies—an era almost as complex as today's—presented its own legacy to the incoming first president.

To begin the study of Washington's foreign policy at the time of his inauguration in April 1789 would, therefore, miss the frightening significance for his administration of the European balance of power that emerged from the Seven Years War in 1763. Each of the three nations most interested in North

America during that conflict—Great Britain, Spain, and France—maintained its high level of interest even after the United States won independence. Their diplomatic maneuvers, Washington feared, would make his country "the sport of Europe's politics." Each nation, moreover, viewed the American republic in the light of its own relationships to the other two. As a result, when Washington became president he inherited a set of problems with each of the three European great powers, problems that were unnecessarily complicated by their rivalries and manipulations against one another. How their actions affected the United States was to them of secondary concern.

Adding to the confusion, and certainly enmeshed with it, was the persistent question of Indian relations along the entire American western frontier, a problem Washington insisted on considering as part of his foreign policy. Because an event at one location might trigger a reaction at another, both adversely affecting the United States, it was difficult and sometimes almost impossible for Washington—and for the modern observer—to separate America's interests with one nation or one Indian confederation from the intricate web of eighteenth-century international power politics.

I have attempted to sort out this diplomatic interplay by tracing individually United States relations with Great Britain, Spain, and France, even though this meant some back-tracking in time and an occasional repeated reference to a specific event. Washington's negotiations with each of these countries, although clouded by frustration and failure, are reasonably discernable during his first administration. They come together conveniently enough in his second, when the first war of the French Revolution brought a new focus to the international setting. It is during these four years that the lasting significance of Washington's foreign policy becomes apparent, for the initiatives he took after the frustrating four years of his first term become important precedents in the American diplomatic tradition.

Presenting all of this within the framework of a short monograph for the general reader set the parameters for my work. My purpose was to focus on Washington's contribution to the development of the American foreign policy tradition. Yet Washington could not appear on every page nor be the central figure of every chapter; there were too many powerful forces at work that had to be taken into account as influencing his decisions. To make these forces understandable I synthesized the writings of others, added the results of my own documentary research, and then presented my own conclusions. I have not, as a result, offered a scholarly discussion of the many and often conflicting interpretations of this highly complex era, especially those concerning the valuable contributions of both Thomas Jefferson and Alexander Hamilton.

Instead, I have relied as much as possible on Washington's own writings and where appropriate let him speak his mind in his own words. This was not always as easy as it sounds, for too often he masked his feelings behind a formal, stilted writing style. To preserve that style, as well as the flavor of his times, I have quoted Washington and his contemporaries exactly as they wrote, without acknowledging their errors in spelling, punctuation, and grammar to avoid interrupting the flow of the narrative. For the same reason I have not cited the sources of quotations, hoping the context would be clear enough. I offer as compensation to the interested reader an extensive bibliographical essay describing the materials consulted.

For me the study of history has always been enjoyable and exciting, regardless of where in time I might poke around exploring some half-forgotten event. Many people shared my excitement as I unraveled the complex tangle of Washington's presidency. I am deeply grateful to several of them for encouragement and support: to the TCU Research Foundation for two research grants which made it possible for me to delve into the public and private archives of Edinburgh, London, Paris, and The Hague for this and another project; to James Newcomer, former director of the TCU Press, who asked me to write this volume for his series and whose patient understanding permitted me to deliver the manuscript a year later than promised; to Kathryne McDorman for her comments on several chapters; to Dr. A.M. "Aggie" Pate, Jr. whose life-long interest in the American Presidency inspired the series and encouraged the publication of this book; in particular to Donald Worcester, friend and adviser, for the years of his professional and personal inspiration that I appreciate more than he will ever know; and finally to Kay, my wife, who shared some of the investigations with me and who understands what it means to be a lonely scholar.

Frank T. Reuter

Prologue

I behold the surest pledges that the foundations of our National policy will be laid in the pure and immutable principles of private morality; and the pre-eminence of a free Government, be exemplified by all attributes which can win the affections of its Citizens, and command the respect of the world . . . since the preservation of the sacred fire of liberty, and the destiny of the Republican model of Government, are justly considered as deeply, perhaps as finally staked, on the experiment entrusted to the hands of the American people.

"PRIVATE MORALITY . . . FREE GOVERNMENT . . . affections of its citizens . . . respect of the world . . . experiment." These were the key ideas expressed in Washington's first inaugural address. Perhaps more than any other American he saw clearly what his country needed as it stood on the threshold of a new age. The Republic of course was an experiment in free government. If the experiment were to succeed, it must earn the affection of American citizens and the respect of the world. If it failed, the glorious promises of the Declaration of Independence would fail too. So humbly but hesitantly George Washington accepted the unique new responsibilities of presidential leadership thrust on him by his fellow Americans, knowing full well that it was his duty to see that the experiment did not fail.

To look once again at the accomplishments of the first president seems a redundancy, merely a confirmation of what every schoolboy already knows: the "Father of His Country" was "First in War, First in Peace, and First in the Hearts of his Countrymen." Indeed, almost every Washington biographer, struggling to separate the myth of tradition from the fact of history, has acknowledged these long-cherished evaluations of the first president. After two centuries, Washington is still considered the greatest of all Americans, exemplifying more than any other the most accepted values of United States citizenship—integrity, competence, diligence, and devotion to duty.

Hero-conscious Americans too often have sought a re-affirmation of these values in some new hero. At no time has this need been more true than as their nation begins its third century. They are still bitter over a faulty foreign policy that led their country into an embarrassing war in Southeast Asia. Watergate made them cynical about the integrity of leadership in general and mistrustful of the presidency itself. These twentieth-century Americans elect new leaders and then almost immediately turn against them as crisis after crisis appears to go unsolved. The United States suffers from a "crisis of leadership," in essence, no leadership at all.

Yet the same cry has been heard by every generation since the founding of the Republic. Other periods were marked by cynicism and distrust. The modern citizen, if he is willing to do so, can discover how American society overcame its challenges and strengthened the nation by making the government more responsive to its people. Reviewing each crisis of the past can give some perspective on the present and revive hope for the future, because these earlier trials produced leaders capable of solving satisfactorily the problems of their time.

No challenges the nation has faced have been greater than those at the beginning of its national experience when cynicism, regional jealousies, local self-interest, and foreign intervention threatened to destroy the newborn country. By modern definitions of the term, the United States in the truest sense was an emerging nation—the first to throw off the shackles of colonialism and to seek its own national identity and national purpose. It shared problems of nation-building similar to those of the more than ninety new countries which emerged from colonial rule following the Second World War. Like these modern embryonic states, it was weak and divided. Its first government under the Articles of Confederation was deliberately decentralized to give vent to a variety of state or local interests. Its only real bond of unity was anger—hatred to a degree—for the common enemy, Great Britain. When the Revolutionary War ended, bringing formal recognition of independence, national unity began to dissipate. Like most of the emerging nations, its government was challenged from the left by populist uprisings of overtaxed and under-represented farmers and from the right by an elitist clique of ex-military officers. Like them too, its economy was underdeveloped, almost totally devoid of investment capital and for years in humiliating bondage to foreign creditors.

Obviously, comparisons between the United States of the eighteenth century and the emerging nations of the twentieth can be carried too far. Americans of the Revolutionary Generation had assets and advantages that the citizens of most of the new modern states lack. Americans shared an English cultural tradition of Protestantism, constitutional government, and, perhaps of greatest importance, respect for the common law. Even the scattered handful of Scots, Scotch-Irish, and Germans accepted and defended this tradition. Until they were finally forced to opt for independence itself, the vast majority of the revolutionists claimed that their actions were to defend their rights as Englishmen under the English constitution, "the most perfect form of government." These early Americans shared a unity that originated in England itself.

But from the very beginning, the frontier experience gave

Americans a unique character. It started when Governor John Winthrop warned the first Puritan settlers of Massachusetts "wee shall be as a citty upon a Hill, the eies of all people are uppon us." In 1630 Winthrop meant to promote God's "Kingdom on Earth" through a Puritan theocracy as the only way a people should live and be governed. Even though this Puritan "errand in the wilderness" failed of its original purpose, it contributed the Yankee tradition of a special American mission in world affairs. Time and again the Founding Fathers reiterated these ideas of a new and different role for the United States. One hundred fifty years after Winthrop, Washington himself insisted that "with our fate will the destiny of unborn Millions be involved."

Washington did not pen these words out of arrogance but rather from his sense of the new nation's unique destiny. And this is why he looms so high during the era of the founding of the Republic. His faith and determination contributed immeasurably to keeping the United States alive. If he had done nothing but lead the Continental Army to victory, his premier place in American history would be secure. But his return to the center of the American drama by assuming the presidency of the new federal government in 1789 was the logical culmination of his role as leader of the Revolution. He had watched for six years while the ineffective Confederation almost let forces beyond its control ruin the experiment in democratic republicanism. He saw all too clearly that this coalition of state governments was dominated by selfish local interests and influenced by equally self-serving European kingdoms. National independence was gravely threatened. And as the former commander in chief of the national army and an outspoken critic of confederation weaknesses, he began to symbolize American nationalism as he had symbolized the War for Independence itself. By the mid-1780s he was the rallying point for ardent nationalists seeking a strong central government. By then, the

Mount Vernon farmer easily could have proclaimed a monarchy with himself as its king. But he did not. Instead he waited, renewing his faith in the ability of his fellow citizens to find an acceptable way to preserve their republic.

This does not mean that Washington was the most optimistic, the most dedicated, or the most creative of early American leaders. He was not a complex man, but his era was terribly complex as the new concept of popular government was tested in a hostile world. His biographers have long wrestled with the meaning of his contribution to this process. The myth-making of Parson Weems, the adulation of John Marshall, and the exaggerated deletions of character faults by Jared Sparks reflected an early nineteenth-century view that cast him in a super-heroic mold. This view met the needs of a society still groping for a national identity, and, for the most part, still survives in schoolboy characterizations of the first president. The more recent, careful scholarship of Douglas Southall Freeman, James Flexner, and Bernard Knollenberg has sought to describe realistically his humanity and its application to the challenges of responsible leadership. Despite these excellent studies, however, Washington's true role is still difficult to perceive. Against the backdrop of on-rushing events and the magnificent intellectualism of Franklin, Adams, Jefferson, and Hamilton, he too often appears more a catalyst than a leader, sometimes trapped by events or at other times nudged into action by those around him.

In truth, Washington was a genuine national hero; his place in history did not require the exaggerations of the myth-makers. His strength, endurance, and physical appearance made him a natural leader of men. A towering six-feet-two, he was a striking figure, almost a head taller than his contemporaries. In uniform or on horseback, even in his youth, he radiated a special charisma that commanded both attention and respect. At twenty-two he became a wilderness legend in the opening days of the French and Indian War. Through the years his quiet dignity and intense loyalty to friends and subordinates added to his reputation and inspired confidence in his abilities. Perhaps a bit shy among large groups of people, he nonetheless enjoyed the company of men and of women as well. He often recorded in his diary, "I danced with the ladies"—and they adored him for it.

The great man had his limitations too, and he was well aware of them. Not a creative thinker nor as well educated as most of his famous contemporaries, he was forced to evaluate and rely on the ideas of others. He regretted this dependence but never resented it. Short of temper, he was oversensitive to political criticism, taking much of it too personally. Although he had long experience with politicians, some of it disastrous, he never fully understood the political process; the factionalism within Congress amazed and angered him. He was stiff and formal to a fault, sometimes creating awkward situations for himself in public. A few unsympathetic historians have accused him of being a dramatist whenever he was able to turn these awkward moments to his favor. Yet other observers have noted his nervousness in public, his stammering when forced into an extemporaneous speech, and his insistence on reading from a prepared text. At official functions he was ill at ease, and formal levees and dinners at the executive mansion were invariably dull.

It was, nevertheless, this war-hero-on-horseback, this gray-haired father figure that the American people trusted to organize their government. They had an almost blind faith in him and his abilities. If his presidency was to succeed he had somehow to transfer this respect for himself to the Constitution and the federal structure it created. His administration had to win for the new system the support of a skeptical citizenry still unaccustomed to national independence under republican institutions. These three million people scattered loosely along the Atlantic seaboard had to accept this new government as their own, to give national ideals precedence over local parochial interests.

But in an era when the vast majority of Americans lived in rural isolation, many in semi-frontier conditions, written constitutions embodying new theories of government were meaningless of themselves. The people had to know that their national government "worked." In a practical sense, as examples, they had to know that currency earned in Boston would be accepted for purchases in Philadelphia and Charleston, that the products of their farms and factories could be shipped securely on ships flying the American flag, or that they might migrate safely to the fertile river valleys of the western territories. Obviously the old Confederation of States had not worked well, at least for most men. If the Constitution served them no better, the American union would probably break up into independent regional or state units, a balkanization that would invite and facilitate European intervention. The destiny of the United States and with it the true meaning of the rights of its individual citizens depended on how well the federal government was able to "establish justice, insure domestic tranquility, provide for the common defense, promote the general welfare, and secure the blessings of liberty."

George Washington's responsibility as first president was to make real these general aims expressed so hopefully in the Preamble to the Constitution. His administration's practical solutions to practical problems did make the Constitution work. When he retired from office the government he established survived him and became the people's own—and this would be his greatest achievement. He used his enormous popularity, his good judgment, and his shrewdness in analyzing the opinions of others to translate theories into practical realities. In the context of this process he can be viewed more clearly and appreciated more fully. Each time he, with his advisers, solved specific issues, he fleshed out the framework of government outlined in the Constitution and established precedents that are still observed. Nowhere is this more apparent than in his approach to the creation of a United States foreign policy. By seizing for the executive the direction of relations with other countries he established long-term practices and attitudes in American external affairs that have continued well into the twentieth century.

When he became President on April 30, 1789, Washington confronted four major foreign problem areas. The war-bred friendship with France that helped win American independence was deteriorating into disillusion and acrimony. From Great Britain came increasing pressures to revise the terms of the treaty ending the war and even greater attempts to retain the United States as an economic satellite of her empire. Spain, a most reluctant ally during the Revolutionary War, tried desperately to alter the boundaries dividing her colonies from the new republic. And on the north, the west, and the south the Indian nations living in the vast unsettled territories beyond the Appalachians, encouraged by both the English and the Spanish, refused to accept American sovereignty over their lands. The United States was surrounded by potential enemies—Britain on the north and northwest, Spain to the south and west. And no European monarch wanted the American experiment to succeed. These external threats had weakened the old Confederation, but their continued presence forced the American people to try once again to achieve unity and national purpose.

Like a juggler Washington kept in constant motion the often conflicting American relations with Britain, Spain, and France and simultaneously carried on continuous negotiations with the Indians. During his first administration he concentrated on removing these European pressures on his country's territory and economy. If he did this effectively he expected the

Indian problem to diminish and probably disappear in time. But before he could bring any of this to fruition, war broke out again in Europe and set each of his problems into a different context. He was forced to spend his entire second administration doggedly working to preserve American neutrality. He correctly feared that any involvement in that war would tear apart his still divided and uncertain nation. Yet despite his efforts the United States was inescapably caught up in the interplay of European power politics.

Europe's great powers had "discovered" America and for more than a century had competed in the race to exploit its wilderness resources. The appearance of a newly independent state in North America did not end that race; it merely changed the rules and the opportunities for the competitors. It was this long and intense rivalry among the Europeans that facilitated achievement of American independence. And this same rivalry continued, but with a resentment for the very existence of the United States. The European jackal world of international politics confronted Washington with the greatest challenges for his presidency.

TRIALS and TRIUMPHS

CHAPTER ONE

"The Sport of European Politics"

WASHINGTON'S FOREIGN POLICY problems originated among the ashes of the Seven Years War, the war which launched his military career and gave him his first experience of leadership. Known in the American colonies as the French and Indian War, it began insignificantly enough in the summer of 1754 as France and Britain clashed over control of the headwaters of the Ohio River, but it quickly widened into a titanic struggle for empire.

Winston Churchill called it the First World War, and indeed it was. The Seven Years War was the culmination of a century of challenge by the late-coming English to the established commercial empires of the Dutch, the Portuguese, the Spanish, and the French. In the century before 1750 aggressive, cocky English navigators, merchants, and colonists had pushed British commercial opportunities in North America, in the Caribbean and the South Atlantic, on the coast of West Africa and the Indian sub-continent, among the Spice Islands of the East Indies, and across the length of the Mediterranean. At each of these locations the English had been preceded by their European neighbors, who more often than not tried to drive them away. The result was a long series of wars interspersed with shaky, often-violated periods of truce. During that hundred years the English had allied with the Portuguese, destroyed the Dutch as commercial rivals, and simultaneously developed a successful maritime commerce and an even more successful navy to protect it. By 1750 England's only remaining commercial rivals were Spain and France.

Behind all of this aggressiveness lurked the specter of mercantilism, a century of Europe's outreach for the world's trade and natural resources. Each of the major countries was convinced that its power and prestige required national economic self-sufficiency; none could risk dependence on neighbors or potential enemies for commodities essential to its livelihood or defense. Instead, national policy dictated a searching out and control of the sources of these vital items wherever they might be found. Such areas of production, most often overseas and variously called "factories," "plantations," or "colonies," were to become economic satellites of the mother country, supplying her with raw materials and, in turn, buying her manufactures. To ensure the effectiveness of this relationship between the mother country and her dependents, the whole was integrated through navigation acts, formal commercial regulations, cash subsidies, trade monopolies, and custom duties. In theory, at least, a successful mercantilist empire guaranteed the home country a continuous supply of vital and profitable commodities, an assured market for its own produce, and enough surplus in raw materials and processed goods to give it a favorable balance of trade with the rest of the world. The difference in the trade balance, of course, was to be made up by gold and silver. The more successfully the nation ran its empire the greater was the inflow of precious metals to underwrite the costs of its status as a great power. No wonder then that in a great competitive urge tens of thousands of Europeans poured out to secure for their own countries economic footholds on every portion of the world.

Thus was a century of overseas commercial rivalries closely intertwined with the development and maintenance of the European balance of power. Each nation's empire provided it with the strength for active involvement in European power politics. Spain already had proved this axiom by dominating sixteenth-century Europe as a result of fantastic wealth drawn from her huge American empire. Meantime the Dutch, although not militarily powerful, had reached levels of cultural achievement and a standard of living unequaled elsewhere in the continent in the seventeenth century. For the European statesman or entrepreneur the overseas world existed to be exploited for the benefit of Europe. For him there were really "two worlds": Europe, the heart and nerve-center of inter-global affairs, and the "other world" existing to supply Europe's needs. By the eighteenth century these needs were growing.

In North America the Europeans had created rival spheres of commercial expansion. The Spanish, secure in the heartland of Mexico, maintained in Florida their toehold on the Atlantic coast and had expanded northward into California and northeast into Texas. The French, finally abandoning their fruitless search for a northwest passage to China, discovered instead great wealth in furs and hides. Mounting a two-pronged thrust toward the best fur resources, the Great Lakes region, they pushed west from Montreal and north from New Orleans. It would be only a matter of time until these two prongs joined to give France control over the vast riches of the interior.

In the meantime, the English had established a series of colonial beachheads along the eastern seaboard, from Maine to Georgia. With their settlements scattered among the great bays and natural harbors of the Atlantic coast, these Anglo-Americans clung to the edge of the continent. But they faced out across the Atlantic, considering themselves a westward extension of a British North Atlantic community. The Atlantic, with its bays and the rivers flowing into it, was their avenue of communication and commerce. To their backs loomed the Appalachian Barrier, protecting them yet isolating them from the rich potential of the rest of the continent. Only after the effects of over-population and soil depletion became apparent by 1750 did they decide to peer over the mountain ranges to see what new opportunities lay further west.

By mid-century Spanish and French and British commercial forces were pushing at one other in North America and in other potential friction points around the globe. Simultaneously the European world itself was about to erupt in a major confrontation as a result of deepseated nationalistic and dynastic rivalries. Two petty conflicts, the War of Jenkins' Ear and the War of Austrian Succession, raised the curtain for the major encounter to come. Those nations with overseas empires had to rely heavily on colonial resources for the success of their European diplomacy. The stage was set for a multinational clash of interests at a dozen different locations and for a dozen different reasons.

When twenty-two-year-old George Washington hacked his way through the primeval forest of western Pennsylvania, he unwittingly strode onto this shaky stage of international politics. Sent to warn the French to abandon Fort Duquesne, he pinched one of the exposed nerve-endings of an already nervous world. From this new outpost strategically located at the forks of the Ohio, France was asserting her claim to the interior of the continent and denying Britain access to it. Fort Duquesne closed the gap in a ring of fortifications and trading posts encircling the English settlements within a great arc that extended from Quebec to New Orleans. The fort gave France control of the entire length of the Ohio, the only natural avenue for British expansion westward. More significant than the posts themselves, however, was the impact they had on the Indians. Through a successful system of military and trade alliances with the tribes, the French exerted an influence that radiated up to two hundred miles around each of their forts and channelled the highly profitable fur trade into their hands. With the aid of the Indians France had mastery of the St.

Lawrence-Great Lakes-Mississippi basin. The British could not ignore so great a prize, and France could not expect her claims to go unchallenged.

Other challenges elsewhere were moving the world inexorably toward war. In Europe the cupidity of Frederick of Prussia for the Austrian province of Silesia sparked the conflict, and formal war broke out in 1756. Among the great powers an unusual pattern of alliances pitted France, Spain, Austria, and Russia (for a time at least) against Prussia and Great Britain. Prussian armies carried the burden of the land war on the continent, while the British navy alone confronted the fleets of France and Spain in the North Atlantic, the Mediterranean, the Indian Ocean, and the Caribbean. British troops carried the war into India, into the East and West Indies, and with the assistance of colonial militia, to North America.

Great Britain's strategy, engineered and directed by William Pitt, was to destroy both France and Spain as Britain's commercial rivals. The King's Redcoats captured both Manila and Havana as hostages to future Spanish policy, destroyed French influence on the Indian subcontinent, and drove French military presence forever from North America. Pitt's policies almost succeeded, but their very success was their undoing, for his was an arduous, costly war. Despite brilliant victories, the price in blood and money was too high for the English people to bear. The war became increasingly unpopular, and English taxpayers groaned as new levies became heavier and heavier. Bowing to these pressures and piqued by his own jealousies, England's new king, youthful George III, was willing to accept peace overtures from his enemies. The great war came to a close. Britain was victorious, but Pitt's strategy of total victory was not fulfilled.

The Treaty of Paris, formally ending, in 1763, the great war for empire, gave to England a pre-eminence among Europe's great powers that she had never enjoyed before. It confirmed England's worldwide empire—India and vital African trading ports, control of Far Eastern and Mediterranean sea lanes, and domination of the West Indies. Her sovereignty in North America extended over all the lands east of the Mississippi from the Florida Keys to the Arctic Circle. Her domain was so vast, so varied, and so complex that some contemporaries likened it to the old Roman Empire. Her problems perhaps would also have rivalled Rome's.

Britain's success, however, was only partial. She had not destroyed her ancient enemies, France and Spain—although the balance of power tilted dramatically in her favor. European nations feared that another such victory in yet another war might destroy the balance entirely and permit the British to threaten the very security of their neighbors. In addition, George III had blundered seriously when he abruptly ended the war, for he had abandoned Frederick the Great, his only continental ally, earning for England Prussia's enmity as well. Great Britain had emerged victorious from the Seven Years War, but she had few friends left to share her joy.

Louis XV's foreign minister, the Duc de Choiseul, found the Peace of 1763 humiliating for France. Long accustomed to seeing Frenchmen stride across Europe as representatives of the continent's cultural and political leader, Choiseul found it galling that France should be in second place to a nation of shopkeepers and sailors. Devious as well as angry, he realized that, though France had been beaten, she was not broken and that her ally Spain had kept its empire intact. He decided too that the Peace of 1763 was just a truce and no long-term settlement for the permanent discomfort of France. He shrewdly assessed the enormity of England's problems in governing such a vast imperial scattering of real estate, and then plotted long-range policies designed to add to those problems. Almost blind to other significant realities, Choiseul grimly planned for the day when France would get her revenge.

Britain soon provided Choiseul his opportunities. As he had foreseen, English leadership confronted a complex of difficulties concerning administration, government, taxation, defense, land policies, native affairs, and commercial regulations. The costly war had left an enormous national debt and an equally enormous land tax. Millions of natives and a world wide scattering of hundreds of thousands of English settlers had to be governed, and the sea lanes connecting all these units to England had to be patrolled and defended. To have any value at all the commercial potential of this extensive new empire had to be integrated into an effective economic structure. Yet with an ineptness that historians have not successfully explained, England's statesmen applied seventeenth-century mercantilist doctrine to their eighteenth-century empire and attempted to channel its divergent interests into a centralized system with leadership, direction, policy, and power emanating from London. Their singleness of purpose was as narrow as Choiseul's, and so they stumbled into an imperial disruption that gave him what he sought.

To the English, and to the French as well, the thirteen North American colonies were the most productive, the most prosperous, and therefore the most valuable part of the British Empire. Compactly settled between the Appalachians and the Atlantic, each had developed a stable local, semi-autonomous government and each had enjoyed the protection and prosperity of the imperial connection. Their combined population of two and a half million, about a third of that in England itself, had a general standard of living higher than the English and a much stronger voice in local affairs than did their fellow subjects back "home." Although their militia in the late war had marched side by side with the Redcoats, their contributions in men and money were ever so slight in comparison to those of the English. Logically these prosperous and seemingly happy people should be willing to assume their share of the burden of maintaining and defending the Empire, an empire from which they had benefited so well.

Parliament labored under this naive assumption until it was too late. Goaded by the King's ministers, it churned out legislation providing for new regulations of commerce, new taxes and more customs officers to collect them, added responsibilities for quartering troops, and extensive plans for control and exploitation of the lands beyond the Appalachians. The colonists quickly woke to the prospect of losing local control of their own destinies; they denied the legality of taxation levied on them by a distant legislature in which they had no representation. They underscored their position by a widespread and violent reaction to the Stamp Tax of 1765, which they literally nullified, and forced a reluctant Parliament to repeal. Obviously colonial logic had a different view of the purpose of empire.

Choiseul, ever watchful, saw this family quarrel between Mother England and her recalcitrant children as a possible crack in the British imperial structure, a crack that might be widened to the advantage of France. Unwilling, however, to risk his international ambitions on a mere spat, he tried to determine the depth of colonial dissatisfaction, eagerly devouring any concrete, specific intelligence coming from North America. He dispatched his own agents in 1764, in 1765, and again in 1767 to ascertain the colonies' potential to sustain a successful rebellion. Cautioned that as yet there was no apparent sentiment for independence, he nonetheless committed himself to developing policies that would encourage independence. Convinced that in the next war between France and Great Britain the American colonies could be used to advantage, he plotted accordingly.

Not totally ignorant of French interests in their problems, colonial malcontents gradually broadened the base of popular support for their struggle against tighter imperial controls.

Aided by the appalling inability of English leaders to understand their American cousins, these potential rebels organized successful economic boycotts of British manufactures and simultaneously wrote hundreds of pamphlets filled with impassioned arguments defending their rights as loyal subjects. Yet back in England their loyalty *was* questioned. Increasing numbers of Redcoats marched into Boston to ferret out the disloyal and to enforce the King's laws. Crisis situations were unavoidable, and when the King's troops confronted Massachusetts' militia on Lexington Green a wedge was driven into the very unity of the British Empire.

While the march of events from Lexington and Concord led inexorably to the Declaration of Independence, the French government watched closely behind a flimsily disguised indifference to England's distresses. Choiseul had left to his successor in the foreign office, the Count de Vergennes, both his plan and his ambition to take every advantage of the British. As soon as Vergennes learned in the summer of 1775 of the bloody confrontation, he dispatched yet another French secret agent, this time to the Continental Congress, the only instrument of united government the rebellious colonies had. In the meantime he successfully convinced his young monarch, Louis XVI, that French encouragement to the Americans would prolong Britain's difficulties, seriously weaken her military strength, and permit France the opportunity of starting another war with England but a war of her own choice as to time and area of combat. Although hesitant to offend the British openly, the king did agree to the organization of a fictitious private company as a front for supplying aid to the Americans. Working also on the assumption that Spain would certainly benefit from a weakened Britain, Vergennes sought to draw in Spanish support for the rebels.

What appears amazing at this point is that two of the most absolutist monarchs in Europe, the King of France and the

King of Spain, would have any interest at all in the rebellion of a third monarch's overseas subjects. Certainly neither should want to encourage a successful colonial rebellion, for the disease of anti-colonialism could spread and all too easily threaten their own empires. And with even more certainty neither monarch would tolerate republicanism, a system totally antithetical to their concept of rule. Both Louis XVI and his Spanish counterpart would later learn with finality the importance of the American example. Their hatred of Britain blinded them to the risks, and both secretly aided George III's republican colonial rebels.

Neither France and Spain on their side nor England on hers truly understood the nature of the thirteen colonies. These three European governments saw thirteen separate political entities each with its own colonial history full of internecine strife over boundaries, fishing grounds, and exclusive fur trading zones. The English saw no American unity at all and little popular support for the rebellion. Their military strategy was to blockade and isolate New England, thrust at the principal central ports of New York and Philadelphia, and ravish the south; then the rebellion would collapse. The French saw American unity only as a common hatred for Britain, and believed that, with independence won, the "united" colonies would resume their traditional quarrelsomeness, all, of course, under the protection and guidance of France. Only Spain dimly foresaw the disaster to her American empire if these British rebels should succeed. So her government hesitated, unwilling to make an open commitment.

American military reversals in the year following the Declaration of Independence cooled French enthusiasm for the American effort and caused the Spanish to withdraw even their tacit support. American emissaries in Madrid and Paris became increasingly frustrated in their attempts to get additional material and monetary aid from both governments. Even the flamboyant Benjamin Franklin, darling of the Parisian salon circuit, found difficulties in maintaining his semi-official contacts with the French government and was denied the opportunity to speak to King Louis. Franklin was becoming an embarrassment to the French, and his cause needed a miracle.

Franklin got his miracle and turned it to the Americans' advantage. The rebels had successfully thwarted a British attempt to cut off New England from the rest of the union. An army led by General "Gentleman Johnny" Burgoyne, advancing south from Montreal, was itself cut off and defeated at a wilderness farm just outside Saratoga, New York. On October 17, 1777, Burgoyne surrendered himself and his five thousand troops to a delirious American combination of Continentals and militia. Not only had the Americans sustained their war effort through an entire campaign season but they had climaxed it by capturing intact an entire British army!

This dramatically significant news reached an excited Franklin in December, and with it he quickly rekindled Vergennes' enthusiasm. Eager to milk every advantage from Britain's distress, Vergennes emphasized the significance of the American victory in urging Spain to ignore the risks and join France in behalf of American independence. "If," he wrote Spain's Foreign Minister, "the two Crowns brought about that separation it seems they should not regret that war, whatever the issue may be."

Dismayed by Spain's hesitation to precipitate an open break with England, Vergennes began hasty negotiations with the Americans, convinced that "the power that will first recognize the independence of the Americans will be the one that will reap the fruits of this war." All official barriers to formal contact between the French government and the American commissioners disappeared, and within two months France openly and formally committed itself to the American cause. On February 6, 1778, on behalf of King Louis two treaties were signed officially recognizing the independence of the United States.

These two treaties were highly significant for the future of the fledgling nation. One, the Franco-American Alliance, was essentially a long-term military alliance that pledged France to maintain "the liberty, sovereignty, and independence absolute and unlimited of the said United States," while it similarly committed the United States to guarantee all present and future "possessions of the Crown of France in America." If France entered the war both nations would make common cause and neither would conclude truce or peace with Britain without the consent of the other. The second agreement, A Treaty of Amity and Commerce, was perhaps equally as far-reaching. It opened the ports of France and of the United States to each other's commerce and accepted the broad American definition of neutral rights on the high seas, including the important concept that "free"—neutral—ships made "free" goods. Each granted to the other most-favored-nation status, thereby promising any future commercial advantages that might be conferred on any other country.

Dropping her mask of neutrality and indifference, France wedded herself to the cause of American independence. It was a marriage of convenience to be sure, for she expected the American government to accept not only her protection but her advice on policy as well, advice intended to augment and benefit her own policies. To make certain this would happen, Vergennes dispatched Conrad Alexander Gerard as France's first minister to the United States. But France also expected to draw to herself the lucrative American trade that had been such a profitable underpinning of Britain's commercial success. The United States could serve well as a junior partner in promoting a return to French grandeur.

Britain now was faced with a dilemma. The shock of Burgoyne's defeat gave George III's ministers second thoughts on the American issue and made them willing to compromise with their colonial cousins. Otherwise they risked the loss of a substantial portion of their empire to French influence, a long-term danger to British security. To prevent this from happening, a peace commission headed by Lord Carlisle was sent to New York to treat with Washington and with the Continental Congress. In effect Britain decided to outbid the French for the affection of the Americans, offering every concession short of complete independence. Carlisle was thus forced to race across the Atlantic to reach the Americans ahead of Gerard and before the Continental Congress ratified the official French treaties and bound itself to France. Unfortunately for Britain, Carlisle arrived too late with too little to offer; he had to return home empty handed. Britain had no choice but to declare war on France, and the truce of 1763 came to an end.

Half of Vergennes' policy had been carried forward successfully, but the other half resisted implementation. Spain steadfastly declined to join the alliance against Britain, failing to see any advantage for herself in American independence. Vergennes could not afford to let France fight Britain alone, and he needed the Spanish navy as well as Spanish ports for the convenience of French fleets. It took a year of frustrating negotiation before he persuaded the Spanish government to enter the war, which it did reluctantly in May, 1779. His bargaining point was a French promise to help Spain recover Gibraltar. The famous rock fortress had been ignominiously lost to Britain in 1704, and Spain had tried desperately ever since to get it back. Vergennes was again playing "two world" diplomacy. If he remained true to his words in both his separate commitments to Spain and to the United States, he had, in effect, tied the Rock of Gibraltar around the neck of American independence.

Once again war erupted in widely scattered theaters, and the British fought it with an ineptness and indifference they had not shown twenty years earlier. In North America the American War, as English statesmen called it, was poorly prosecuted and was becoming increasingly unpopular at home. The idea of Englishmen killing other Englishmen, regardless of what they called themselves, somehow seemed unnatural. A peace movement arose among English subjects and especially among the Parliamentary opposition. If it had not been that the Empire was again fighting its ancient enemies, France and Spain, popular discontent in England in all probability would have collapsed the entire war effort. When Cornwallis blundered into the cul-de-sac of Yorktown and was forced to raise the white flag on October 19, 1781, almost four years to the day after Saratoga, the King's ministers decided to open secret negotiations with American representatives in Europe.

Lord North, the King's own choice as war-time leader, fell from power in January, 1782, and a new ministry dominated by the more enlightened Lord Shelbourne took on the task of ending hostilities. Despite claims that loss of the colonies would reduce England to a second rate status, Shelbourne was convinced that an independent United States, strong and secure through a generous peace, could be made a friend to Great Britain rather than a weak protegé of France. Fortunately for England he also had a few negotiating assets. The British navy was dramatically successful in the Caribbean, while the British army repulsed a combined Franco-Spanish attack on Gibraltar. If handled properly, Shelbourne reasoned, a peace settlement would strip away only a little of British power and prestige.

Negotiations for the Treaty of Paris of 1783 turned on the question of the future of the United States of America. Each of the three major European powers had its own ideas of what that future should be, while the Dutch, whom the British forced into the war in 1780, sat on the sidelines hoping for a share of American commerce. Although Great Britain was forced to return East and West Florida to Spain, Lord Shelbourne nonetheless maintained his ideas of laying the basis for future Anglo-American friendship and cooperation. British negotiators offered the United States a surprisingly generous land settlement, far more extensive than many realistic Americans could have expected. Extending westward from the Atlantic to the Mississippi, bounded on the north by the great Lakes and Canada, and on the south by the Floridas, the vast region was larger by far than the combined areas of all the other nations involved in the war.

The Spaniards were aghast at the prospect of an independent United States fronting on their North American possessions. Protesting vehemently and smarting from their inability to recapture Gilbraltar, they forced the French to support their demands that the United States be confined to the area between the Atlantic coast and the eastern slopes of the Appalachians. Time after time French and Spanish negotiators redrew the map already accepted by the British and Americans, each time trying to create a buffer area between American and Spanish territory. France readily fell in with this scheme, for a belt of Atlantic coastal states would be too weak and too quarrelsome to survive without French protection. France could again be involved in North American affairs, and the immense wilderness to the west would be open for a return of her own ventures in the fur trade. More than a few Frenchmen even flirted with the will-o'-the-wisp of a French reconquest of Canada.

Britain adamantly rejected Spain's demands on the simple grounds that the areas in question had never been effectively won from her and she could dispose of them in any way she wished. Spain then appealed to British cupidity by offering to split the vast trans-Appalachian region into two zones as protectorates over the Indian hunting and fur-trading regions, the British north of the Ohio River and the Spanish to the south. This idea had some appeal to the English, for already their fur companies were warning Shelbourne that he was about to give away some of the most valuable fur resources in the world. But such a cession of territory from the Americans would defeat Shelbourne's long-term policies. So the British remained firm and the western boundary line was drawn officially down the middle of the Mississippi.

Britain was, however, less generous in other matters of vital national interest to the Americans. She refused to grant them the "right" to fish off the Grand Banks of Newfoundland, the rich source of cod for the New England fishing industry; instead, after John Adams' emotional arguments, she conceded it as a "liberty." She also insisted that British creditors would "meet with no lawful impediment" in the collection of pre-war debts owed to them by American merchants and especially by Southern planters—altogether about five million pounds. She was equally adamant in demanding compensation for the approximately 80,000 Loyalists who had lost their properties and been driven from their homes because of their support for George III. Such compensation was a bitter pill for the Americans, but they accepted a compromise in the treaty by which Congress would "earnestly recommend" that the states restore property taken from Loyalists. Britain's negotiators were also unwilling to discuss a commercial agreement which would permit the United States to continue its lucrative pre-war pattern of trade in the British West Indies.

Neither France nor Spain was pleased with these British concessions to American nationhood. Despite the Anglo-American debates leading to compromises in the treaty, both the French and Spanish governments saw the United States emerging as a more powerful nation than either had expected—or wanted. When the definitive treaty was signed in Paris on September 3, 1783, both countries were forced to reassess their foreign policies in terms of this new American nation and to ascertain its effect on the European balance of power. Their two-world concept was seriously endangered because these transplanted Englishmen had successfully established a sovereign state in the American portion of the "other" world.

Back home, the Americans showed no such cynicism as they wildly celebrated their new status with fireworks, bonfires, patriotic speeches, and public days of thanksgiving. Their city governments and state legislatures ordered victory medals struck and the erection of statues of war heroes. And together they feted their victorious Commander in Chief in a triumphal procession that set out December 4, 1783, from war-damaged New York City, and ended Christmas Eve at the candle-lit doorway of Mount Vernon. Like their citizen-general, Americans enjoyed the taste of victory after eight and a half years of war. They were more naive than he, for they saw in the treaty not only a guarantee of their independence but also a guarantee of their freedom to build their nation the way they wanted it.

But history records no such guarantees.

Events quickly caught up with the Americans, and by the end of 1784 the sweet taste of victory began to sour as England, France, and Spain completed their assessment of American independence. In London, the generous and farsighted Lord Shelbourne fell from power—precisely because he had been generous and farsighted. As might be expected, a reaction set in among the defeated English; they would live with Shelbourne's treaty, but they would make no further concessions nor interpret it generously. Urged on by mercantile groups most likely to suffer from a restoration of an aggressive American economy, the new ministry replaced Shelbourne's vision of post-war Anglo-American cooperation with a policy of retribution. The Americans simply were not to be rewarded for stepping out of the empire. In fact, if the President of the Board of Trade had his way, enough economic pressure would be put on the individual states that one by one they would seek return to

Mother England. English producers were encouraged to swamp the American market to be sure that 150 years of colonial dependence on British merchandise was not shifted to French or, worse still, to American manufacturers. The significantly important New England carrying trade supplying fish, food, and timber products to the British West Indies was denied. And the New England cod fleets found their "liberty" to fish along the Grand Banks so seriously restricted that many faced bankruptcy.

As a more direct threat to American sovereignty the British indicated second thoughts about the expansion of American territory into the Northwest, that triangular region bounded by the Ohio, the upper Mississippi, and the Great Lakes. English fur-trading interests had seen merit in the Spanish ploy at the peace negotiations to create a British protectorate over the Indian hunting grounds. They considered the treaty a surrender of a rich part of the trade in skins and pelts to American entrepreneurs. Succumbing to their argument, the ministry delayed, and then refused, recalling its troops from the fortified trading posts south of the Canada-United States boundary. Scattered in a giant sweep from the eastern edge of Lake Ontario to the northern tip of Lake Michigan, these posts controlled the fur trade in the area and exercised considerable influence over the Indians who by tradition had resented the westward pressure of American settlement. By staying in position at these strategic locations, the British blocked the migration of Americans into a large portion of their own national territory. The vast region would be empty of Americans and left open to fur-traders operating out of Canada. Masking their real reason, the British excused their policy by blaming the Congress of the United States for not fulfilling its commitments made in the peace treaty. Loyalists were not welcomed back home nor compensated for their confiscated property. And British creditors were finding it difficult if not impossible to

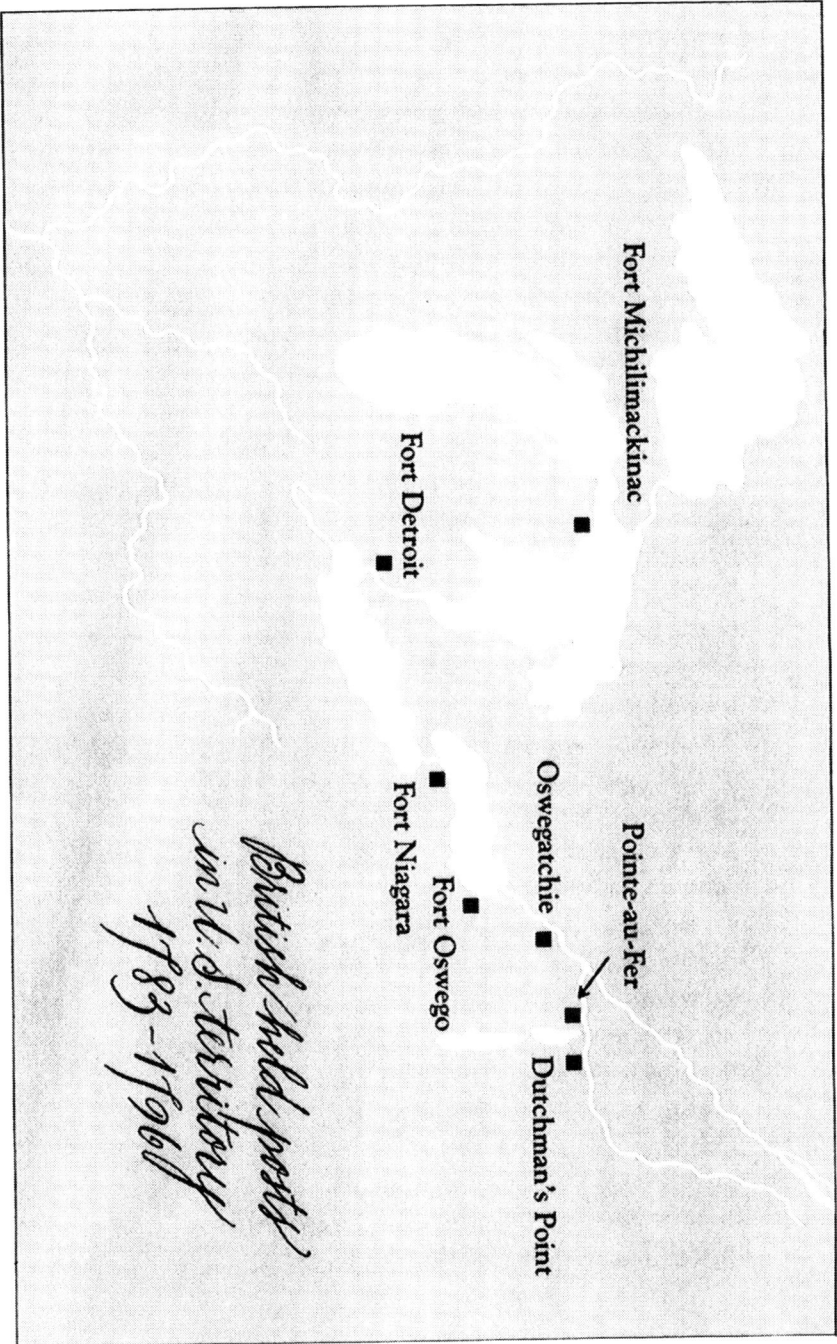

Fort Michilimackinac

Fort Detroit

Oswegatchie

Pointe-au-Fer

Fort Niagara

Fort Oswego

Dutchman's Point

British held ports
in U.S. territory
1783–1796

present their claims in the state courts for collection of prewar debts. Congress was powerless to enforce both of these commitments on the individual states, and the British knew it. They suspected as well that Congress was too weak to dislodge them from the posts; the Continental Army had been disbanded, and state militias certainly would not be sent in any effective force into the wilderness north of the Ohio.

To salt the wounds already inflicted on American nationhood the British also refused to participate in an exchange of ministers, the final act of formal diplomatic recognition of American independence. Although they begrudgingly accepted John Adams as the first United States minister to London, they did not consider it necessary to accredit their own minister to Congress, preferring instead to permit minor diplomatic problems to be handled by their consuls at the major American port cities. This meant, of course, that any attempts by the government of the United States to solve outstanding differences would have to be made by Adams in London. And in London Adams was treated shamefully—often ignored, occasionally insulted. His primary assignment was to get a commercial agreement, but British officials were unwilling even to discuss the idea.

Meanwhile Spanish reassessment of the United States created another set of problems for American sovereignty south of the Ohio River. Despite its reluctant acceptance of the Mississippi River as the western boundary in the Treaty of Paris, the Spanish government deliberately tried to interdict American settlement west of the Appalachian mountains. In 1784 the King prohibited American travel on the Mississippi River, making it impossible for the settlers to float their surplus goods downriver to New Orleans for shipment to markets on the Atlantic coast. This effectively cut out the economic basis for these western settlements. Simultaneously, Spanish colonial officials negotiated treaties with the Indian nations of the re-

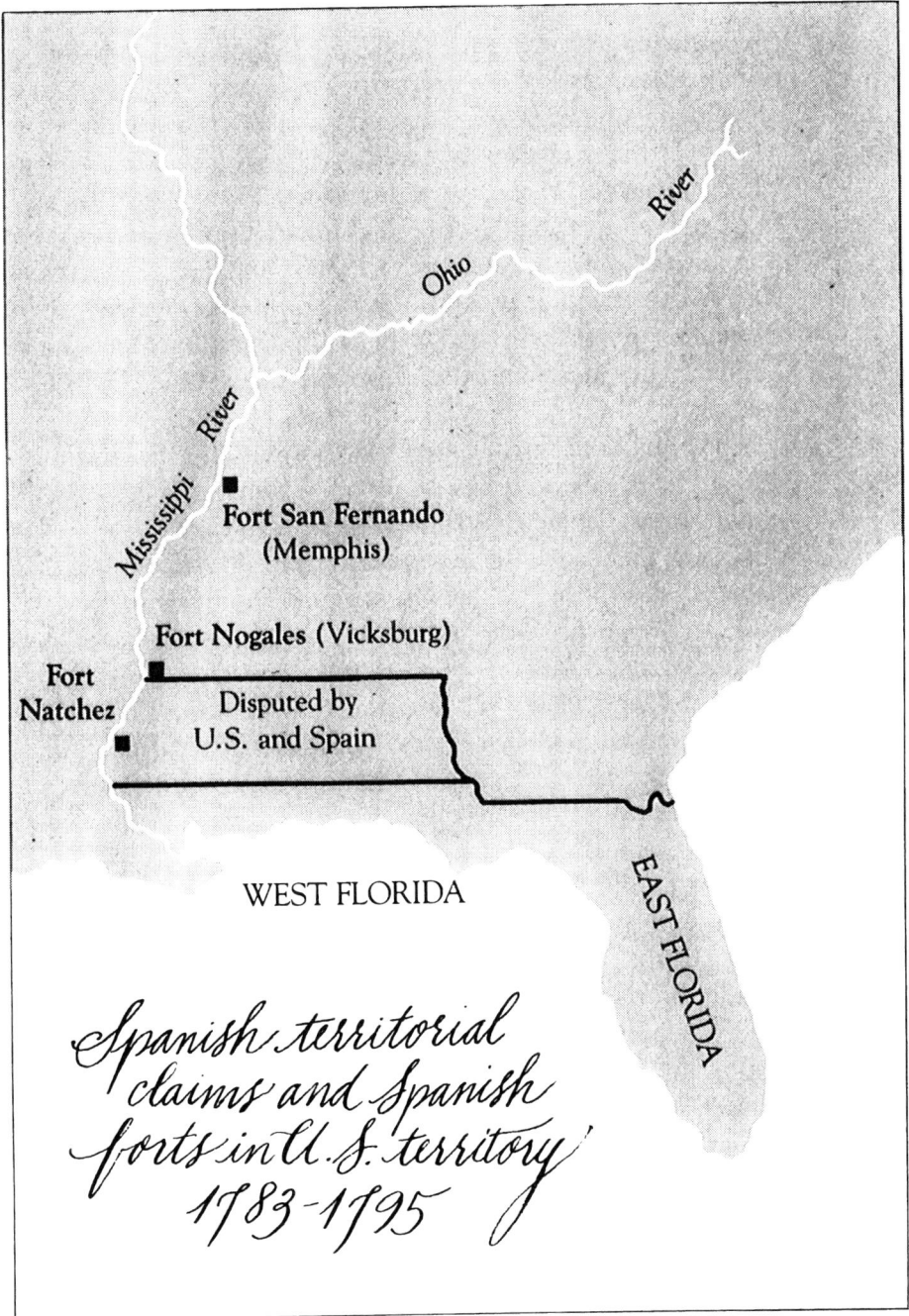

Fort San Fernando
(Memphis)

Fort Nogales (Vicksburg)

Fort
Natchez

Disputed by
U.S. and Spain

WEST FLORIDA

EAST FLORIDA

*Spanish territorial
claims and Spanish
forts in U.S. territory
1783-1795*

gion, encouraging with gifts of trade goods, guns, and ammunition their resistance to the advancing Americans. The government also arbitrarily extended the northern boundary of western Florida some two hundred miles above the 31st parallel, the line both the Americans and the British had understood to be the official border. To enforce this advanced position they built forts at Natchez, Vicksburg, and, briefly, even as far into American territory as the site of Memphis. Spain in effect had nullified the authority of the government of the United States in the entire southwestern quadrant of the new country.

Having done so, she set about transforming the region into a buffer zone between the United States and her own possessions in Texas, Florida, and Mexico. Her policies sowed dissension and fear along this western fringe of American settlement, and she sent in agents, some of whom were Americans, to bribe, threaten, and cajole the settlers. She offered generous land grants on the western side of the Mississippi, hoping to depopulate the eastern area by promising Spanish protection from the Indians and complete freedom to trade and travel on the river. Since few Americans wanted to resettle, Spanish agents encourged separatist sentiments among the log villages scattered along the Kentucky and Tennessee valleys, promising protection and commercial privileges if these frontier farmers would declare thier independence and then profess loyalty to the Spanish king. The United States thus was left with little or no influence over the Southwest.

While Britain and Spain were sowing dissension and discord in the West, France was evaluating her experiences with the new republic. The French government had met only limited success in manipulating American domestic and foreign policies through her minsiters sent to Congress during the war. Foreign Secretary Vergennes also had attempted to draw American commerce closer to France when in 1784 he induced

Franklin to sign a consular convention in effect accrediting French consuls to the individual states rather than to the government of the Confederation. Congress had rejected this arrangement as too blatantly subordinating American interests to those of France and granting too much independence to French merchants resident in the United States. And Vergennes' aborted domination of the peace negotiations was yet another endeavor to maintain the United States as a French protegé. France was realistic enough to recognize American reluctance to stay firmly in the embrace of the Franco-American marriage of convenience.

Nonetheless Vergennes' long-term plan to draw American destiny closer into the French orbit continued long after the War was over. A new consular convention negotiated in 1788 with Thomas Jefferson, Franklin's successor in Paris, still gave France considerable influence over American commercial affairs. It acknowledged the sovereignty of the United States of America, but it included the right of consular courts to exercise civil jurisdiction over French nationals, a denial of that sovereignty. Although technically reciprocal, this stigma of extraterritoriality was a tacit admission of the weakness of the American system of confederation; there were no national courts, and the thirteen varieties of state judicial systems made impossible a consistent policy concerning foreign nationals. The new agreement may have improved the relative position of the United States, but it certainly did not dispel American suspicions of French intentions.

Taken altogether, French policies regarding the United States were mixed with both successes and failures. By assuring American independence France had weakened the British empire and British prestige, but the price was a long, costly war that had driven her own precarious finances dangerously close to ruin. She had helped create a new nation and a potential friend in the world balance of power, yet these new Americans were suspicious and preferred the isolation of their own distant continent. She had encouraged Americans to free their economy from British mercantilism, expecting it to interlock with her own; but as soon as the war ended, she witnessed an almost complete return of American preference for British products and almost none for French. American independence in the guise of a weak, divided, inadequate confederation was a frustration for France simply because it was unreliable as an ally, customer, or friend.

With American independence causing second thoughts in London, worries in Madrid, and disappointments in Paris, the United States could not escape the environment created by other nations. Its people had begun bold experiments in both state-building and representative government, experiments that required time and patience for careful reflection and gradual maturation. But in the hothouse of international politics neither time nor patience was available. Europe's self-interest aggravated the inherent internal weaknesses of the American union, and the critical years following 1783 were crammed with threats to the country's stability and security. Independence of itself could not guarantee the American experiment in nation-building, yet without a strong nation independence could not be guaranteed either.

Despite the cloak of unity provided by the Articles of Confederation, thirteen state sovereignties did not constitute a nation. The governmental system of the Confederation had not overcome state jealousies, eliminated individual state tariffs on interstate trade, provided a national revenue, created a western defense against the Indians, or presented a respected face to the rest of the world. The internal weaknesses of the system invited, even encouraged, external pressures that could bring down the great experiment. No wonder Washington clung to the sentiments of his prophetic, morose query of 1783 when he wondered if the American Revolution would be a "blessing or a curse."

But Washington and men like him who had invested heavily in the Revolution were determined not to squander that investment. They had risked being hanged as traitors as well as financial ruin to expend the time and effort necessary to fight the war. Too much had been asked—and given—to win independence to allow it to be jeopardized by distrust, dissension, and disunion. Their solution was the Constitutional Convention at Philadelphia in 1787, a reanalysis of the American purpose and a restructuring of government necessary to accomplish that purpose.

The Constitution did what the Articles of Confederation could not do. It still maintained the entities of the several states, but it created the federal government as a suprastate whose laws and treaties transcended those states. It gave this government the right to tax, to declare war, to make peace, to negotiate treaties, to issue a national currency, and to maintain a national military establishment. And perhaps most importantly, it created a strong executive through whom the nation could develop responsible leadership for national policies. Creation of this new federal structure, however, did not of itself assure national survival any more than did the old Confederation. Yet the nature of the structure was such that the chances of survival were far greater, for a more unified nation was stronger, and with that strength a single executive could earn for his country the respect of nations.

Now the country's future depended on the qualities of leadership provided by its first chief executive. It was an awesome responsibility that faced America's first president, for to a large degree the future of the nation depended on how he solved the domestic and foreign problems the Confederation had failed to solve. He could no longer tolerate policies and practices which Washington claimed were "exposing us to become the sport of European politics." Instead, he must create an administration with enough strength and purpose to meet the needs of his people while earning the respect of the community of nations.

CHAPTER TWO

"Integrity and Firmness is All I Can Promise"

WASHINGTON ASSUMED HIS LEADERSHIP role with considerable reluctance. When he resigned his commission as Commander in Chief in 1783 he made it quite clear that he was through with public service, and five years later he brushed aside Alexander Hamilton's hope that he would become president. "You know me well enough," he wrote Hamilton, "that I am not guilty of affectation, when I tell you, that it is my sole desire to live and die, in peace and retirement on my own farm." At fifty-seven, in an era when winning revolutions and conquering wildernesses were the work of younger men, he felt too old and too inadequate for such new responsibilities. He confided in Henry Knox, the Secretary of War for the Confederation, "I am without that competency of political skills, abilities and inclination which is necessary to manage the helm." Yet as a good citizen deeply dedicated to the success of the Republic he could not ignore his country's call, admitting "nothing but a conviction of duty could have induced me to depart from my resolution of remaining in retirement." A proud man justifiably enjoying the well-earned admiration of his fellow Americans, Washington was reluctant because of his fear of failure, a fear that caused him to lament, "I greatly apprehend that my Countrymen will expect too much of me. . . . So much is expected, so many untoward circumstances may intervene in such a new and critical situation, that I feel an insuperable diffidence in my own abilities."

This new and critical situation justified all of the General's anxieties. He would become the president of the world's first emerging nation, and any astute observer would have to agree that presiding over the process of nation-building would be sailing through "an Ocean of difficulties." The United States was not yet a nation, and it was the president's responsibility to see that it became one. While other countries had evolved from dynastic holdings, his had developed from thirteen separate colonizing efforts carved from the raw North American wilderness. Despite the fact they shared a common English cultural and constitutional tradition, each of the colonies had established its own concepts of local rule, its own vested commercial interests, its own petty politics. When they declared their independence, the thirteen united colonies had not really tried to form a nation. Instead, their major bond was the war against England, and even then their individual contributions toward ultimate victory were often inadequate, directed more toward protecting parochial interests than promoting the common goal. During the difficult period following the war, centrifugal forces of disunity almost overcame the forces of cooperation. Indeed, the strong and sometimes violent debate on the Constitution itself reflected the popular apprehension that a national government would suppress local liberties. Ratification of the new federal system was barely achieved in just eleven of the states at the time of the President's inauguration.

Washington shared some of this apprehension. His experiences with the Continental Congress during the war embittered him with its lack of national focus and authority to make and carry out decisions. As early as 1783 he called for "an indissoluble union of the states under one Federal Head" and warned again that a weak union would "expose us to becoming the sport of European politics." During the mid-1780s he watched nervously from Mount Vernon as weaknesses in the union became increasingly apparent. He personally promoted interstate cooperation between Maryland and Virginia for joint development of the Potomac River as an access to the West. The uprising of debt-ridden farmers in western Massachusetts in 1786 convinced him finally that a stronger system of national government had to be established or national independence itself could be lost. By 1787 he was willing, if hesitant, to represent Virginia at the Philadelphia Convention. Although the Constitution this meeting produced had some items "which did not full accord with my wishes," Washington "was convinced it approached nearer to perfection than any government hitherto instituted among men."

This was not the naive observation of a visionary revolutionary, but the assessment of a hard realist who knew both the strengths and weaknesses of his own people. Washington, like so many of his fellow patriots, had long since been convinced that the American Revolution had a unique place in history. He constantly referred to the special destiny of the American people and did homage to divine providence, to "that invisible hand which so often interposed to save our country from impending destruction." When it became apparent that the Constitution would be accepted, he wrote General Benjamin Lincoln that he rejoiced "at every step the people of this great Country take to preserve the Union, establish good order and government, and to render the Nation happy at home and respectable abroad."

Happiness at home and respectability abroad would be the keystone of any first administration. One was essential to the other, and neither could be promoted without an effective but benevolent national government. But in the last quarter of the eighteenth century, in a world ruled by ancient monarchies and entrenched aristocracies, the American experiment in self-government commanded little respect at home and none abroad. So different in concept and traditions, the European power system was anathema to both colonial independence and democratic republicanism. The long colonial experience had taught the Americans how they could be used to promote the interests of that power system and not their own. Even during the brief period of euphoria following formal recognition of independence, it was obvious to them that European nations had no serious interest in the long-term survival of the United States or those troublesome concepts of individual rights embodied in its Declaration of Independence. Washington adamantly hoped, therefore, that "the United States of America will be able to keep disengaged from the labyrinth of European politics and Wars; and that before long they will, by the adoption of a good national government, have become respectable in the eyes of the world so that none of the maritime powers shall presume to treat them with insult or contempt."

Obviously, then, the new American government must achieve two essential goals. First, the people of the several states had to become truly American and accept as their own the new federal government. Second, the European countries must be made to accept the United States as an entity, a sovereign state to be respected as a legitimate member of the world community of nations. It was not obvious, however, how closely intertwined these two goals really were. Domestic tranquility and prosperity at home would assure popular respect for the new government, but this could not be achieved until the physical security of the nation had been guaranteed and its overseas commerce promoted and expanded. On the other hand, European empires threatening both the security of the United States and its commerce would not treat seriously with it until they came to respect its strength and the consistent policies of its government. The dual task for the first president was to provide both the sense of acceptance at home and the focus of American leadership to the international community.

It was clear that Washington was the only American who could do this. To his fellow citizens, as well as to many

Europeans, he symbolized the Revolution. Having held together the Continental Army through eight difficult years, he emerged from the war as the most popular person in the United States. And his prestige soared when he voluntarily surrendered his military responsibilities to the civilian authority of Congress and refused on subsequent occasions to take them up again. During his "retirement" he was inundated by correspondence from prominent Americans and Europeans seeking his advice, opinion, and action. Mount Vernon almost became an executive mansion as he hosted a steady stream of the important and not so important—some came merely to gawk at him—visitors who wanted to discuss significant issues, paint his portrait, or ask favors. Indeed he would record in his *Diary* those rare evenings when he and Mrs. Washington sat alone at dinner. He politely rejected right wing pressures to overcome the nation's problems by establishing a military dictatorship. His lack of personal ambition was most refreshing to an age when the jumble of state governments encouraged grasping aspirations. In a period of peace the country still was enamored of its greatest war hero.

Washington's enormous reputation did more to gain ratification of the Constitution than any other factor. "I think that were it not for one great character in America," commented a member of the Virginia ratifying convention, "so many men would not be for this government." Summarizing this popular trust in the General's judgment, one writer asked, "Is it possible that the deliverer of the country would have recommended an unsafe form of government for that liberty, for which he had for eight long years contended with such unexampled firmness, consistency and magnanimity?" By his participation in the Philadelphia Convention and his feverishly active endorsement that followed, Washington had transferred this trust in him to trust in the quality of the document that had emerged. "If the plan is not a good one," wrote the

Pennsylvania Herald, "it is impossible that either General Washington or Dr. Franklin would have recommended it." And if the plan were a good one, why not the General as the chief executive to put it into operation? By mid-summer 1788, while Virginia and New York were still hotly debating ratification, Independence Day orators were calling for his unanimous election to the presidency.

But what exactly would be a president of the United States? The Founding Fathers were well aware they could not determine every aspect of the chief executive's role. And, more importantly, as they wrote the document they increasingly saw Washington as the only person qualified to be first federal president. Despite their deep historic suspicion of strong executives, they trusted his integrity and wisdom to establish correct precedents to make the position function successfully, yet not abusively. By listing only a few specific duties and still fewer formal limitations, they allowed wide latitude for his development of presidential leadership in both domestic and foreign affairs. Their particular concern for the significance of America's international problems was clearly manifest in more detailed specifics for presidential conduct of foreign relations. He was to be commander in chief of the armed forces and could call up state militias; he was empowered to negotiate treaties but could not ratify them without two-thirds Senate concurrence; he was to appoint and to receive ambassadors, ministers, and consuls. Because the Constitution was thus deliberately vague, the first incumbent was expected to be the actual creator of the office.

Americans, however, had to wait a year and a half before this creative process started; ratification of the Constitution came slowly. Despite Washington's strong endorsement, no overwhelming majorities sprang up to demand its quick acceptance. Instead, long and often heated public debates were necessary to overcome suspicion of the new government in state after state. It was not until late summer of 1788 that the last two major states, New York and Virginia, finally ratified, bringing the total to eleven, just in time for the November elections. Even so, of the total eligible voters only a bare eighteen per cent actually bothered to cast ballots for candidates to the House of Representatives. In truth, there was no popular mandate for the Constitution and the federal government it established. There were also delays in getting Congress organized. Newly elected senators and representatives were unconscionably slow drifting into New York City to provide necessary quorums for both houses. By then, it was more with relief than excitement when on April 6, 1789, before a joint session of Congress, the ballots of the Electoral College were counted and General George Washington was formally elected President of the United States.

Meanwhile, Washington roamed the fields of Mount Vernon and waited unhappily for news from Congress. Each passing day his anxiety grew as he received premature well-wishes from friends and neighbors. Although his election was a foregone conclusion to everyone but himself, he was trapped by his own sense of propriety and would say or do nothing in preparation for his new task until he received official notification. Rumors about the causes for the delays in New York merely added to his irritability, but all he could do was wait.

Then on April 14, an almost breathless Charles Thomson clattered up to Mount Vernon's door. Because he had been Secretary of the Continental Congress, Thomson was selected by Congress as a gesture of continuity with the past to carry the news to the waiting Virginian. Seeing the plantation's proprietor in the doorway, he wasted no time in preliminaries. "Sir," he said, "I was honored with the commands of the Senate to wait upon your Excellency with the information of your being elected to the office of President of the United States of America."

The General had had weeks to prepare for this moment and so he was ready. Giving no indication of the deep turmoil within him, he replied, "Whatever may have been my private feeling and sentiments, I believe I cannot give greater evidence of my sensibility for the honor they have done me, than by accepting the appointment."

With this simple but formal exchange the history of the United States shifted dramatically.

Two days later, after having confided to Henry Knox "that my movements to the chair of Government will be accompanied by feelings not unlike those of a culprit who is going to the place of his execution," Washington set out for New York. Still denying his fitness for office, he reminded Knox that "integrity and firmness is all I can promise." To his pleasant surprise the spirit of gloom was dispelled by an outpouring of public acclaim he had not expected. At Alexandria, Georgetown, Wilmington, Philadelphia, and New York, and many places in between, the people hailed him as the hero they meant him to be. Uniformed cavalry escorted him from town to town over pathways strewn with flower petals; the roars of thirteen cannon saluted him; children's choirs serenaded him; city councils feted him at banquets; toasts of thirteen "huzzahs" honored him. And on the 30th of April, his inauguration at New York's newly-designated Federal Hall was an appropriately simple ceremony as befitting the beginnings of a republican government and was climaxed by the most elaborate fireworks display in that city's already long history.

Just as he had symbolized the Revolution, Washington now became the symbol of the Constitution itself. If it were to grow in popular esteem, this respect and trust in the General had to be transferred to the new federal system it established. And the task would not be easy, for, in truth, the spirit of republicanism did not yet run deeply in the hearts of most Americans. In an age when peoples still identified government

with the trappings of kings, nobles, and bishops it was difficult
for the Americans to accept genuinely and permanently a government of their own creation staffed by officials of their own
selection. Government *for* the people was what they wanted of
course, but government *by* and *of* the people was a terribly new
concept. As a result, the first president's chief role was to assure
long-term acceptance of the federal government by providing a
transition from the familiar traditions of monarchy to the new
practices of democracy. As he presided over the creation of the
federal bureaucracy and set its policies in motion, each step was
important, each action might well be a precedent. Washington
reminded himself of this a year after he assumed office, when he
wrote, "in a government which depends so much in its first
stages on public opinion, much circumspection is still necessary for those engaged in its administration."

Fortunately for the President his first administration was
relatively quiet, a period of surprisingly easy transition from the
multiplicity of state sovereignties to the central national jurisdiction. He had ample opportunity to use his "circumspection"
to gain the support of public opinion. The second administration, on the other hand, suffered from enough discord and
controversies in both domestic and foreign matters that its
chief was profoundly embittered when he finally left office in
March, 1797. Yet the causes of these difficulties existed all
during the earlier period; their significance only became apparent following the outbreak of war in Europe in 1793 when
foreign policy questions intruded themselves into domestic
politics.

During the first administration problems of foreign relations could not be dealt with, however, until the essential
integrity of the national government had been determined.
The First Congress in 1789 re-established the "great" departments—State, War, Treasury—and from these a federal administration emerged. By rejecting a proposed fourth, or

"Home" department, Congress gradually added duties beyond the more traditional foreign affairs functions to the State Department; it was to take the census, grant patents and copyrights, prepare commissions, and publish the laws. The Department of War was vested with power concerning land and naval forces, ships and supplies, military commissions, and the management of Indian affairs. The Treasury Department was given even broader authority, including collection of national revenues, disbursing federal payments, executing the sale of public lands, and superintending all public accounts. Its secretary was to report to Congress on "plans for the improvement and management of the revenue and the support of the public credit." In time, Treasury assumed such wide-ranging additional responsibilities as maintaining the country's first marine hospital and paying military pensions. During these early formative years when administrative responsibilities were not clear cut, each of these departments—and their chiefs—would have significant influence on the formation of foreign policy.

Filling these and other federal posts Washington considered the "most irksome" of his burdens. Given his customary integrity he refused to make any commitments before taking office and determined his own criteria for appointments. Each nominee must have "fitness of character," implying that the candidate have both competence and standing in the community. Prior "services and sacrifices" to the country, especially during the war, should be recognized as well as the claims of incumbents in office when the new government was established. Whenever possible equitable geographic distribution of the major positions and local residence for the lesser ones had to be considered. Above all, appointments would not be influenced "by ties of blood or friendship." Aware of the importance of prior experience to the success of his own administration, the President also hoped to maintain a degree of continuity from the previous government, particularly among principal officeholders. He was delighted when General Henry Knox, the Confederation's Secretary of War, agreed to continue on in the same position. Knox, the Boston book-seller-turned-artillery-officer, knew more than anyone else about Indian affairs on the frontier, and this information would be vital for bringing security to the western settlements. Washington also would have preferred John Jay to continue on as Secretary of State even though Jay was not overly popular in the South as a result of his 1786 negotiations with Spain on the Mississippi Question. Jay, whom the President considered worthy of any federal post, preferred instead to become the first Chief Justice of the Supreme Court. Washington then decided to offer State to fellow Virginian Thomas Jefferson, still in 1789 the American minister to France and the only remaining top-level diplomat in active service. For Treasury he turned to Alexander Hamilton, now actively engaged in New York business interests and one of the country's most outspoken proponents of the Constitution. And he chose Edmund Randolph for his Attorney General, a post originally intended as a part-time legal adviser to the president.

Of these top-level appointments Hamilton's would turn out to be the most crucial, for his ideas on the public credit laid the basis for achieving the domestic prosperity and respect of nations so much desired by Washington. Hamilton already had earned an enviable reputation for his well-reasoned approaches to fiscal and business matters. Both the Congress and the President would grow to rely heavily on his carefully prepared plans and proposals to establish a strong, viable system of national credit and finance. An unabashed admirer of British practices in banking and commerce, he was convinced that the American government should pattern its fiscal system after that of the English to assure the internal stability so essential to earning the respect of the American people. With a government promoting benevolent economic policies at home the nation would then be in a stronger position to protect its commercial interests abroad. In addition, Hamilton believed a system of stable national finance would overcome America's embarrassing inability to meet its obligations to foreign creditors.

Hamilton was encouraged and supported in these ideas by Washington, who unjustly denied his own competence in such matters. With additional backing from a wide distribution of vitally interested businessmen whom he deliberately cultivated for the purpose, the Secretary in 1790 and 1791 pushed through Congress a package of significant legislation that established the long-term fiscal stability of the federal government and simultaneously stimulated the growth of a viable national economy. The accumulated war-time debt of some 77 million dollars owed by the national and state governments to both domestic and foreign creditors was refunded at par. The national debt that resulted was to be serviced by new national revenues drawn from tariffs on specified imports and from the sale of lands in the public domain; eventually excise taxes on certain luxuries, including distilled spirits, were added. A mint was established, and the dollar designated as the official American currency. And finally, Congress chartered for twenty years the Bank of the United States, a semi-public agency intended as a commercial bank and as a receiver and disburser of federal funds. Both the Bank's notes and the new federal securities were negotiable and circulated at full value as a medium of exchange. Thus, in perhaps the greatest long-term contribution of Washington's administration, Hamilton's fiscal plan provided the country tariff protection for its infant industries, much needed capital for its underdeveloped economy, and sufficient and regular income for meeting its financial obligations.

With this new plan the American government could now pay off the nagging debt that had so engulfed the old Confederation. Having established good credit it could, if necessary, borrow easily and cheaply to meet future contingencies. With bank notes and federal bonds being used as money, there was for the first time currency acceptable in all parts of the Union. American merchants were able to pay off their own debts and re-establish credit with European suppliers; in fact by 1800 almost half of United States securities were held by Europeans. The new tariff overcame the fractionalizing of state and local preference and created a truly national common market. Behind this wall of protectionism and stimulated by investment capital available from the Bank of the United States, American manufacturers arose to meet the needs of the domestic market with products ranging from ships to copper kettles. The broad national market so invigorated American agriculture that by the end of 1790 most commodity prices were higher than they had been before the Revolution. Collectively, and surprisingly for a country where 90 percent of the population drew its income from farming, the new legislation laid the basis for modern American capitalism. A truly national economy was emerging.

But the new system was fragile. Its long-term success depended upon internal stability, a continued expansion of overseas commerce, and, clearly, continued peace with actual and potential foreign customers. Any disturbance caused by domestic political dissension or drastic shifts of international relations could destroy its effectiveness. A war could interfere substantially with imports and drastically reduce the revenue from customs duties. Without this income the debt could not be serviced, the value of federal securities would drop, the government's credit would evaporate, and with it citizens' respect for the whole federal structure. Obviously, a substantial portion of American mercantile and manufacturing interests was vitally concerned with maintaining and expanding existing commercial contacts with their best foreign customers and suppliers. The success of their economic position depended immeasurably upon the direction of American foreign policy. The fragility of the new system was all too apparent.

For Washington, then, it was vitally important to establish a realistic and workable foreign policy. Yet, because of his heritage from the Confederation, he was not totally free to create fresh initiatives of his own. Thus far the republic had a poor history in managing its affairs with other nations. It was this dramatic, if brief, tradition that had prompted the Founding Fathers to be more specific as they wrote out the areas of presidential responsibility in foreign relations. As colonists the Americans had had few such experiences of their own; Mother England had always done this for them. But on the eve of independence it was necessary to look squarely at the importance of foreign aid to the success of their cause. The Second Continental Congress, called in 1775 to protest British government excesses, recognized quicky the inability of achieving anything singlehandedly. That year it organized the Committee of Secret Correspondence to set up clandestine contacts with unofficial representatives of France. When the actual commitment to independence was made, Congress changed the name to "Committee of Foreign Relations." Headed originally by Benjamin Franklin, the Committee drew up the ambitious "Plan of 1776," an idealistic statement of long-term American goals. And it wrote the instructions for its militia diplomats, including Franklin himself, who were sent to Europe to seek support from England's potential enemies. Initially, Congress had intended to manage all of the affairs of a country at war through such committees, keeping control of fundamental policies and even detailed activities in its collective hands. The sheer and obvious burden of detail was so frustrating that most policy direction drifted for years. Congress itself was often distracted by changes in its own membership, conflicts stemming from local and state interests, and the clumsy attempts by the French ministers to manipulate affairs. In a desperate effort to pinpoint managerial responsibility, Congress in 1781 established three administrative departments: War, Finance, and Foreign Affairs.

Although the Continental Congress had retained ultimate responsibility for setting policies, its new arrangement provided executive control for greater efficiency than had previously existed. Superintendent of Finance Robert Morris staved off national bankruptcy through his hard but realistic restructuring of fiscal procedures. Benjamin Lincoln, the Secretary of War, despite his occasional bungling, brought a degree of order out of the chaos of supply to the long-suffering Continental Army and its frustrated commander. The first Secretary for Foreign Affairs, Robert R. Livingston, introduced professional standards for his amateur diplomats and created the nucleus of a true Foreign Service. His successor, John Jay, capitalizing on his own bitter experiences in Madrid, injected a sense of realism into American relations with Europe's great powers. It was this sytem of bureaucratic structure and the equally important tradition of Congressional responsibility for policy that were part of the legacy for the new president.

Washington also inherited the philosophy for the conduct of foreign affairs embedded in the "Plan of 1776." Drawn up in late summer of 1776, the Plan was a guide for future American relations with other nations. Created out of the obvious and desperate need for foreign aid in the struggle against Britain, it provided a set of principles for negotiations before expediency overcame common sense. Based on a century of colonial dissatisfaction at being pawns in the European diplomatic chess game, it restated, but from an American viewpoint, the European "doctrine of two worlds." The United States was to isolate itself in the security of the Western Hemisphere from involvement in European power politics, yet it also called for the opening of American ports to the commerce of all nations. During the colonial era each colony's economy had relied on the export trade, and as a nation the United States could prosper only with an expansion of that trade. More significantly, however, the Plan intended to promote world free trade, a concept unheard of in the age of national monopolies until the publication of Adam Smith's *Weath of Nations*. These Founding Fathers were enthusiastic if somewhat naive in their belief that trade brought national prosperity and therefore world free trade could make all nations prosperous. In particular they hoped to convince the continental countries that Britain's power came from her domination of the world's trade and that the strength of each of them would grow if it opened its ports to one another and to the United States. By promoting the principles of free trade, Americans were offering Europeans an opportunity to break Britain's monopoly of North American commerce.

Underlying the Plan of 1776 was the basic American fear of becoming embroiled in international power politics. Ties to other countries should be commercial, not political. Commerce guaranteed mutual prosperity, but political connections most assuredly would lead to ruinous wars. In case of war the Plan invoked some additional new concepts concerning the rights of neutral commerce, including a very narrow definition of contraband. Promoting what were known as "small navy" principles, it was an undisguised attempt to win the sympathies of European neutrals who had consistently suffered from the arrogance of Britain's "large" navy. Considered as reflecting the "new" diplomacy, these principles nonetheless were incorporated in the Treaty of Amity and Commerce with France in 1778 and were followed closely in subsequent negotiations for commercial agreements with The Netherlands (1782), Sweden (1783), and Morocco (1787). Taken altogether, as a statement of long-term national goals, the Plan of 1776 was as bold and revolutionary to the eighteenth-century world of international relations as were the electrifying concepts on human rights enunciated in the Declaration of Independence.

Thus it was that Washington assumed the presidency with established national traditions existing in both the philosophy and the conduct of foreign affairs. He was not inclined to break with either tradition as he charted his own course. Only events themselves would dictate changes that ultimately would be seen clearly as his own. Events would indeed force him to seize the initiative and establish new directions for presidential leadership that would involve him—and most of his successors— in continuous conflict with Congress. But at the start he would avoid if at all possible any such conflicts—that is, if Congress would let him.

Unfortunately the first Congress, a year before it actually debated Hamilton's new fiscal measures, almost made them impossible to achieve and handed the President his first constitutional dilemma. Ardent nationalists in the House, still clinging to the philosophies of the Plan of 1776, were convinced that the United States now had its best opportunity to show the rest of the world how to break the monopolistic stranglehold of mercantilism. Influenced by the economic liberalism of the Enlightenment and especially by the ideas of Adam Smith, they wanted to set an example of how international trade ought to be carried out. The United States under the Constitution was now strong enough not only to protect its own commercial interests but to carry on successfully a trade war against those nations that still held it in disrepute. Led by James Madison they proposed a schedule of tonnage duties in American ports that deliberately discriminated against the shipping of those countries which refused to make commercial agreements with the United States. The schedule would levy a rate of nine cents per ton on American owned ships, 30 cents on those from countries, such as France, in commercial agreement with the United States, and 50 cents on ships from all others.

Clearly directed against Great Britain, the proposed tonnage act manifested the American perception that Britain remained the villain in the game of international politics. Britain's cavalier refusal to honor the terms of the peace treaty left Redcoats still occupying pieces of American territory. Her government continued in its refusal to discuss a commercial treaty, revealing that same insulting reluctance which frustrated John Adams during his three years as minister in London. Her manufactures, thanks to the advanced technologies of her industries, were again preferred by Americans more than any others, including their own. And her mercantile and banking houses were the only ones capable of advancing long-term credits to American merchants. As a result, by 1789 the ex-mother country had re-established pre-War patterns of trade between herself and her former children, but at higher levels. By then she was supplying nine-tenths of America's needs in manufactured goods and three-fourths of all its imports, but taking only half of its exports. The resultant trade imbalance continued the United States in the subservient role of colonial dependent.

Madison's proposal in effect was the first part of an economic declaration of independence. But the implied trade war that might result considerably frightened a majority in the Senate. With the economic leverage Britain enjoyed, she would win such a war all too easily. Those Senators representing states with considerable overseas trade recognized quickly that discrimination in favor of France would bring little benefit to the United States. The Franco-American commercial treaty of 1778 had not lived up to expectations, for there had been little of mutual advantage in the commerce between the two countries. And the commercial agreements with other nations had been mere token recognition of American political independence; they offered no significant economic advantage for the

United States. American prosperity obviously depended upon a regularization of trade with Great Britain.

Hamilton, as Secretary of the Treasury, saw this clearly, and was well aware that any disruption of the trade with the English would jeopardize plans he and others might have for laying the foundation of a stable American economy. He needed time to work out his ideas for a sound fiscal policy, and his own proposals could not be presented until the next session of Congress opened in January, 1790. So he and likeminded Senators worked against Madison's bill. Even Madison's fellow Southerners thought his strong nationalistic stand a bit unrealistic and pointed out that discrimination would place their plantation commerce in the hands of northern shipowners, a prospect that cheered them less than the more familiar dependence upon the English. Because of these arguments, the upper house produced as a compromise the Tonnage Act of 1789. It did discriminate in favor of American shippers by assuring them of almost exclusive domination of inter-coastal trade, but it treated equally the ships of all other nations.

As the first major piece of economic and foreign policy legislation, the Tonnage Act made the President furious. His anti-British nationalism was as strong as Madison's, and he had favored the discrimination in the original bill. But in the act sent to him for his signature, Congress had established a policy of which he did not approve. Yet in his view of the separation of powers between the legislature and the executive, Congress was to legislate and he was to execute that legislation. As President he felt he should not attempt to influence Congress; his time for decision would come when legislation was presented for his signature. Admitting that the Tonnage Act "was so adverse to my ideas of justice and policy," he seriously considered letting it become law without his signature rather than vetoing it outright. Only after several Senators assured him that they contemplated more effective ways of promoting the

American economy did he sign the bill into law. But the lesson on the responsibility for the origination of policy, especially in matters concerning foreign relations, was not lost on him.

This experience troubled Washington's sense of what was proper in his relationship with the Congress. The Constitution complicated it by the stipulation that the President should seek "the advice and consent of the Senate" on matters concerning nominations and treaties. He read this clause literally as calling for regular two-way communication between himself and the Senate. But the Senate, without explanation, had rejected Benjamin Fishbourn, one of his nominees for a federal post. Perplexed and somewhat angry, he reprimanded the Senate. Acknowledging the legitimacy of its reasons "such as you deemed sufficient," he suggested that future questions about nominations ought to be referred back to him for more information before a final vote was taken. It was apparent from the Fishbourn incident that a clearer definition of the connection between executive and Senate was necessary, and a senatorial committee was delegated to call on the President to determine "the mode of communication."

While these discussions were in progress, he hoped he had found a solution in the necessity to meet a crisis over the Creek Indians in the Southwest. Part of the legacy of the old government to the new, the still unsettled status of these Indians was aggravated by policies of the State of Georgia. During the Confederation, Georgia had signed treaties with them to determine the boundary between its settlements and their hunting ground. Unfortunately the treaties were vague; both sides violated their terms, and a border war was imminent. Complicating the situation further was the question of the extent of United States jurisdiction over a large portion of the Southwest. This region, the modern state of Tennessee, was at the time an extension of North Carolina, and that state had not yet joined the Union. Since Washington considered the Indian confederations as nations, new negotiations would be a federal matter and not that of the individual states. At Washington's request Congress had already appropriated $20,000 to send a commission to confer with the Creek chieftains and if necessary negotiate a new treaty. But the situation was both difficult and dangerous because of its ramifications: an expensive Indian war could result, or an extensive string of fortifications might be needed, or a substantial slice of territory purchased. Congressional action would be necessary to meet any—or all—of these contingencies.

At this point Washington badly needed advice. To get it, he interpreted literally the "advice and consent" clause of the Constitution and arranged a meeting between himself, Secretary of War Knox, and the Senate. He hoped in this way both to improve his method of communciation with Congress and to get the sense of the Senate on the Creek negotiations. In preparation he had Knox draw up a draft treaty and a list of issues that required examination. But his hopes for a give-and-take discussion evaporated immediately when he and Knox entered the Senate chamber.

The day was warm and the rumble of street traffic coming through open windows permeated the room. Worse still, Vice President Adams treated the visit as a state occasion, obliging the President to give an extemporaneous speech. Adams then read point-by-point the entire treaty draft and the list of issues; too frequently he could not be heard over the street noise and he was forced to reread the entire list. As Adams finished the second reading, the Senators were so confused and uncertain of their responsibilities that they sat in an embarrrassed silence. Finally, Senator William Maclay, a west Pennsylvania democrat with a reputation for criticizing the majestic trappings of the executive, protested against immediate action and asked that the matter be referred to a committee which would consult the President at a later date. Although Washington's temper flared in disapproval, he quickly recognized he could do little else but wait. Red-faced and angry he stomped from the room mumbling "this defeats the very purpose of my coming here." Two days later, however, he received from the Senate its sense of what ought to be done, and he instructed the commission in its direction of negotiations.

Neither Washington nor the Senate recognized the constitutional significance of this irritating episode. Had the Senate accepted the role vaguely implied in the Constitution and sought by the President, it might have established the basis for becoming a council of state and gradually assumed executive functions of government. But as the upper house of the legislature, it was also trying to determine its proper functions and was jealous of what were expected as its own prerogatives. The Senate did not wish to be part of the executive and was clearly interested in maintaining the separation of powers intended by the framers of the Constitution. And had Washington met success with his discussion in the Senate he might have unwittingly surrendered some of his own prerogatives, limiting presidential discretion in control of foreign policy. By refusing to discuss with the President the details of the Creek treaty, the Senate was setting a precedent for executive leadership in such matters, reserving for itself only the constitutional mandate to give or to withhold its "consent" to whatever the president had negotiated. But the situation was confusing for both President and Senators. This constitutional dichotomy for ultimate responsibility in the final approval of treaties would continue to vex Washington and every one of his successors.

Unfortunately the episode with the Senate did little to answer the practical question of how the president should get necessary advice. Washington learned quickly to use written communications with both houses of Congress. But with the exception of a handful of friends who were members and whose opinions he trusted, he made no further attempts to consult

formally with either house. Although the Constitution nowhere refers to a "cabinet" or set of presidential advisers, to
be practical he turned to those closest to him, those whom he
had appointed to head the administrative departments—
Hamilton, Knox, and, when he finally took up his duties,
Jefferson. But because open debate often embarrassed him, he
tended at first only to ask for written opinions on specific issues
that were under his consideration. Usually he kept his own
counsel, examining the opinions submitted to him, and then
made his decision. Obviously the complexity of new national
issues required more discussion than what was available in
written reports, even though some of Hamilton's exceeded
10,000 words. The President conferred individually with his
advisers, often asking one to comment on another's report. In
time he would ask them all to meet with him, often for break-
fast or luncheon, and even occasionally at dinner. Only gradually did he institute formal meetings for broad discussion of all
issues under his consideration. Slowly his practices evolved
into the basis of a modern cabinet system.

One practice, however, was quite apparent in Washington's approach to advice: he let no one counselor have exclusive domain over a specific matter. Always a little unsure of
himself and a bit fearful of depending on just one set of ideas, it
was typical of him to seek opinions from as many as possible of
those most directly interested in a particular issue. He had
followed this practice in the Continental Army, relying heavily on the collective wisdom of his staff before making his final
decision. Now with even larger issues to consider it was even
more important for him to do so. He meant, of course, no
disrespect for any single adviser. But he shrewdly observed that
a variety of special interest groups had emerged in the new
nation. Solutions to major problems had too many ramifications that could adversely affect any one of these, and their
outspoken opposition might destroy the still delicate policies

he was trying to initiate. Without a political party structure to channel opinions into a campaign platform, it was vitally important not to overlook a significant reaction from any group before reaching a final decision. This is why, for example, he often sought advice beyond "my own department," his reference to the executive branch. During the early years he called in particular upon fellow Virginian James Madison for help. Through his leadership role in the House, Madison contributed more than any other to the organization of the First Congress and to working relationships between both houses and the executive. Until Madison began to differ with presidential support of Hamilton's fiscal program, especially the Bank of the United States, Washington looked upon him as one of his most valuable counselors.

Probably Thomas Jefferson was more uncomfortable with this practice of the President than any of the other secretaries. Because of delays in returning to Virginia from Paris and his desire to settle personal matters first, he did not come to the State Department until March, 1790, almost a year after Washington's inauguration. He quickly observed that several foreign policy initiatives were already in train. And in his absence Washington had already developed the habit of getting a broad spectrum of opinion on foreign affairs from Madison, Jay, Knox, and especially Hamilton, who was seeing a significant interdependence between internal economic policies and external relations. It soon became apparent to Jefferson that the President considered foreign affairs so over-riding to the success of his administration that he had assumed the responsibility for foreign policy himself. In actual practice he was his own foreign minister. In time Jefferson found his position untenable and, with a growing sense of frustration, he resigned. As the first Secretary of State, nevertheless, he contributed significantly to the establishment of long-term American practices in the conduct of relations with other nations, and his influence on Washington was far greater than he himself believed.

With Jefferson's belated arrival in New York, Washington's official family was complete, but he was still confronted by a serious administrative problem. The United States government was totally isolated from formal official contacts with other governments, for by his appointment of Jefferson the President had withdrawn the last remaining American from a major diplomatic post. He had been so angry over the insufferable treatment John Adams had received in London that he refused to consider sending a replacement. And in the autumn of 1789 the only European minister in the United States, France's representative, the Comte de Moustier, returned to Paris. True, Britain and France had consuls in American ports, and the United States had a small delegation under a chargé d'affaires in Paris. But no recognized government-to-government exchange of official representatives existed anywhere, an intolerable situation for a new nation facing momentous international difficulties.

During its first session Congress did nothing to alleviate the situation. It took no initiative in directing the President to formalize relations with other governments or in appropriating the necessary funds. On the contrary, support in the House for Madison's nationalistic attempt to establish discrimination in tariff and tonnage duties reflected the strong sentiment still continuing from the Plan of 1776 to remain politically isolated from Europe. If a specific problem arose necessary contacts could be made through the existing 1778 ties with France. Among many of the Senators the feeling was the same. One of them had growled his opposition to "all this kind of gentry, ministers, ambassadors, chargé d'affaires, etc." and demanded "no political connection whatever with any other country whatever."

As strongly nationalistic as any Congressman, Washington nevertheless let his common sense dictate a different approach. Most of the outstanding and more serious difficulties for the United States were with Great Britain. It was inconceivable to postpone their solution by remaining diplomatically isolated from her government. Goaded by his own feelings of national pride, the President did not want his country to appear as a humble petitioner begging at the Court of St. James's. Yet encouraged by strong praise for the Constitution appearing in English newspapers and such comments about him personally as "that most illustrious character," he decided to initiate an informal contact with George III's ministers. He was also encouraged by the arrival in New York of Major George Beckwith, aide to Lord Dorchester, the Governor of Canada. Obviously the King's government itself sought at least an informal contact of its own to bridge the chasm between the two countries. But its intentions were suspect.

So the President decided to send his own personal representative to test the sincerity of British motives. At the urging of Jay and Hamilton (Jefferson was still in France), but without consulting Congress, he dispatched an urgent request in October, 1789, to Gouverneur Morris in Paris. Morris, a New York merchant traveling in Europe on private business, was asked to proceed to England and ascertain "the Sentiments and intention of the Court of London" toward the United States. Morris seemed ideal for the President's purpose. An outspoken Federalist and long-time friend, he was already carrying letters of introduction from Washington and his orders to purchase items for use in the presidential residence. And Washington credited him, too much it would later appear, with sufficient tact and knowledge to speak candidly and privately with the King's ministers about affairs of the new American government. He was expected to determine British willingness to negotiate the still unsettled terms of the Treaty of Peace of 1783, the prospects for a commercial agreement, and the possibility of an exchange of ministers. As the first private and personal presidential representative, Morris could lay the groundwork for a formal and official American diplomatic structure in Europe.

American foreign policy, however, needed something more permanent than the personal diplomacy of a private citizen. In April of 1790, after Jefferson took charge of the State Department—he had two secretaries, two clerks, and a part-time translator—he and Washington began the reorganization of the foreign service. The previous summer the President had sounded out Madison's thoughts on getting "the sense of the Senate" on sending official representatives to Europe. At that time Madison suggested, and now Jefferson and Jay agreed, that the Senate had "no Constitutional right to interfere" with a presidential decision for diplomatic missions. The Senate's only proper role was to confirm or deny specific nominees for appointment, and both houses of Congress, of course, had to appropriate the necessary funds. To press the point further with the legislature might set a dangerous precedent that in the future could hamper presidential initiatives. Such thoughts agreed with Washington's, although he was aware of strong feelings in Congress against such permanent diplomatic missions. He did not want to create unnecessary antagonisms between himself and the Congress, but he was convinced that the power of leadership in foreign affairs had to be in the hands of the executive. This raised yet another and related problem.

What did it actually cost to maintain a mission in a foreign capital? What salaries would be necessary to attract the best qualified individuals to assume these posts? Relying again on the collective opinions of Jay, Jefferson, and Adams, all of whom had had actual experience in the field, he pulled together a budget for the foreign service and sent to Congress a request for an appropriation of $49,000, an amount he considered a bare minimum. Congress established its own pinch-penny precedent by appropriating only $40,000, setting maximum salaries and expenses at $9,000 for a minister, $4,500 for a chargé d'affaires, and $1,300 for a minister's secretary. Congress thus imposed its own influence on foreign policy and obliged the President to trim the extent of his initiatives. With some chagrin but within budget limitations, he sent his first list of nominees to the Senate. This experience taught him some more of the realities of politics within the Congress, and he decided to "intimate to a member or two of the Senate" where he contemplated sending diplomats. Within a year he had the funds necessary to establish missions in Paris, London, Lisbon, Madrid, and The Hague.

While organizing formal government-to-government relations, the President also created the consular service, a structure vital to his hopes of expanding American trade. Since the Revolution the United States did not have at any one time more than two or three consuls with semi-official status in foreign ports, a serious handicap for the merchants of a country with an extensive sea-borne commerce. Under the revised Consular Convention that Jefferson had negotiated with France in 1788 the United States was entitled to more consuls in French continental and West Indies ports than it actually had. But ratification of this agreement had been deliberately delayed by the old Congress of the Confederation, and it literally waited in New York for action by the incoming president. Although he too saw problems lurking in its special privileges for French consuls in America, Washington accepted its terms as the best available under the circumstances. As one of his first official acts he sent it on to the Senate for approval. To implement this agreement and also to expand additional protection for American merchants and ships in foreign ports, in June, 1790, he nominated fourteen men for appointment as American consuls in Europe and the West Indies. In this case, however, he did not have to go to Congress for an appropriation; consuls received no salary. Usually selected from among men already resident in foreign ports and carrying on their own business affairs or from overseas employees of American mercantile houses, consuls received remuneration from fees charged for their services. By confirming this unfortunate practice, Washington unwittingly encouraged procedures that would become embarrassing for the United States throughout the nineteenth century. But it was a common practice for most countries and one that would not add strains to the already delicately balanced budget of the fledgling nation.

Despite the surety of his constitutional position, the support of public opinion, and the structure of a diplomatic service, Washington could not carry out a successful foreign policy without the necessary military power to back up his commitments. This was especially true along the 1,500 mile western frontier where continued Indian depredations had been the most open scandal of the old government. American weakness in the area had been his greatest worry for the survival of the nation. In repeated warnings to friends around the country, he saw the new federal system as the only hope of saving the West. And so his earliest and most vital concern was for the creation of a decent military establishment. The Constitution named him commander in chief, but commander in chief of what? True, Congress in August, 1789, had re-created the War Department, and the Senate had confirmed the reappointment of genial, corpulent Henry Knox as its secretary. At the time, Knox reported that the entire federal military consisted of two companies totalling 76 men, an arsenal at Springfield, Massachusetts, and 596 men stationed at various posts along the Ohio and the Wabash. Washington needed much more than this if he were to assert American sovereignty over the western territories.

But the most Congress provided was authorization for him to call up state militias in case of national emergencies; at best these were unevenly organized, trained, and equipped. He and

Knox wanted a stronger force, and in his first State of the Union Address in January, 1790, he admonished, "To be prepared for war is one of the most effectual means of preserving peace." This first Congress nevertheless still reflected the traditional national distrust of standing armies, fearing perhaps what an ex-general (even one beloved by his people) and a large army could do to their liberties. Congress also reflected the realities of an almost bankrupt government; it balked at Knox's price tag of $1.1 million for 5,000 men as totally impractical. The permanent army would remain small. In the future Washington could expect Congress only to support individual requests to fund specific military operations.

Creation of a foreign service, an organized military establishment, and a national fiscal policy advanced Washington's administration considerably toward its goal of building national unity and earning the respect of nations. Tactfully and cautiously the President grasped the reins of leadership, establishing the traditions of a strong American executive. No great dramatic flourish accompanied this process. Rather, in keeping with his serious-mindedness, Washington followed a methodical, almost plodding approach, confronting the issues one at a time. And to be certain the American people realized at last they had a true national government, he let himself be seen as head of that government by personal tours to the northeastern states in October, 1789, and to the South in March, 1791. When recalcitrant Rhode Island finally ratified the Constitution in May, 1790, he went there as well to welcome that state into the Union. Reasonably satisfied with these accomplishments of his first year, he wrote LaFayette in that stilted style that so often concealed his true feelings, "The principal difficulties which opposed themselves in any shape to the prosperous execution of our Government seem in a great measure to have been surmounted. A good temper prevails among our Citizens."

Having thus secured the popular, constitutional, and economic bases for the strength of his leadership, Washington could turn his attention to the external pressures threatening the security and total sovereignty of his country. The continued geographic encirclement of the United States by a pair of indifferent and antagonistic powers could undo what he and his people had already achieved. The success of his administration, and with it the long-term survival of the federal system, depended heavily on the ability of his foreign policy to dismantle the menace of European influence in the North, the West, and the South.

"... and suffered with Impunity (by J. Britain)"

To see the very real danger to his country and to his administration, all Washington had to do was look at a map of North America. Like the jaws of a giant vise the British to the north and the Spanish to the south exerted tremendous pressure on the territory of the United States. Neither nation had been satisfied with the terms of the treaty that ended the Revolutionary War, and for the following decade both only grudgingly accepted American independence. To the south, Spain continued promoting her goal of an Indian buffer zone between the United States settlements and her own possessions in Louisiana and Florida. Her agents stimulated anti-American hostility among the southern Indians while simultaneously encouraging secessionist tendencies among the settlers on the Tennessee and Cumberland rivers. To the north, along the Great Lakes, Britain clung tenaciously to the trading posts south of the official Canada-United States boundary. British traders kept the Indians of this region in economic bondage to their fur trade by operating out of those posts. Reassured by such protection, roving bands of Miamis and Shawnees raided on both sides of the Ohio, endangering the lives and livelihoods of Americans from Pittsburgh to Louisville. Both countries, with no stated agreement between them, were for all practical purposes engaged in a joint Anglo-Spanish effort to drive the American presence from the entire area west of the Alleghenies. And until the creation of the federal government the United States was too weak to prevent such an event from happening.

Great Britain held the key to open the door for America's control of its own western territory. Although considerably more Americans suffered from Spanish harassment in the Southwest, the British threat north of the Ohio was significantly stronger. Thanks to Britain's superiority in commerce, manufacturing, and naval power it was obviously the senior partner in the unspoken anti-American alliance. If the United States and Great Britain were to settle their outstanding differences, Spain would find herself standing alone; her resistance to America's authority in its own Southwest would crumble. If the United States was to prove to a doubting world the effectiveness of its new government, it must first gain the respect, however reluctant, of its most potent adversary. To do so successfully Washington and his advisers had to have a clear understanding of both the strengths and the weaknesses of post-war Britain.

As might be expected, Great Britain was a poor loser in the war for American independence. But the haphazard coalition of powers arrayed against her had barely beaten her, and her commercial empire was still intact. When the mild-mannered and generous Shelbourne fell from power in 1784, his policies of accommodation with the United States were abruptly repudiated. Under the influence of Lord Sheffield, at the time chairman of the Board of Trade, the British government developed a hard line of reaction to the Americans. His pamphlet, *Observations on the Commerce of the American States*, aroused the English people from their doldrums with well reasoned arguments on the superiority of British commerce and manufacturing to effect a quick recovery. He predicted, and for a time he was correct, that pre-war American dependence on the British economy would quickly reassert itself and Britain would suffer no serious commercial loss. He also predicted, and once or twice he might have been correct, that the American union was so weak that pieces of it would break off and seek readmission to the Empire. Sheffield touched a vein of popular reaction, and his ideas gained widespread acceptance.

Official concurrence with these ideas came from England's new prime minister, William Pitt the Younger. Second son of Lord Chatham, "the Great Commoner," Pitt was trained for politics by his father, who saw quite early the boy's natural abilities. Accepting office at the age of twenty-three, the younger Pitt had by the mid-1780s developed a successful working relationship with George III that was to last, with but one brief interval, for twenty years. His aim was to rebuild Britain's commercial empire and to extend it into every corner of the world. In the process, significantly, the British navy would be strengthened in its ability to defend the empire against any and all challenges. Pitt surrounded himself with a cabinet dedicated to the same purposes.

His administration attempted to push its nation's commerce into totally new endeavors. Thanks to the explorations of Captain James Cook, British seamen and merchants soon realized the fantastic trade potential of the Pacific Ocean. Huge herds of whales were sighted throughout its southern waters. Along the northwest coast of North America from San Francisco to the Aleutian Islands, an enormous population of seal and sea-otter waited to be slaughtered for their skins, so highly prized by the Chinese. With the British toe-hold in India already expanded to a tentative control of the entire subcontinent, the China market now beckoned with its lure of even greater profits. East of China more profits waited in the untapped resources and underdeveloped markets of the archipelagoes scattered from Australia to Japan. Pacific trade would easily offset losses resulting from American independence, and exploitation of its vast potential assured the continued growth of the imperial economy.

Visions of similar commercial profits fascinated other European nations as well. Spain occupied the Philippines; Portugal held tiny enclaves on the Asian coast; France operated from strategically located ports. French merchants had begun their century-long penetration of Siam and Cochin China. And Dutch merchants, dominating the Indonesian islands, monopolized the spice trade and enjoyed the only European contact with Japan. Dutch possessions straddled the sea-lanes to China, most significantly the important route from India to Canton through the Strait of Malacca, that vital narrow waterway between Sumatra and the Malay Peninsula.

Pitt's commercial ambitions were most threatened by the Dutch position in the Pacific. By themselves the Dutch were not dangerous, but their friends were. Allied with France in the recent American war, the United Provinces of the Netherlands still continued under strong French influence. And in the always present possibility of another Anglo-French war, French troops could easily occupy the Dutch East Indies and quickly throttle Britain's Pacific trade routes. To hedge against this possibility Pitt wanted from the Dutch an island off Malay at the eastern end of the Malaccan Strait. Here Britain could open a new door to East Indian commerce and develop a safe harbor on the way to Canton from India.

But to accomplish this Pitt's ministry was forced to fish in the muddy waters of Dutch politics. A convenient civil war broke out in the United Provinces as discontented unemployed workers backed the hereditary Stadholder's challenge to the leadership of a pro-French clique of merchants and bankers. By tradition the Stadholder's family had been pro-English, and the civil unrest in Holland presented a golden opportunity to advance English policy. Aided by a Prussian army, the English intervened. The result was an Anglo-Prussian-Dutch treaty guaranteeing the Stadholder's position and with it a pro-British direction in Dutch foreign policy.

Meanwhile the English watched nervously as another ambitious monarch, Catherine of Russia, embarked on a new war with Turkey. Intending to drive the Turks from the Black Sea, her dream was to establish a Russian puppet empire at Constantinople. From here Russian influence could pour out into the Eastern Mediterranean and compete with the English in Egypt and in the rest of the Middle East. This worried England because a weak and compliant Turkey was an effective shield for British commerce in the area. Fortunately, for Pitt's government at least, bad wheat harvests in the Ukraine cut short Catherine's southward advance. Yet the vision of the awakening Russian bear haunted the dreams of the British lion.

While Pitt's government tried to hold off potential competitors and push British commerce into totally new areas, it also encouraged expansion of its historic contacts in other parts of the world. Attention was refocused on the west coast of Africa and especially on the strategically located Cape of Good Hope. On the other side of the south Atlantic increased pressure was exerted to break up further Spain's theoretical monopoly of Spanish American trade. British ship captains continued their challenge of Spain's paper control of the Gulf of Mexico and the Caribbean Sea, especially in the lucrative mahogany trade of the Honduran coast. And in the Floridas, given back to Spain after the treaty of 1783, an English company, Panton & Leslie, actually expanded its traffic with southern Indians for hides and deerskins. Britain saw no reason to concede Caribbean commerce to the Spaniards, or, for that matter, to the Americans.

Behind this resurgence of England's commerce stood her retrenched and revitalized traditional system of mercantilism, now made stronger by more efficient navigation acts designed to prevent future recurrences of the debacle of the American Revolution. American secession had meant the loss of approximately a third of the British merchant marine, and with it the loss of a substantial number of sailors available for wartime navy service. Frightening thoughts of a weakened navy forced Pitt's government to fall back on the time-honored doctrine in traditional mercantilism that a strong merchant marine was the nursery of seamen for the navy. Encouraged by the rational but reactionary arguments of Sheffield, it took stringent steps to insure the British mercantile fleet would continue as the exclusive carrier of intra-Empire trade. Through specific acts of Parliament it prohibited all foreign shipping from calling at colonial ports, redefined British ships as those built in English shipyards, and set up a central registry in London for all vessels larger than fifteen tons. This last was an indirect acknowledgment of the genius in smuggling of American ship captains who carried both American and British registry.

With an eye to its own opportunities within the American market and without a formal commercial treaty with the United States, Pitt's government granted most-favored-nation privileges to American ships carrying American produce from the United States into English ports. It also permitted the sale of American goods in colonial ports, but in keeping with the spirit of the navigation acts, these products had to be carried in British bottoms. Despite such minor concessions the restrictive dogmas of mercantilism pervaded British commerce again by the mid-80s. Even the surprisingly liberal Eden Treaty, a reciprocal trade agreement negotiated with France in 1786, strengthened trade controls elsewhere.

With such global imperial interests at stake, Britain's problems with the United States would seem as nothing more noxious than a swarm of gnats. And to an extent this was true; there were far more significant issues elsewhere. George III's adamant refusal to accredit his own minister to the United

States indicated what a low opinion he and his government had of the new republic. Yet almost every action the British took somehow exacerbated the still unstable peace between the two countries, heightening anti-British sentiment in the United States as well as anti-American disgust in England. In a variety of areas and in a multitude of ways British policies increased the friction existing as an expected and normal legacy for the war. Each slight seemed to the Americans to be a deliberate attempt to antagonize them. And each must be seen as contributing to the impossibly low level of Anglo-American relations at the time Washington became President.

Britain's attempt to overcome her embarrassing dependence on the American whaling industry was one such policy. Before the war the English market for spermaceti oil was supplied almost exclusively by American colonials encouraged by a protected market and a generous imperial bounty. Operating out of New England ports, these Americans developed specific ship design and unique nautical skills quite different from other forms of seamanship. England herself had less than thirty whaling vessels, manned mostly by foreigners; whaling was not an effective art of England's maritime industry. Yet spermaceti oil was becoming increasingly important to the English economy, both as an illuminant brighter and more efficient than candles and as a lubricant for the new machines of its expanding number of factories. To remove its reliance on foreign oil, anathema to mercantilist dogma, the British government sought to create a domestic whaling industry. It withdrew the subsidy, closed the home market to foreign importers, and through a new set of subsidies sought to attract European and American whaleboat owners and their crews to settle in England.

The effect of this policy was disaster for the American whaling industry. Hundreds of whaleboats rotted at their wharves while thousands of seamen were u~ ·mployed. On

Nantucket Island, where the entire population of 5,000 depended on the industry, the economic depression was complete. In desperation some of the islanders seriously considered secession from the Union, but only a handful migrated to England. Britain's shortsighted policy wrecked the American whaling industry and did little to create one of its own. The heavy duty on imported oil raised the price in the English market but did not stimulate domestic production, while the government subsidy to lure foreign whalers to England was far more expensive than was originally intended.

Unfortunately for Anglo-American relations, Pitt's government followed similar reasoning in its solution to the problem of supplying the British West Indies. In the process it almost bankrupted the islands' sugar economy. For over a century the West Indian islands had been one of the major objects of the international scramble for colonies. Their extensive production of cane sugar molasses was shipped to the mother country to be refined into coarse brown lump sugar or distilled into rum, a valuable exchange item in the African slave trade. Because profits were high, the islands, regardless of who owned them, developed a one-crop economy and depended heavily on outsiders for provisions. Needing lumber for building, barrel staves to ship the molasses, cheap grades of salted fish and meat for the slaves, and better quality foodstuffs, furniture, and textiles for the white population, they found their biggest suppliers were colonial New Englanders. Indeed by the eve of the Revolution, the Yankees had an almost exclusive monopoly of this trade with the British islands and, when no governing official was looking, that of the Spanish, French, and Dutch islands as well. A substantial part of the New England economy—its shipping, its fishing, its shipyards—rested solidly on the West Indies trade. Some American ports developed specialized services for this trade. Connecticut, for example, had a sizeable fleet of ships especially designed to carry livestock; even much of her agriculture was devoted to the breeding of carriage and riding horses to be sold to the sugar cane planters.

After the war, England shut off this trade to the Americans with catastrophic effect on the New England economy. Similar to conditions in the whaling industry, the depression hit the fishing fleets, the merchantmen, and the shipyards. Even concessions for American shipping to the French islands provided under the Franco-American agreement of 1778 were not enough to offset the losses from the much larger trade with the British planters. New England's John Adams, America's minister in London, pleaded desperately for a commercial treaty which would reopen this vital trade to the Americans.

While they were a reassertion of traditional mercantilism, Britain's new policies, nevertheless, created economic chaos in the sugar islands themselves. Without the necessary supplies from New England the sugar economy quickly broke down, forcing the powerful West Indies lobby in London to challenge the government and demand relief. In response, Pitt's ministry effected a two-pronged compromise. For the short-term, through an Order-in-Council, the King permitted some American ships to enter the trade for emergency relief. The volume of American shipping would be at the discretion of the individual islands' governors, who could more easily ascertain local needs. And for the long term, the government planned to develop Canada and the maritime provinces of New Brunswick and Nova Scotia to replace New England as suppliers to the West Indian plantations. Quebec's governor, Sir Guy Carleton, raised to a peerage in 1786 as Lord Dorchester, rashly promised that with encouragement from the Imperial government in three years Canada would be able to supply all of the West Indian needs. Thanks to the over-exaggerated reports on Canada's potential, neither Dorchester nor his superiors in London recognized that it would take thirty years, not three, to develop the Canadian economy sufficiently. In the meantime, Orders-in-Council permitted temporary infractions of the navigation acts and slightly reopened the trade to Americans. But the trade was so tenuous that New Englanders continued to press for a formal agreement regularizing their position. Despite this, it was sufficiently profitable that enough American shippers were sucked into the practice to cause an eventual crisis in Anglo-American relations.

In still another area Britain's attempts to overcome mistakes of the past and foster more stringent controls over vital industry stimulated additional dissension within the United States. She sought to monopolize the lucrative fishing industry along the Grand Banks off the coast of Newfoundland. For generations English fishermen and their North American cousins, with some competition from the French and Scandinavians, shared this almost inexhaustible resource of food. Together they supplied the colonial and English domestic markets as well as a substantial portion of the European, especially in the Catholic countries of the south. Fishing along the Banks, however, also meant beaching the fishing boat in a convenient bay or inlet and on shore cutting, curing, salting, and packing the fish to be carried to the consumer. With unlimited access to these bays as well as to the fishing grounds themselves, the colonial fishermen through the years competed successfully with their counterparts in England. After independence, the British government intended to restrict or eliminate the New Englanders, and at the same time prevent the rise of any new colonial challenge to the English fisherman's monopoly. The Peace Treaty of 1783 promised the Americans the "privilege" of fishing in the area but said nothing about access to ports, bays, and inlets. So British policy aimed at restricting American access to shore facilities, a policy the Americans considered as harassment and violation of their "right" to make a living from the sea.

Such attitudes were the natural result of Pitt's aggressive leadership for the rebuilding of the British Empire. His global perspective committed the British boldly and sometimes courageously to poke into every corner of world affairs while in the process of reasserting their role as the leading commercial nation. Putting his policy and program into practice naturally aggravated poor relations with other countries as well as with the United States. But what might appear as relatively minor issues to his government were of momentous importance for the young nation. Even as reviving the principles of mercantilism tended to shut out American commerce and fishing, other attempts to promote British self-interest were equally damaging to American national security. Nowhere else were these more apparent than in the raw North American wilderness separating His Majesty's dominions from those of the United States.

Insisting that the United States had not fulfilled its part of the treaty of 1783, Britain's government refused to honor its commitments as well. At that time her negotiators in Paris were adamant that British creditors be allowed to collect debts from Americans. Most notably from Maryland and Virginia tobacco planters, these debts had accumulated to them during the years before the war. And in a rare humanitarian impulse the King had wanted the Loyalists returned to their homes or compensated for their confiscated properties. The miserable fate of some 50,000 of these hapless refugees angered the English, who believed the Loyalists had been the victims of overzealous American patriots merely on the basis of principle. Actually only a few had actively opposed the Revolution, and the King felt a strong moral obligation to protect their interests.

In accepting the peace treaty, Congress had promised to recommend to the states that no "impediment" should prevent creditors from suing to collect their legitimate debts or for Loyalists to recover their property. Unfortunately, under the Confederation, the treaty was not necessarily binding on the individual states. Almost from the beginning British merchants complained bitterly that they did not receive fair treatment in state courts, and state legislatures refused restitution for the few bold refugees who dared return or attempt to recover their property.

Despising a government too weak to enforce its own treaty obligations, the British ministry retaliated. It refused promised compensation to American planters for several thousand slaves British armies had captured in the South during the War. These slaves were not returned after the peace was signed, and their loss was a severe financial hardship to many of the farmers, some of whom were also the same planters in debt to English creditors. The value of the slaves was far less than the total amount of the accumulated pre-war debts, and until the latter were paid no consideration would be made for the former.

More menacing, however, was Britain's equally adamant refusal to hand over to the Americans with "all due speed" the seven fortified trading posts clearly located within territory granted to the United States. On the contrary, they strengthened the garrisons at these posts and later built another south of Detroit. Located on the southern side of the St. Lawrence-Great Lakes boundary between Canada and the United States, these posts were vital to the fur trading system centered in Montreal. Indian tribes in the area were completely dependent on this trade. Doing their trapping within United States territory they exchanged pelts with English and Scottish traders at the posts for necessary English-made items, including traps, guns, and ammunition. British influence over the Indians radiated beyond each of the posts and was so pervasive that American sovereignty was nonexistent along the vast, northwestern frontier that stretched from Lake Champlain to Lake Michigan.

Voluble fur merchants in London, fearing substantial losses, caused the government to have second thoughts about this liberal territorial cession to the Americans which contained such profitable fur resources. According to James McGill, the principal trader at Detroit, of the £180,000 in furs taken through Montreal "£100,000 value I think is brought from the Country now within the American Line as fixed by the late treaty of Peace." With encouragement from their Canadian partners some of the London merchants visualized an Indian hunting ground extending south to the Ohio River and protected from the ravages of advancing American settlement that would surely destroy the natural environment and with it the fur trade itself. A generous few even proposed a joint Anglo-American administration of the region, suggesting that merchants from both countries could trade freely. The British government did not go that far, but it did excuse the delay in withdrawing on the excuse that the Americans obviously were unable to take over effective responsibility of the posts. Maintaining peace and stability on both sides of the international boundary would require American garrisons at the posts and American traders to continue the flow of trade goods to the Indians. The bankrupt Confederation had no troops available for this duty, nor was there a sufficient American fur trading industry to supplant the British. Pitt's ministry knew if it did withdraw its troops it would create a political and economic vacuum causing the Indians to go on a rampage. It waited, therefore, to see what the Americans would do, and in the meantime enjoyed the profits of the trade. Unless its government could gain sufficient strength, the United States risked losing a quarter of its territory by default.

Farther east along the border Britain's threat was almost as severe. While the British were fishing in the troubled waters of Dutch politics, they also wetted a line in those of Vermont. An anomaly for the United States, Vermont was neither state nor organized territory. Caught up in the vagaries and inaccuracies of the antique colonial charters of New York and New Hampshire, the region was claimed by both states. Settlers from one state armed with land grants or bills of sale from their own state government poured into Vermont valleys often to discover their land was already occupied by immigrants similarly armed from the other state. Claim jumping and forcible dispossession were bringing the countryside close to civil war. Since neither state moved in to establish jurisdiction and Congress was unable or unwilling to interfere, Vermonters took matters into their own hands and the movement for separate Vermont nationalism was born. Led by Levi, Ira, and Ethan Allen, those Revolutionary War heroes whose Green Mountain Boys had flanked into disaster Burgoyne's invasion of New York in 1777, negotiations were opened with the British in Quebec and then in London.

As early as November, 1784, Ira Allen had appeared in Montreal claiming that the freemen of Vermont had declared "an independent and sovereign state." He proposed a commercial treaty between Vermont and Great Britain. The idea intrigued Canada's Governor, who was increasingly embarrassed because of Canadian inability to fulfill his brash promise of replacing New England as the supplier to West Indies plantations. On the contrary, bad harvests had forced Canadians to import food from the United States. Although not wanting to give "umbrage to the United States," colonial officials treated Allen "with attention and civility." Governor Dorchester, unsure of himself and worried about growing instability all along the border, kept the door open over the next two years by conversations with all three Allen brothers. While waiting instructions from London, his Legislative Council bent British navigation laws enough to permit commerce from Vermont to come up Lake Champlain and down the Richelieu River to Montreal.

Pitt's ministry, under pressure from London merchants trading with Canada, followed a policy of watch and wait. It confirmed Canada's limited trade with Vermont but not by a formal agreement, even after Levi Allen arrived in London in late 1788 to press the issue. It considered a separate treaty "entirely out of the question," while it evaluated the process of ratification of the new American Constitution. And it ignored Dorchester's encouraging opinion of October, 1788, that the inhabitants of Vermont, well aware of the potential change of government in the United States, "seemed determined to remain in their present unconnected situation and if hard pressed they will defend their country by arms."

Yet the prospect of new British trade with the growing number of interior settlements could not be ignored. After several years of investigation, the Lords of Trade as late as April, 1790, reported to Lord Grenville, then Britain's Home Secretary, that an agreement with Vermont could easily offend the United States but "in a commercial view it will be for the benefit of this country to prevent Vermont and Kentucke, and all other settlements now forming in the Interior part of the Great Continent of North America from becoming dependent on the Goverment of the United States . . . and to preserve them on the contrary in a state of independence and to induce them to form Treaties of Commerce with Great Britain." Despite this arrogant advice, Pitt's government hesitated too long and lost its opportunity. While the Allens were away intriguing in Montreal and London an anti-Allen faction pushed through the Vermont legislature a resolution to seek admission to the American Union.

To the east of the hotbed of Vermont, Anglo-American interests also clashed over the Maine-New Brunswick border. At best a vague line running along misidentified rivers flowing through the thick forest wilderness, the border was under dispute as a result of inaccurate geographic descriptions used for the peace treaty of 1783. The issue was not so much land itself, but potential use of good harbors and the ambitions of unscrulous land speculators from both Nova Scotia and Massachusetts trying to promote settlements in the disputed area. Although the problem was complicated and took years to solve, its significance paled compared with more fundamental national differences. But continued dissatisfactions in Halifax and in Boston added to the growing distrust in the relations between the two countries.

Britain's adamant refusal to negotiate all of these issues and many others affecting the American economy fitted her overall scheme of retrenchment following the war. No wonder John Adams bitterly considered his mission in London a failure. Lord Sheffield and his cohorts in England's business community had done their job well. Their ideas, expressed in newspaper articles, pamphlets, committee reports, and petitions to cabinet and Parliament, had convinced the English people that commercial expansion protected by strict mercantilist policies would restore national prosperity. Sheffield's own facts and figures cited in his *Observations on the Trade with the American States* were remarkably accurate forecasts of how conditions in the American economy would benefit Britain's prosperity. The Eden Treaty, an Anglo-French reciprocal trade agreement negotiated in 1786, was meant to open for England new markets in France and on the continent. How successful it would have been will never be known; within three years France was plunged into an internal political crisis that violently unhinged her economy. The Eden Treaty was not a break with traditional British mercantilism but an answer to the seemingly dangerous American ideas of free trade among nations.

To say the least, by 1789 Anglo-American relations had deteriorated dangerously for both American economic prosperity and national security. When Adams returned in disgust to the United States to participate in the new government, all formal contact between the two countries was broken off.

President Washington inherited this legacy of bitterness and misunderstanding in Anglo-American relations. Too American to look objectively at British policies, he shared the general dislike and distrust of British intentions. He was delighted when in its first session the House of Representatives passed anti-British discriminatory tariff and tonnage duties, and furious when the more rational Senate refused to concur. Yet he was too shrewd, too full of common sense, to beat his breast in defiance of the British predator. Instead, he recognized all too clearly the inherent weaknesses of the American position, even now under the potentially strong but untried new federal system. He moved so cautiously that he often exasperated his most ardent supporters.

He saw clearly, too, that the Indian threat along the western frontier was strong because it received encouragement from both Britain and Spain. He recognized easily that both European countries were able to promote their own interests in the American West precisely because the Indians checked the advance of American settlement. The Indians would continue to hold the advantage as long as the Europeans exploited the absence of American authority west of the Alleghenies. Closely tied to the Indian problem and of even greater significance was the fact that the American people would not respect their new federal government until its authority extended to the farthest corner of American territory and the governments of Britain and Spain were forced to recognize that authority. The interlocking interests of the two European powers and the Indians of the American West were the greatest threat to the survival of his country.

For Washington this must have appeared to be an insurmountable problem. Because Congress had not and at the time could not give him sufficient military forces to exert the government's jurisdiction over the West, the Indian confederations could defy that authority with impunity. This is why he warned in his first State of the Union message, January 8, 1790, that "to be prepared for war is one of the most effectual means of preserving peace." And at the same time his inability to coerce the Indians made dim the prospects of any successful negotiations of outstanding differences with the governments in London and Madrid. In his diplomacy with the Indians and with the British and the Spanish, he was operating from an unenviably weak bargaining position.

Proud and sensitive as an American, he was not intimidated by the hopeless situation. Nor did he share the haunting fear of many Americans that overt action against the Indians might engender retaliations from the British or the Spanish or both. Instead, with no grandiose overall plan in mind, carefully but quickly he moved American diplomatic and military policy simultaneously in two directions.

First, his government began negotiations with the Indians to effect an armistice in the continuous border wars between red raiding parties and white settlers. It considered the Indian confederations as nations instead of bands of savage interlopers on American soil. He hoped through diplomacy, tact, and flattery to work out a series of treaties clearly defining boundaries between Indian hunting grounds and American agricultural settlement. To reach such an accommodation the government would offer to buy large slices of land from the Indians and make these areas available for controlled American settlement. By sending General Benjamin Lincoln to the Creek villages in the autumn of 1789 he started this slow and patient process of treaty-making. Then he instructed General Josiah Harmar at Fort Harmar (Marietta, Ohio) to reopen negotiations with the Shawnee, Miami, and other tribes north of the Ohio for a specific line in that region.

Second, the President set out to find the means of establishing—or re-establishing—normal diplomatic contacts with Great Britain. He took the first step in September, 1789, through Acting Minister of Foreign Affairs John Jay, who formally requested permission from Lord Dorchester for an American surveyor to enter Canada to make astronomical observations for an accurate survey of the Canadian-American border. Neither Jay nor Washington was aware of the positive reaction of the surprised Dorchester, who reported to London "the President's disposition to promote an Interchange of friendly Offices between the two Nations." Jay's polite and friendly request had the desired effect in smoothing somewhat the turbulence separating the two countries.

Unwittingly, perhaps, the British aided Washington in deciding on the next step. Worried about the long-term impact of Madison's aborted attempt to secure passage of anti-British commercial legislation, the government requested from Sir John Temple, its consul in New York, information about the American economy, population, and attitude toward Great Britain. Temple was shrewd enough to see this request as the ministry's possible opening for establishing formal relations with the American government, and so he reported the substance of the request to Jay, who in turn informed Washington. In the meantime Dorchester was equally uneasy over possible intentions toward Canada of the new leadership of the United States. Jay's letter on behalf of the American surveyor quieted his immediate fears but did not remove his apprehension.

Like Washington, Dorchester was governing from a semi-rural capital and had responsibility for the defenses of a far-flung scattering of isolated settlements. He also suffered from agonizing delays in getting accurate information, most of which came to him via London. Rumors about conditions along the Canadian-American frontier traveled much faster through the wilderness than did official reports. If the new Washington administration had hostile or aggressive designs toward the British position on that frontier, he needed to know, and his need to know prompted him again to send his aide-de-camp, Major George Beckwith, to New York.

Returning to Canada through the United States after a leave in England, Beckwith landed in New York in late September, 1789. Ostensibly one of the many foreign officers traveling about the new country to satisfy their own curiosity, Beckwith secured comfortable lodgings and settled in for a longer stay than most tourists. Almost immediately he began contacting important Americans he knew were friendly toward Britain. To them he carried a warning from Home Secretary William Grenville that commercial retaliation might result if Madison's ideas on discrimination were adopted. Meeting with Alexander Hamilton he also let it be known that the British government wanted to minimize its differences with the United States. Freely admitting he was Lord Dorchester's confidential agent, Beckwith found several sympathetic Americans who were willing to discuss Canadian-American problems and who hoped that his reports to Quebec might reduce the apprehension and distrust between the United States and its northern neighbor.

Most of his contacts did not know that Beckwith was an experienced intelligence officer rather than an innocent messenger. During the Revolutionary War he had been coordinator of the British Army's intelligence operations in New York for Dorchester, then General Sir Guy Carleton, the Army's commander. In 1787 he had returned to New York when Dorchester worried in Montreal about unconfirmed rumors of an organized invasion north of the Ohio by armed Kentucky settlers. Beckwith was to find out if there was a genuine anti-British threat within the Confederation's government. When he came again in September, 1789, the issue was Washington's known open hostility to British occupation of the frontier posts. This time, because of the stronger federal government, the concerns for Britain were far more important than Canadian-American border problems. For information, Beckwith ingratiated himself with a small group of Congressional and administration officials who in time would become leaders of the Federalist party in House and Senate. Their candid expressions of pro-British bias so startled him that he felt it necessary to identify his informants by code in his dispatches to Dorchester. On his initial interview he gave each individual a number, and in all subsequent references he identified each informant by this number. When he left New York in early November he had already made nine such designations. Dorchester was equally startled at Beckwith's successful penetration of the inner councils of the American government, and he sent copies of the Major's reports to Secretary Grenville, including a separate letter marked "Private" that gave the key to the number code. With surprising ease over the next two years Beckwith would in this fashion identify twenty-three prominent Americans as sources of information. His ability to gain the confidence of the "right" people in the United States was so important that he returned briefly to New York in the Spring of 1790 and for a much longer stay the following July, when he would play out his true role as the British king's spy at the court of the American president.

Washington was also deceived about the true nature of Beckwith's purpose; at least he gave no indication of being suspicious. He remembered meeting the Major in New York in 1783 when arrangements were being made for the final withdrawal of the British army after the war. He met him again only twice, briefly, in October 1789. At that time the President was designated "Number 3" on the coded list of conversations. Even when Beckwith bobbed up again in 1790 Washington still considered him the personal representative of the Canadian governor. The President never knew of the long series of intimate conversations his own Secretary of the Treasury had

with the British major nor that private discussions of his cabinet would be quickly reported to London. He viewed the man's
appearance in New York as an example of the way he might
begin establishing formal diplomatic contact with Britain.
Shortly after Beckwith's arrival in New York, Washington decided to send his own personal representative to London.

When he asked Gouverneur Morris to assume this task,
the President had followed the advice of Jay and Hamilton, but
rejected that of Madison. Because Washington had already
nominated Thomas Jefferson as Secretary of State, Madison
cautioned him that an important contact in London, even
though informal, should be directed by the State Department.
He also warned that if he were to name a minister to England,
Morris would have a prior claim and expect the appointment.
But waiting for Jefferson would mean postponing action for at
least six months. Washington did not want to delay that long,
for he was most anxious to determine the British government's
attitude toward his new administration. He did not, furthermore, see as clearly as Madison what was happening within his
official family. Hamilton and a group of commerce-minded
northern Senators and Congressmen were pushing a pro-
British direction in American foreign policy. Whether from
personal conviction or simple naiveté Washington let this happen. The Morris appointment was the first step in that direction, for the New Yorker's background, experience, and thinking fitted into this pattern. Actually, Washington wrote both
Jefferson and Morris on the same day, October 13, 1789, asking
them to accept their respective appointments; obviously he was
not concerned for Jefferson's opinion on this particular matter.

In his instructions the President asked Morris "to converse with his Brittanic Majesty's Ministers" to determine
"whether there be any and what Objections to now performing
those Articles in the [Peace] Treaty, which remain to be per-
formed on his Part: and whether they incline to a Treaty of

Commerce with the United States on any and what Terms." In a separate and more confidential letter he urged Morris to inform the King's ministers that the new American Constitution created a system of courts where British creditors finally could get adjudication for their legitimate claims. He insisted this "removes the objection heretofore made to putting the United States in possession of their frontier posts." In these letters Washington's tone was certainly not a hard line toward Great Britain, but rather an expression of his willingness to establish relations with "perfect and mutual Good Faith."

Morris delayed in Paris and did not reach London until late March, 1790. His first meeting with Foreign Secretary Carmarthen, now the Duke of Leeds, on the 27th was cordial and held out the promise of positive achievement. In later sessions, however, he overemphasized what he considered American advantages and too lightly tossed off still significant British concerns. In particular he ignored their insistence that new federal courts did not necessarily guarantee payment of all the pre-war debts. He was, moreover, indiscreet. Even before he met Leeds, Morris had called upon the French Ambassador, Chevalier La Lucerne, and during his six months in London he was often in the company of members of the Opposition, seemingly enlisting their support for his mission. None of this endeared him to Pitt and Leeds, and their willingness to deal with him as a negotiator gradually dissipated. Because of his narrow pro-American stand he misread British intentions toward the United States. He saw in their refusal to discuss in detail a commercial agreement or the withdrawal of troops from the frontier posts an indication, as he reported to the President in September, of their unwillingness "to treat with us at present."

Morris' inability to understand the British position was in part caused by the unfortunate timing of his mission. His appearance in London coincided with an awkward moment in Anglo-Spanish relations, a situation fraught with potential danger to the United States. Morris arrived at the start of a war scare that was to heighten in intensity until midsummer. Under the circumstances the British government did not want an antagonist to threaten one of its colonies, but rather an ally to assure the safety of that colony. His almost belligerent attitude appeared to Pitt's cabinet as an American attempt to take advantage of Britain's looming crisis.

Spain had challenged Britain's commercial thrust into the Pacific at a region far distant from London, Madrid, or New York. In an isolated inlet on the west side of Vancouver Island, known as Nootka Sound, a Spanish man-of-war seized an English merchantman trading with the Indians for seal and sea-otter skins to be used in the China trade. Three times previously the Spanish navy had warned off British traders, insisting that the entire Pacific coast of North America belonged to their king. But through direct intervention at Nootka they now risked war to protect a claim staked out 200 years earlier by Spanish explorers on behalf of Philip II. War became an increasing possibility as "Nootka" was heard as a rallying cry for British national pride.

Not only an affront to British nationalism, it was a setback to Pitt's ambitions for a commercial empire in the Pacific. The Spanish government had already strengthened its hold on part of the coast by encouraging Father Junípero Serra in the building of his famous chain of missions extending northward from Baja California to San Francisco Bay. If left unchallenged, Spain's antique claims might prevent English exploitation of seal skins as a popular item needed to pry open the door to trade with China. Pitt was, therefore, willing to take risks, and he received the first report of the incident at Nootka in mid-March, only a few days before Gouverneur Morris arrived in London. By May the angry ministry ordered a press of seamen for the Navy, the first step in mobilization.

In New York, an apprehensive American government

faced the horrible prospect of a war between its northern and southern neighbors. Too many possible actions of the belligerents could easily threaten the United States. As usual, the greatest threat was posed by Great Britain. Unconfirmed rumors from the West reported increases in British garrisons at the frontier posts. Because of historic British ambition to control the Mississippi Valley, the possibility of Redcoats massing in western Canada for an invasion to seize New Orleans was ominous. Even worse, what if an aggressive British navy seized the Floridas from Spain? In answer, the most pessimistic analysis saw a successful Britain totally encircling the United States along its entire continental boundary. Even the most optimistic agreed that a war between Spain and England would be fought in part in the American West. The simple incident at remote Nootka triggered anew the century-old rivalry between the British and Spanish empires, and the United States was caught in the middle.

Haunted by this threatening situation, Washington sought advice from the most knowledgeable Americans in government. Would British troops in Canada invade United States territory to attack Spanish garrisons on the lower Mississippi, or would they ask American permission first? In either case what should be the American response? If Spain invoked the Bourbon Family Compact and forced France into the war, would the United States be dragged in under the terms of the Franco-American Alliance of 1778? These hard questions could not be answered easily. Unfortunately, Washington's advisers, Hamilton, Jefferson, Knox, Adams, and Jay, did not agree on what to expect from the British or how the United States should respond. They offered divided counsel and left him with the lonely conclusion that any decision he made would be difficult and cause dissatisfaction with many groups within the Union.

While Washington fretted about his options, in July, Major Beckwith reappeared in New York. Almost immediately he contacted Hamilton and intimated that Great Britain was willing to negotiate a commercial agreement and an alliance. When questioned about his authority for such a bold proposal, Beckwith rather arrogantly replied that Lord Dorchester knew the wishes of the British cabinet. When Hamilton reported the interview to Washington and Jefferson, the President was suspicious and refused the British bait. The last thing he wanted was to become entangled in a European power struggle, and the offer confirmed his distrust of the British. Although he and his Secretary of State were now convinced that English perfidy had tied the much desired commercial treaty to an unwanted anti-Spanish alliance, both were misinformed as to British intentions. Either Beckwith had exceeded his instructions from Dorchester, or Hamilton had misreported them. Beckwith's unofficial status prevented him from meeting with the President, and he met only casually with the Secretary of State. So the flow of information between Beckwith and Washington came only through Hamilton, a situation that Jefferson found increasingly intolerable.

It was obvious now even to Washington that Beckwith's role was something more than that of a personal agent of Canada's governor. It was equally obvious that Pitt's cabinet in London did not want to deal with Gouverneur Morris. The ministry's procrastination from March to July in answering Morris' questions on policy greatly frustrated Washington's efforts at normalizing relations. Instead of the proffered semi-official channel of communication, Morris-Jefferson-Washington, they preferred their own, totally unofficial but safer and more sympathetic line, Dorchester-Beckwith-Hamilton-Washington. Beckwith's surprising success in insinuating himself among the Federalist leadership in the autumn of 1789 had been repeated the following March when he returned to New York to reassure Dorchester on the purpose of American troop concentration in the Ohio country. By mid-summer of 1790 his well-cultivated contacts were too valuable for the British to ignore for determining future directions of American policies. Accordingly he was ordered to remain in New York as long as he would be of "use to the King." In essence, until the British ministry determined otherwise, Beckwith functioned as a non-accredited minister to the United States, a situation satisfactory enough to meet all of Britain's current needs.

President Washington accepted Beckwith's presence but did not like it. He would have been even more apprehensive had he known how well the Major was penetrating his administration. While he worried about possible British invasion of American territory, he would have been surprised to know that Dorchester agonized over the weakness of Canadian defenses if the United States should take advantage of the Nootka war scare. He did, however, assure Dorchester, through Hamilton and Beckwith, that the United States had no commitments to Spain and no threatening intentions toward British troops in the frontier forts. He was not convinced by Beckwith's denials to Hamilton that the British were not inciting the Indians.

Emboldened by wilderness rumors of war between Spain and England, these Indians felt no restraints on raiding south across the Ohio. They brought death and destruction to Americans on both sides of the river and so unsettled the West that Kentuckians demanded immediate retaliation. If Washington's administration was to mean anything, he had to take action despite the momentary delicacy in international relations and the risk of British misinterpretation. Quietly he directed Arthur St. Clair, Governor of the Northwest Territory, to call up the militia from neighboring states to augment the small contingent of regulars stationed at Fort Washington (Cincinnati). Under the command of General Josiah Harmar these combined forces were to make a punitive thrust at the center of

Indian strength, the Miami and Shawnee villages in the Maumee river region south and west of Lake Erie.

While Harmar's preparations were afoot, the Nootka Sound crisis was solved in Madrid and not in the wilderness of the American West. Spain found herself all alone confronting the might of the British navy. Expected assistance from the French navy was now impossible as her ally weakened under pressures of revolution. France's Louis XVI had far more immediate local concerns than his Spanish cousin's vague territorial claims seven thousand miles from Paris. With no help from any quarter, Spain's irresolute King and his irresponsible government capitulated to British demands. Britain's power in the Pacific was on the ascendant, while Spain's declined to disappear entirely a century later at the hands of the still upstart United States.

Nootka taught each nation involved some hard lessons. Spain's was the humiliating admission of her weakened position in the international balance of power. The United States learned all too clearly that it must assert control over the western territories or some future invasion might prove a national disaster. Britain was forced to recognize the ineffectiveness of informal and indirect contact with Washington's administration in improving American attitudes toward her policies. To the surprise and embarrassment of her ministry, Washington had not even commented on Beckwith's proffered package of commercial agreement and a possible alliance. Despite Beckwith's developing friendship with Hamilton, both he and his government had misread American intentions. The United States wanted freedom of action and would not tie itself to the policies—or ambitions—of any European nation.

As a result, by September, 1790, Foreign Secretary Leeds concluded it was necessary to send an official minister to the United States. He informed Morris of this decision as the

American prepared to leave London. Unfortunately for the expected improvement in Anglo-American relations, British procrastination in making the appointment confirmed Morris' suspicions of their double-dealing, as he reported to Jefferson. Neither Morris nor his superiors in America had any way of knowing, of course, that part of the reason for the delay was the inability to find a qualified man willing to serve his king in the wilderness outpost of New York. Several turned down the appointment while those who volunteered were either inexperienced or incompetent. It was not until the following May that George Hammond, twenty-eight-year-old minister plenipotentiary recently assigned to Madrid, was directed to establish formal diplomatic relationships with the American government at its new capital in Philadelphia. In the meantime, influenced by the cynical reports from Morris, Washington remained sceptical of British intentions. He stubbornly refused to send his own minister to London until the British had sent theirs first.

   While the Nootka war clouds gathered and then dissipated, the President continued his attempts at negotiating with the Indian confederations both north and south of the Ohio River. Although he considered Harmar's northward expedition an essential show of force, he preferred patient careful bargaining to avoid a general frontier war. He still feared that a major Indian war could be a disaster. But toward the Southwest there was more of an urgency in his approach. All during 1790 he received from southern governors, soldiers, and settlers reports of continued Spanish demands on the Indians to put on enough pressure to encourage separatism and disloyalty among the settlements in Kentucky and Tennessee. Washington saw the problem all too clearly as he indicated in his *Diary* "that Spain is playing a game which, if not counteracted, will depopulate that country, and carry most of the future emmigrants to her territory." As the year wore on, it was obvious that

Spanish colonial officials, if not the Spanish home government itself, were taking advantage of the Nootka crisis to promote their own interests at the expense of the United States.

The American government thought it had met some initial success following General Benjamin Lincoln's mission to the Creeks in the autumn of 1789. Because of Lincoln's efforts, thirty Creek chiefs met the President in New York to negotiate a settlement of differences. Here, on August 13, 1790, the Creeks signed the Treaty of New York formally ceding away the disputed territory in western Georgia between the Oconee and Ogeechee rivers and acknowledging American sovereignty over a portion of Creek country. Washington congratulated himself on the success of this peaceful settlement by writing Lafayette that "the basis of our proceedings with the Indian Nations has been, and shall be justice, during the period in which I may have anything to do in the administration of this government."

Although these negotiations with the Creeks are more properly detailed as part of the broader issues in Spanish-American relations, they had considerable ramifications on affairs with England. Washington was well aware that British agents, particularly the infamous James O'Fallon, were circulating through the Kentucky, Cumberland, and Tennessee settlements, presumably under indirect orders from London. Washington did not know, of course, that England's Lords of Trade had recommended a policy encouraging independence sentiment among these frontier villages with the purpose of forming commercial treaties with them. Such information would not have surprised Washington, however, for he recognized that Britain as well as Spain would benefit from the chronic instability in the Southwest. The key to potential British successes throughout all of the West was the continued hostility of the Indian tribes to Americans.

Washington meant to overcome this hostility when he

sent General Harmar against the Shawnee and Miami villages. Their location at the rapids of the Maumee River, some twenty miles upstream from Lake Erie, was strategic. The Maumee was separated near its source from the southerly flowing Wabash by only a short portage (Fort Wayne, Indiana). That portage, the Maumee rapids, and Niagara Falls were the only breaks in a continuous watercourse connecting Montreal to New Orleans, a natural avenue for interior commerce. Under the terms of the Peace Treaty of 1783 British traders were permitted to move freely along these rivers. With such easy access and close trade relations with the Indians, British commercial aspirations in the western American settlements would be fulfilled. Harmar's expedition was intended to lessen these possibilities.

Harmar's northward thrust would, however, go dangerously close to British-held Detroit. If misinterpreted in London it could undo all of Morris' efforts for Anglo-American talks. To avoid this risk, Washington ordered Governor St. Clair to inform the Redcoat commander at Detroit, Alexander McKee, that the American expedition was not a threat to the British. McKee, however, did not play by Washington's rules; he warned the Indians that the Americans were coming. Because forest rumor had exaggerated the size of the invading force, the Indians abandoned their villages and refused to meet Harmar head on. Instead they hung on his flanks, watched his every move, and waited their opportunity. With 320 regulars and 1,100 militia he easily destroyed five empty villages and a cache of 20,000 pounds of corn. But when two detachments penetrated into the forest to make contact, they were quickly surrounded and cut off from the main body of troops. Both times a smaller number of Indians swooped out from behind trees and so frightened the militia that it broke and scattered, leaving the regulars to be hacked to pieces. Because of these two blows and the approach of an early winter storm, Harmar had no choice but to gather up his stragglers and retreat to the

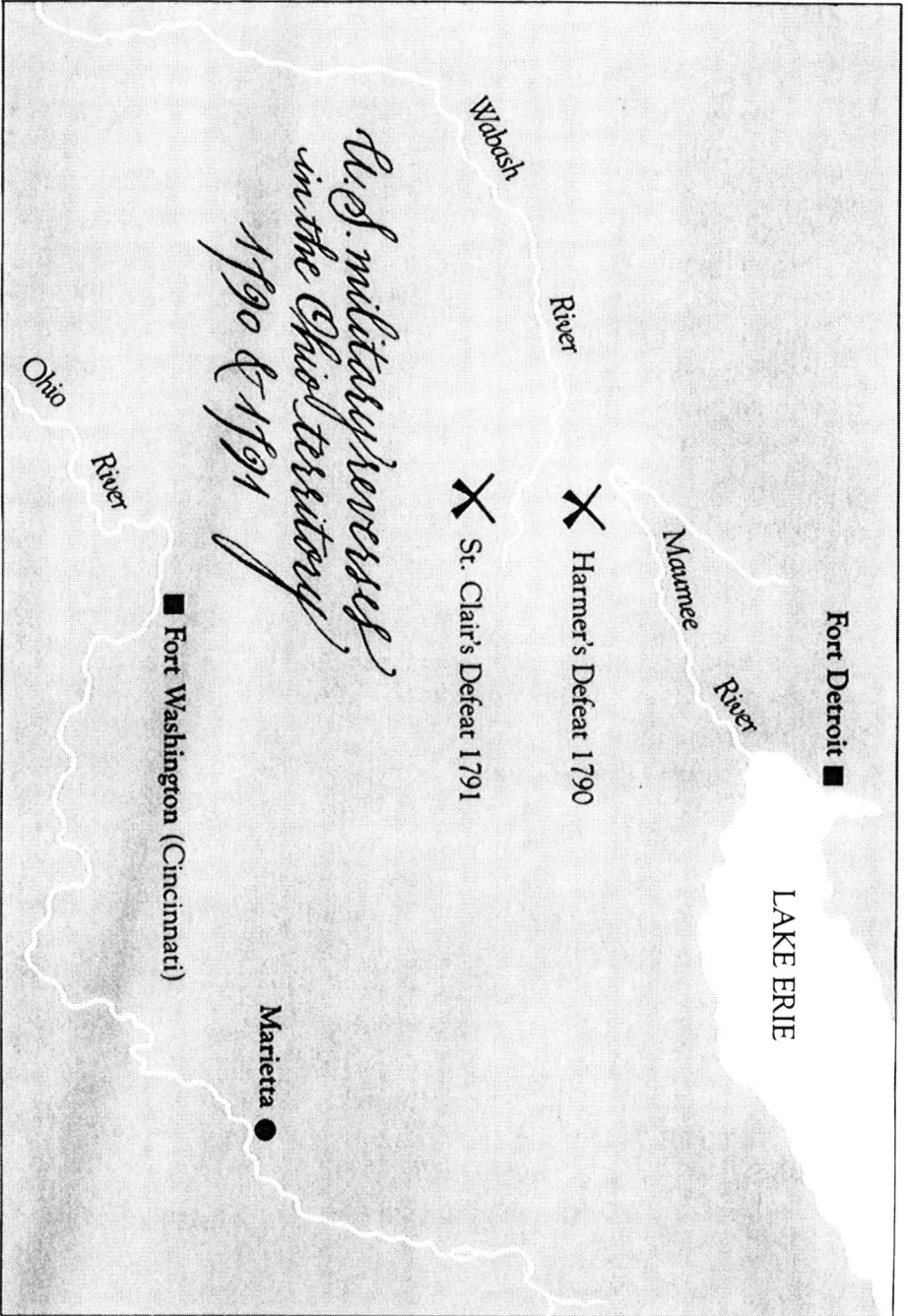

U.S. military reverses
in the Ohio territory
1790 & 1791

Wabash River

Ohio River

St. Clair's Defeat 1791

Harmer's Defeat 1790

Maumee River

Fort Washington (Cincinnati)

Marietta

Fort Detroit

LAKE ERIE

safety of Fort Washington, where he finally counted up his loss of 183 men. Harmar's expedition did nothing but prove the uselessness of untrained militia against smaller but better organized forces.

Emboldened by this easy success, the tribes gathered at the falls of the Maumee to assess the meaning of their victory. Here they rejected a warning from Dorchester's representatives to make peace with the Americans and preferred instead the advice of McKee, who warned they would never be safe until the Americans were pushed back across the Ohio. Under their leader, Little Turtle, a chief unknown to most Americans, these northern Indians committed themselves to accept nothing less than the Ohio river as the fixed boundary between their territories and the United States. In January, 1791, they launched a new series of raids against settlements on both sides of the river. One of these was so daring it was watched in horrified impotence by migrant New Englanders from the walls of their fort at Marietta. It caused their most prominent citizen, General Rufus Putnam, to beg Washington for help, pleading "our situation is truly critical."

Again wilderness rumor outran official information as the frustrated President waited weeks, with mounting pessimism, for Harmar's report. When he received it, he convinced himself that finding a solution to problems with the British was almost impossible. In December he wrote Morris "it is not only useless, but would be derogatory to push them any farther." And the continued disturbances on the frontier, he insisted, were "instigated thereto I am persauded by the british traders." In February he carried this pessimism into his message to Congress by declaring British unwillingness "to enter into any arrangements merely commercial" or "to fulfil what remains of the Treaty of Peace to be fulfilled on their part." He then ordered Morris "to discontinue his Communications with them." If Anglo-American relations were to improve, Britain would have to take the initiative.

Having broken off his own attempt to deal with Great Britain, the President concentrated once again on asserting his government's authority over the Northwest. He received support in this effort from a now angered and fearful Northeast. The report of Harmar's ignominious defeat was quickly followed by news of imminent danger to the former New Englanders at Marietta. Previously, eastern Congressmen had been indifferent to the insecurity of the distant West. But with violence and death threatening relatives and former friends, worried representatives from New York and New England took the lead in pushing through Congress Washington's requested authorization and funds for a much stronger military drive against the Indians. Washington gave responsibility for organizing this new campaign to Arthur St. Clair. Commissioned a major general, his old rank in the Continental Army, St. Clair would remain Governor of the Northwest Territory and thus would be in better control of all aspects of the whole operation.

In April, still smarting from Harmar's failure, Washington brooded during a vacation at Mount Vernon. Finally he wrote Jefferson to contact the Governor of Canada "to prevent the Indians receiving military aid as supplies from the british posts or garrisons. The notoriety of this assistance has already been such as renders enquiry into particulars unnecessary." Masking the anger in that observation, he suggested Jefferson might find Beckwith "the channel of an indirect intimation" to inform "in such manner as to reach Lord Dorchester, or the Officer commanding in Canada, that certain information has been received of large supplies of ammunition being delivered to the hostile Indians, from british posts, about the commencement of last campaign. And that the United States are equally surprised and disappointed at such an interference by the servants or subjects of a foreign State." Beckwith had tried to prevent Washington from reaching this conclusion by showing Hamilton eyewitness evidence to the contrary. Obviously Beckwith had failed his master, for the President refused to accept his denial and wanted no future repetition of British perfidy. Not too privately Washington laid the blame for Harmar's defeat at the feet of Canada's Governor General.

His plans for another attack on the Indians were strengthened when Vermont and Kentucky were admitted into the Union. Significantly, the decisions of their citizens to join came only after long and heated debates on complex questions. What long-term advantages would there be to becoming independent and drawing closer to Britain or to Spain? Or would their futures be brighter and safer as full-fledged states within the larger American nation? By opting for union they undercut anti-American sentiment in both Northeast and Southwest, relieving one of Washington's greatest worries. Even more remarkably, the smooth way Congress welcomed its newest members proved the effectiveness of the Constitution as a system of government for an expanding society. The lesson was not lost on other isolated groups of settlers debating their own futures. Little by little American nationalism began its march across the continent and in the process enhanced the prestige of the administration. The addition of two more states was a compliment to Washington's perseverance in coping with the instability along the fringes of his country.

During this rare moment of self-satisfaction, the President unfortunately but unwittingly damaged his own attempts to improve relations with Great Britain. His February report to Congress on the failure of Morris' mission to London excited latent Anglophobia in the House. This sentiment was also aggravated when the French complained that American tariff policies denied most-favored-nation treatment to their vessels entering American ports. The point had been made in the

1778 Treaty of Amity and Commerce as fundamental to the process of drawing closer together the economies of the two countries. Pressured by the French protest and angered by Washington's report, a majority in the House, as in 1789 and 1790, again pushed through anti-British discrimination in tariff and tonnage duties. Jefferson, however, although sympathetic to France, could not support the technicality of the French argument and thereby weakened the pro-French faction. As before, the Senate blocked the legislation. The United States would continue its practice of equal treatment to all foreign shippers.

Nevertheless, George Beckwith sounded an alarm in London. Recently rewarded for his services by promotion to lieutenant colonel, Beckwith reported the gathering strength of the pro-French faction. Although his fears had some basis in fact, they were exaggerated and misinterpreted, for he foolishly relied on information drawn exclusively from Americans strongly sympathetic to Britain. Like most foreign observers, and for that matter quite a number of Americans, he saw only a simple schism of pro-French or pro-British factions developing in American politics and missed the appearance of a purely nationalist sentiment that fell into neither camp. His alarms, therefore, caused him to follow Dorchester's worried orders to save time by communicating directly with England's Home Secretary, William Grenville. His letters of March, April, and June warned that even in the Senate "the French party obtained an occassion of strength." And he further damaged Morris, informing the Secretary "from a respectable quarter here" that Morris had a long and intimate acquaintance with France's minister in London, La Lucerne, and had disclosed to the Frenchman "the nature of his objects in England." He predicted that anti-British legislation would probably pass in the next session of Congress if Britain did not send a minister to the United States.

England's cabinet was forced to listen more attentively to its secret agent by the summer of 1791. Other valid, perhaps more significant, factors were supporting his warnings. Despite their mutual popular antagonisms, the trade between the English and the Americans had reached new highs since the creation of the new federal government. Customs house records showed that in the year from August, 1789, to September, 1790, Britain took almost half of American exports and supplied four-fifths of American imports. Also, the Lords of Trade had admitted Dorchester's promise to make Canada the provisioner of the West Indies appeared impossible to fulfill. Closer to home, hard facts indicated each year that England herself was no longer self-sufficient in production of food grains. Since reliance on Europe for food was dangerous and on Canada improbable the Lords were forced to conclude that if crops failed in England "the Deficiencies can only be supplied from the Harvest of America." Meanwhile English private investors were finding the developing economy in the United States an inviting opportunity. Their capital had long sustained the credit base for profitable trade with the American market, and now it was finding its way as investment in the American national debt. At various times Englishmen held twelve to fifteen percent of the total of United States government securities. Balance sheets in London pointed to the need to draw British interests closer to those of the United States.

Pitt could delay no longer formalizing relations with the American government. Obviously personal diplomacy had failed for both countries. Once the Nootka crisis had subsided, neither Pitt nor Leeds maintained a pretext of negotiating with Morris, and Beckwith's effectiveness was diminishing. Sir John Temple, British consul in Philadelphia, had cautioned Leeds in April that Beckwith's prolonged stay had "indeed disgusted not a few who heretofore leaned towards Great Britain." Beckwith could only "be considered in no other light than as a petty Spy."

Knowing that Washington desired to exchange ministers but would not take the initiative, Leeds had no other choice. He finally recalled the youthful George Hammond from Madrid to London for instructions and then dispatched him on to America.

Hammond arrived at Philadelphia, the new seat of government, in October, 1791. Despite his age he was an experienced diplomat with prospects stretching before him of a successful career in His Majesty's foreign service. But he was the wrong man to send to the United States. His temperament, prior experiences, and faulty knowledge of the country as well as the narrow instructions given him by Leeds limited his effectiveness. Under existing circumstances too much was expected of him. He was surprised, however, at the friendly reception given him as the first official representative of that old tyrant George III. Most Americans seemed genuinely eager for better relations between the two countries. Even Washington of the long memory greeted him with "politeness and respect" at the formal presentation of his credentials as the King's minister. Only Jefferson hesitated. The Secretary of State simply did not trust the British, particularly when he determined that Hammond was not empowered to negotiate a commercial treaty but only to *discuss* outstanding differences. Actually Hammond's private instructions directed him to link evacuation of the frontier posts with some arrangement for securing payment of pre-war debts. By offering British mediation between the United States and the Indian nations of the Northwest, he was to secure American acceptance of an autonomous Indian zone south of the Great Lakes from Lake Champlain to the Mississippi.

Stubborn and suspicious, Jefferson refused to have open, relaxed discussions with Hammond, preferring to deal with him by means of formal written notes and reports. This, too, was a surprise for Hammond and threw him on the defensive.

Already armed with a summary of Beckwith's reports, the young diplomat turned automatically to the friendship offered by the Colonel's contacts, most importantly Alexander Hamilton. Unknowingly Jefferson again had provided Hamilton the means of shunting aside the Secretary of State in the developing diplomacy with England. As he had with Beckwith, Hamilton easily established his own personal contact with Hammond, frequently giving him information that often contradicted Jefferson's formal written replies to the minister's enquiries.

Despite Hammond's intricate arguments tying British troop withdrawal to the payment of pre-war debts, Washington pushed ahead with his project for a military show of force in the Northwest. St. Clair was to gather a sufficient number of regulars and six-month militia to thrust north from Fort Washington into the heart of the Indian country, building a series of forts at thirty- to forty-mile intervals along the way. The plan looked good on paper, but in practice it was filled with agonizing frustrations. Army contractors were all but criminal in the slow delivery and shortages of essential supplies. From necessity the starting date of the expedition was postponed again and again. The authorized militia levies never reached their full strength, and the constant delays caused many enlistments to run out just as the campaign started. Winter was approaching, and depressing memories of Harmar's fate the previous year tended to demoralize the force as it began its march on September 17.

But they built two crude fortifications as they hacked their way northward through the silent forest. When they camped in a snow storm to begin building a third fort, only 1,400 men were left of the 2,600 that had started with St. Clair. In the half-light of dawn the next day, November 4, the cold and underfed army was surprised by 1,500 of Little Turtle's boldest warriors. Disorganized and frightened, only a few stood to fight while many fled to the uncertain safety of the surrounding wilderness. After three hours of violent fighting and the loss of experienced officers, St. Clair, himself ill and unable to mount a horse without assistance, frantically tried to organize a retreat to save most of his men. Abandoning wounded comrades, their own rifles, artillery, and vital supplies, they straggled back along the rough road so recently opened. It was not until days later that St. Clair could assess the totality of the disaster. Just 98 miles from the relative security of Fort Washington he had suffered a catastrophic defeat and the loss of 913 of his men. Once again the United States had been humiliated by the half-savage Indian confederations. As the shocking news spread like a brushfire throughout the West, fear struck the settlers while boldness inspired the Indians. From Pittsburgh to Louisville frontier villages on both sides of the Ohio braced for a renewal of the violence. The Indian challenge to American sovereignty in the Northwest was stronger now than when Washington took office.

The President's western policy was a shambles. Irritated by the lack of intelligence from the Ohio, he was half-resigned to a defeat when it was finally reported to him in mid-December. He could do little else to restore peace on the frontier but make another attempt to negotiate with the Indians, this time from a much weakened position. The government would go as far as humanly possible to bargain with the Indians for the sale of their lands and for an acceptable boundary between them and the settlers.

In case this effort failed, however, he stubbornly set about organizing yet a third striking force to carry American authority north to the Great Lakes. But until this force was ready, and it had to be well organized and carefully equipped, he was forced all through 1792 into a policy of appeasement with the Indian tribes in both the Northwest and the Southwest. In January, through Secretary of War Knox he dispatched two Indian traders into the Miami country to declare American readiness to forget the past and reopen negotiations. He sent warning messages to Governor Blount of the Southwest territory and to St. Clair, still governor in the Northwest, ordering them to keep their troops only in defensive positions and to prevent at all costs (even to their own popularity) any offensive operations against the Indians by the settlers themselves. In late March he entertained at Philadelphia a delegation of friendly Iroquois from western New York and requested them to act as mediators with the tribes farther west. In May, he authorized Knox to send two Kentucky militia officers north to the Miami villages to carry his formal offer for generous peace terms. Tragically these two peace emissaries were murdered and their papers given to the British commander at Detroit. In desperation Washington invited Joseph Brant, possibly his last hope, to meet with him in Philadelphia in June. A Mohawk patriarch, Brant's influence was extensive, and he realistically appraised the necessity for conciliation with the Americans. He agreed to carry the Presidential message of peace to the Shawnees and Miamis and would try to arrange a general conference between the Indian tribes and American negotiators for the next spring.

What Washington feared the most was happening. The successive defeats of Harmar and St. Clair in the north were unhinging the delicate peace with the Creeks and Cherokees of the south. Both Spaniards and Indians were taking full advantage of the weakened United States Army in the Northwest. Any cooperation between the Indian confederations of the two regions would be disastrous. Yet the President had no alternative but appeasement of the tribes. His policy was frightening to the settlers huddled along the Cumberland and Tennessee Rivers as they watched the gathering forces of a new Indian offensive.

Spurning the proffered generous peace terms and with

elimination of all threatening military actions against them, the Indians on both sides of the Ohio obviously wanted no reconciliation with the United States. Aided almost openly by the English and the Spanish, their demands for American withdrawal behind permanent fixed boundaries became stronger. If the federal government granted these concessions, it would abandon all of the Northwest and most of the Southwest below Kentucky. The prospects of an Anglo-Spanish Indian buffer zone were greater now than ever before!

For Washington the only break in the impasse would be a successful show of military force. With remarkable patience and an equally remarkable control of his emotions, he again persuaded a reluctant Congress in March to provide appropriations for yet another army to be sent into the hostile wilderness of the Northwest. This army would be different, however. Consisting of no less than 5,000 men, to be called the American Legion, it would be better equipped, better trained, better organized, and better led than its two predecessors. Washington sought stronger leadership and prudently evaluated the list of available general officers, seeking skills, daring, and, equally important, a sense of national purpose. Finally his choice fell on Anthony Wayne, another Revolutionary War general whose audacity during the war had earned him the sobriquet "Mad Anthony." Ignoring criticisms of his selection, the President gave Wayne detailed instructions and complete support.

Satisfied with his efforts for taking the military initiative against the Indians, Washington still had to deal with the English, who he was convinced were the chief cause of his problems. He was furious in April when he received from Morris a report that the new Home Secretary, Henry Dundas, had strongly suggested the United States accept the Ohio River as its legal boundary with the tribes to the north. Fortunately for the deliberateness in his diplomatic efforts he did not know that Dundas, in May and again in June, directed Alured

Clarke, acting Governor General of Canada, to promote that boundary in the upcoming Indian-American negotiations because "the greatet object to be attended to is to secure such a Barrier against the American States by the Intervention of the Indians." He did know that Grenville, who was now Foreign Secretary, had again instructed George Hammond to offer British mediation and to suggest to Jefferson American acceptance of the Ohio River line.

Jefferson indignantly rejected both Hammond's offer of mediation and his suggestion of the boundary. Then he pushed the British minister hard to find a basis for settling other issues dividing their countries. In response to Hammond's bill of particulars listing case after case of unsettled pre-war debts and unsatisfied Loyalist claims, he penned a remarkable 17,000-word refutation. Considered to be the Secretary's greatest state paper, it freely admitted the weakness of the old Confederation, explained how the new federal courts provided the means for adjudication, and historically argued the American position beginning with the British change of heart following the fall of Lord Shelburne. Clearly the onus was on the British, of course, but now regardless of past events a basis for mutual understanding was both possible and desirable. To his surprise Jefferson never received an official reply to his statement. He did not know, nor did Washington, that Hamilton had confided to Hammond that Jefferson had written only his own opinions and not those of the President, a blatantly false conclusion. The Treasury Secretary's indiscretion indicated how far he had slipped into Hammond's pocket and how deep were the differences over foreign policy dividing Washington's two most important secretaries.

Hamilton's obvious pro-British sympathies could not shake the President's suspicions of Pitt's government and its intentions. Disappointed in the limitations of Hammond's instructions, he nevertheless had to fulfill his part of the reciprocal exchange of ministers. Although he was personally satisfied with Gouverneur Morris, he knew indirectly through Beckwith that Morris was unacceptable in London. He therefore selected Thomas Pinckney of South Carolina as his first official minister to the Court of St. James's and decided to send Morris to Paris as minister to France. Marking the primary importance of the English connection, he ordered Morris to remain in their capital until Pinckney's arrival. Washington had little hope, however, that a new American in London would be any more successful in bringing the English to a better understanding with the United States.

To Washington, hope for success with the British still depended on a strong American stand against the Indians of the Northwest. He carefully watched General Wayne's slow, methodical organization of the American Legion. He hoped to avoid a major frontier war if he could keep the British from interfering. It was "these interferences," as he wrote Morris in June, 1792, "and to the underhanded support which the Indians receive (notwithstanding the open disavowal of it) that all our difficulties with them proceed." Blaming the British for frustrating his efforts at peace by convincing the Indians the United States wanted all their lands, he would nevertheless keep trying to work out an acceptable treaty. But, he added, "if they will not after this explanation (if we can get at them to make it) listen to the voice of peace, the sword must decide the dispute; and we are, though very reluctantly, vigorously preparing to meet the event."

But "the event" was terribly slow in taking place. A Congressional inquiry into St. Clair's defeat made General Wayne more cautious and less vigorous. He slowly and carefully selected his officers and men, organized their training, and established proper supervision of Army contractors. His well-advised caution, however, delayed the campaign against the Miamis for an entire year. This meant the government's bargaining position was non-existent. As a result Washington was forced to continue for another year his very unpopular appeasement of the Indians and accept humiliating conditions for the arrangement of a general peace conference with the tribes.

Entirely influenced by Alexander McKee, Miami and Shawnee chieftains rejected the advice for moderation offered by the Iroquois. Supported now by over a score of other tribes, including the powerful Delaware and Wyandot, they insisted the Americans meet them the following June at Sandusky, away from their villages on the Maumee but also a considerable distance from the protection afforded the Americans at Fort Washington. The British were to be represented officially, in effect putting them in the role of mediators, and were to supply provisions for the conference, a traditional mark of prestige at such assemblies. American representatives could travel to Sandusky only under a British passport and escorted there by British troops. Most significantly, the Indians would consider only the Ohio River as the boundary line.

Angered by these preset conditions, Washington privately wondered if they should be rejected out of hand. After conferring with his Cabinet and informing the Senate, however, he reluctantly agreed that a conference with the Indians, whatever the conditions, was absolutely necessary. On February 28, 1793, Secretary of War Knox sent the Indians an American acceptance of the terms for the Sandusky Conference and selected his emissaries.

By this time, too, Washington had reluctantly accepted his re-election as President. His hopes to retire after one term faded as he realized that too little had been accomplished in solving American international problems. Although relations with Great Britain had been formalized, none of the basic differences between the two countries had been resolved. No commercial treaty opening the West Indies to American shipping had been negotiated. Worse still, British influence over the American Northwest was greater now than when he had taken office four years earlier. Much had yet to be done!

CHAPTER FOUR

"Spain is Playing a Game"

WASHINGTON'S STRUGGLE to clear Spanish influences from south of the Ohio River matched his desperate diplomacy against the British-Indian menace to the north. In the President's mind the Southwest, even more than the Northwest, held the future for the United States. The region, bounded by the Appalachians, the Ohio, the Mississippi, and West Florida, was abundantly rich in the necessary resources to build a great civilization. It was already luring thousands of settlers eager to tap those resources. Of greater importance, the Southwest was for Americans the gateway to the entire Mississippi Valley.

No one saw this more clearly than did the President. All of his life he had been a Westerner at heart. As a young surveyor he had explored much of what is today West Virginia. When he marched with Braddock against the French and Indians in 1754 he again sensed the value of the place. To fulfill youthful dreams he purchased land along the Kanahwa River and invested in other schemes to open the even more fertile lands farther west. During the Revolution he encouraged George Rogers Clark to thrust into the Illinois country as a basis for future American claims to all or part of it. When the war ended he celebrated the knowledge that the Peace of 1783 had set the United States boundary on the Mississippi itself. From his earliest years he corresponded with anyone capable of giving him detailed descriptions of western climate, terrain, and soil fertility. By the time he became president he had developed a wide scattering of western friends on whom he relied heavily for information. By then he knew more about the Southwest than any other part of his country, except of course his own Virginia.

His earlier joy turned to icy fear soon after the war, however, as he watched the quarrelsome states of the Confederation fumble attempts to assert true control over the Southwest. In 1789 American sovereignty south of the Ohio was almost as non-existent as it was to the north. He saw clearly the danger if the Southwest was separated from the Union. The United States would be forever a small nation hemmed in by the Appalachian Barrier, unable to fulfill the great destiny he and his fellow Americans had envisioned.

Washington's hopes for the future greatness of the United States stumbled on the dreams of hundreds of men who had ambitious plans to exploit the Southwest for their own advantage. The region offered an enticing attraction to men of broad vision or of selfish particularism. The gateway to the interior of North America and the crossroads for generations of Indian travelers, it possessed some of the richest soil of the continent, a lucrative variety of timber, a generous climate, a wealth of wild life, and, above all, a system of navigable rivers to give it easy access to the sea. For the ambitious, persistence and hard work could turn dreams into realities, realities that could become luxurious plantations, thriving cities—or even empires. These rich potentialities of the Southwest invited serious challenges to Washington and his government; there were just too many dreams in too many other places to let Americans enjoy exclusively an area that from 1783 technically was theirs.

In France, even after 1783, visions of empire still focused on the American Southwest. From the time the French established themselves at New Orleans in 1718 they staked out a claim to the entire Mississippi River valley with colonists who someday would build an agricultural and commercial empire to be called Louisiana. By 1763 these farmers were tilling the

Illinois prairie at Kaskaskia and Cahokia while their merchants were building St. Louis, a small trading post at the mouth of the Missouri. From here their traders briefly dominated the fur trade eastward up the Illinois to the Great Lakes and had begun their penetration west along the Missouri toward the fantastic fur wealth in the high country of the Rockies. But France's bitter defeat at the hands of England in the Seven Years War shattered her North American ambitions. Forced to cede eastern Louisiana to the victorious British, she saw no advantage and great danger in keeping half an undeveloped empire. So to rid herself of a possible liability she ceded western Louisiana to Spain, her ally in defeat, as compensation for the Spanish loss to England of West and East Florida. Despite this calamity, for the next forty years influential Frenchmen harbored the hope that France would re-establish her glory on the Mississippi, and they agitated French politics continuously to keep alive their dreams.

Spain considered her acquisition of western Louisiana at best a mixed blessing and at worst a debilitating financial drain. But after 1763, with her ancient antagonist Great Britain confronting her along the entire east bank of the Mississippi, she could use the empty new wilderness territory as a protective shield for her more valuable possessions in Texas and Mexico. Moreover, she now held New Orleans and St. Louis, and with them the existing French-manned organization of a lucrative Indian fur trade. This could be developed further, and in time its profits would make the new province economically self-sufficient. Twenty years later, however, Spain's complacency was shaken by the American Revolution. The removal of London's restraints on Indian trade and white immigration uncorked a westward flow of American settlers that frightened the Spanish more than anything else. Pessimistic officials in New Orleans, Havana, and Madrid envisioned aggressive expansionist Americans quickly filling up the eastern half of the

Mississippi valley and then jumping that great river to move inexorably into Texas. To prevent this disaster her diplomats in Paris had labored desperately to have the Peace Treaty of 1783 set the western boundary of the United States at the line of the Appalachians or on the Tennessee River. Having failed in this attempt, Spain was forced to adopt a policy of containing American westward settlement and, if possible, bring it to an end. The twin diseases of colonial independence and republicanism must not contaminate the Spanish empire.

Indians, however, not the French or Spanish, were the real challengers to the American government. Creek, Cherokee, Chickasaw, and Choctaw nations had developed a fairly complex and sophisticated civilization with fortified towns, good farmlands, and structured systems of government. Their contacts with Europeans involved them in a profitable fur and hide trade, but as unfortunately happened to most of the tribes in eastern North America, they became increasingly dependent on trade items manufactured in Europe. From the 1760s they minimized intertribal differences and formed shifting, loose confederations to protect their hunting grounds from the westward encroachment of American settlers who began pouring through the mountain passes after the Revolution. By the mid-1780s they fell under the influence of a young Creek chieftain, Alexander McGillivray, son of a Scots trader and a half-Creek princess. The father, Lacklan McGillivray, had operated a successful business in the Indian trade at Charleston, but his Loyalism during the Revolution cost him heavily.

McGillivray learned much from his father, especially a dislike for Americans. Well educated, knowledgeable in languages, he had a Scot's shrewdness about the intricacies of business, trusted the British, and was willing to use the Spanish when it met his purposes. For him life in the American states was untenable, so he opted to live among the Creeks despite his frail physique and chronic illnesses. His mother's lineage and his familiarity with both cultures pushed him into prominence among the Creek chiefs. Still only in his twenties, he became the focus of leadership against the whites. A cunning and careful diplomat, he played white against white and when necessary Indian against Indian. By 1789 he was the acknowledged spokesman for the Indians of the Southwest.

American pioneers, too, had their dreams for the future of the Southwest. They were the cutting edge of a westward movement that would span the entire continent in less than a century. Pressured by overpopulation and land-hunger in the East, the result of decades of land-butchery and soil exhaustion, they were lured to the West by the rich promise of the fertile valleys of the Kentucky, Cumberland, and Tennessee rivers. By the late 1780s their settlements were concentrated in three areas: along the Holston River just west of the Appalachians, in the bluegrass region of north central Kentucky, and on the southern curve of the Cumberland centering on the fort at Nashville. Besides these indomitable pioneers, the land speculators of the East had their plans for the West's future as well. Plotting in London or in colonial capitals, they formed corporations or joint-stock companies to lobby for huge slices of western territory. Prior to the Revolution dozens of notable Americans, including Franklin and Washington, had invested in this future. Many of the great plantation owners of the Chesapeake sought western fields to replace worn out tidewater farms. When the War was over these same interests took advantage of the confusion over ownership of the trans-Appalachian region and applied pressures on state governments for new grants. The speculators' attention focused on the Muscle Shoals area of the great southern curve of the Tennessee and, farther to the west, on the black soils of the Yazoo River as it flowed into the Mississippi itself. For the pioneer farmer and the eastern speculator expansion into the Southwest was the beginning of unlimited opportunity.

Their opportunities were severely limited by confusion. The area south of the Ohio was unlike that to the North. There the individual states had surrendered their vague and overlapping claims to the nation itself; the entire Northwest was under the jurisdiction of the government of the United States. In the Southwest, however, Virginia, North Carolina, South Carolina, and Georgia hung on tenaciously to old colonial charter grants that gave each of them a frontage on the Mississippi. Their governments succumbed to the interest in western migration and issued grants to unoccupied western lands. In the process they ignored their own treaties with the Indians or those of the national government. Only Virginia had attempted to organize a government in the West; in 1776 it established Kentucky as a county, and four years later subdivided this into three. But the other states almost totally ignored the western settlers. With their capitals located on the eastern seaboard, they were more interested in financial retrenchment to pay Revolutionary War debts than expenditures for Indian defense and local justice in the West. As a result, westerners through primitive democracy and local militias—better described as vigilante committees—governed and defended themselves. In the meantime the United States government of the Confederation was powerless to exert any influence over the area.

This distressingly weak American posture in the Southwest invited Spain's interference. Her government now had the opportunity to push back to the east the official boundary of the United States, what her diplomats had failed to achieve in the treaty negotiations of 1783. The Floridas, indeed, had been restored to her after twenty years of British rule and they provided a springboard for new aggressive policies. Under the leadership of her King's principal minister, Conde de Floridablanca, Spain began in 1784 an ambitious five point plan to strengthen and defend her position in North America. Floridablanca asserted Spain's claim east of the Mississippi as far as the Flint, Hiwassee, and Tennessee Rivers, an area comprising almost two-thirds of the entire southwestern quarter of the United States. By royal order the Mississippi River was closed to American commerce. Effectively choking off the economic development of western settlements, this order denied the settlers their only avenue of trade downstream to waiting merchant ships at New Orleans. Then the Spanish invited remaining Americans to resettle in Louisiana or West Florida under generous terms offering religious toleration, protection from Indian raids, and the same privileges of trade given Spanish subjects. In the meantime Spanish colonial officials were directed to negotiate new treaties with the Creek, Choctaw, and Chickasaw tribes living south of the Tennessee in order to tie the Indian economy to Spanish policy through the hide trade managed under official government auspices by merchant houses in Pensacola, Mobile, and New Orleans. To make all of this palatable to the Americans, Spain sent Don Diego de Gardoqui as Minister to the United States to offer the commerce-starved Northeastern states a trade treaty in return for an American thirty-year self-denial of settlement in the Southwest.

Floridablanca's American policy was really an admission of Spain's weakened position in world affairs in the last quarter of the eighteenth century. The upstart United States should not have been considered such a serious threat to the northern fringes of Spain's American empire. But it was. The once mighty world-wide Hapsburg empire of the sixteenth and seventeenth centuries was on the defensive in the eighteenth. Spain had not recovered from the War of Spanish Succession (1701–1713), a long, costly civil and international conflict that put a French Bourbon prince on her throne. For the next seventy years the cousin kings of France and Spain, through a personal alliance known as the Bourbon Family Compact, ventured in costly attempts to be the arbiters of European politics. Spain's Bourbon kings, notably Carlos III (1759–1788), had tried to overcome local lethargy, centuries of tradition, and religious conservatism to effect modernizing reforms in economics and political structure. But these were at least a half-century too late to make Spain a contender for world markets, economic self-sufficiency, and national prosperity.

Floridablanca's policies regarding the United States were merely a small part of his world-wide concerns. He loyally devoted his entire career in a determined effort to arrest the slide in Spain's prestige. If he had to ally his country to the savages of North America to bring this about he would not hesitate to do so. His policy did almost strike a deathblow to the western settlements, and it caused a deep-seated enmity for Spain that set the entire Southwest in turmoil for over a decade.

By shutting off the Mississippi waterway, the Spaniards effectively eliminated a vital leg of an essential triangular trade pattern that meant success or failure for the frontier farmer. Life was hard enough for these intrepid pioneers, carving homesteads from the unrelenting wilderness. They hunted, trapped, and farmed for most, but not all, of the essentials for survival. What they could not produce they had to buy: gunpowder, iron implements, fabrics—and this took cash. But the Appalachian barrier isolated them from markets on the east coast; dragging their bulky products eastward across the mountains was physically exhausting and economically unfeasible. Their only solution was to load the produce of forest and farm—flour, wheat, tobacco, hides, furs—aboard canoes or flatboats and float downriver to seaport markets at New Orleans or Mobile. It was a slow, weeks-long, hazardous voyage, but at least they could sell for cash or barter with ship captains who carried their frontier products to markets on the East Coast or in Europe. Even their flatboats could be broken up and sold as building timber. With cash in hand they faced two or three more weeks of omnipresent danger walking hundreds of miles back home along the ancient Indian trails, the Natchez Trace being but one, constantly threatened by hostile Indians and bands of runaway slaves. Back at their home villages itinerant peddlers would sell the pioneer farmers what they needed, carried laboriously by pack mules across the mountains from Baltimore or Philadelphia. But the frontier settler needed the cash or else the peddler passed him by.

No wonder the West was aflame with anger toward Spain. By 1785 the citizens of the more developed settlements, especially in Kentucky, were screaming for the state or national governments to do something—or else they would do something themselves. What, no one knew for sure. Angry talk in the settlements proposed pooling efforts to drive the Spanish from New Orleans in defiance of both Spain and the timid governments on the East coast, or creating an independent republic strong enough to stand alone against Spain, or seeking help from the British. Whatever might result, Spanish policy had injected the "Mississippi Question" into Spanish-American relations, and it would plague the United States until the Louisiana Purchase in 1803 eliminated the problem.

To take advantage of this turmoil, Spain's minister, Don Diego de Gardoqui, exploited the Mississippi Question with cunning and cash. Cleverly he probed the weaknesses of the United States and of John Jay, the Secretary of Foreign Affairs. Lavishing attention on Mrs. Jay, he flattered the couple into an intimate friendship. He invited leading members of Congress to small dinner parties at his luxuriously furnished residence and overawed their simple frontier tastes with excellent cuisine and seemingly genuine concern for their personal interests. He did favors for some of them, and for one in particular, Henry Lee of Virginia, he arranged a "loan" of $5,000, a loan that apparently was never repaid. When he discovered that George

Washington was planning to breed mules at Mount Vernon, he got the King of Spain to send the General a jackass as a personal gift. Gardoqui concluded correctly that Washington, still a private citizen in 1785, was the most influential man in America. He needed the General's friendship, if not his outright support.

Gardoqui led the susceptible Jay into a tentative settlement of Spanish-American differences in early 1786. On paper Spain appeared generous. She was willing to open for American shipping her ports at home and in the Canary Islands (but not in Spanish-America) on a most-favored-nation basis. She offered to mediate on behalf of the United States with the British to get them to withdraw from the northern frontier posts. And to alleviate the critical shortage of specie in the United States the Spanish government would purchase for cash American hardwoods as building timbers. Both countries would guarantee the other's territories in the Americas if attacked by a third country. In return for all this support the United States must "forbear" using the Mississippi River for twenty-five years and accept a new southern boundary with West Florida. The line of the 31st parallel (a westward extension of the northern border of the Florida panhandle) was to be shifted north to an east-west line where the Yazoo River flows into the Mississippi (at modern Vicksburg). Dazzled by the prospects of a trade agreement that would materially relieve the severe economic depression in the Northeast, Jay and northern Congressmen took Gardoqui's bait.

But this Jay-Gardoqui Treaty was a serious blunder for the Secretary of Foreign Affairs. He had not expected the vehemence of Southern opposition. Planters and speculators of the South considered the agreement a crass betrayal of their agricultural interests. A "give-away" of any portion of the Southwest would deny the fulfillment of their own dreams of a profitable future. The trade-off of an immediate economic upturn in the Northeast for a twenty-five-year delay in southwestern expansion was unacceptable. And the embarrassed Jay knew it; so he dropped the negotiations even though Gardoqui had received instructions from Floridablanca to offer minor concessions. By 1787, while the Constitutional Convention was sitting in Philadelphia, both the Spaniards and the Americans waited in the limbo of the transition period to see what the prospective new government would do to solve the Mississippi Question. The waiting frustrated Gardoqui and he asked permission to return home to Spain. Although his diplomacy had failed, he succeeded in opening a cut between Northern and Southern interests. It was a wound that would fester continuously in the process of establishing a foreign policy during the early years of the Republic.

In the meantime at New Orleans Estevan Miró, Spain's colonial governor of Louisiana and West Florida, began implementing his part of Floridablanca's schemes for the Southwest. Inching Spanish authority northward along the Mississippi, he strengthened the garrison at Natchez, a small river village some fifty miles above the 31st parallel. Eventually this thrust of Spanish garrisons would extend as far upriver as the site of modern Memphis. The settlers of the Natchez region were primarily Loyalist emigrés from the Revolution with no love for the United States; they welcomed the protection of the Spanish flag. At the same time, the summer of 1784, Miró effectively struck a double blow at American authority. At a pair of Indian conferences held at Pensacola and Mobile he bribed the Creeks, Chickasaws, and Choctaws to accept a Spanish protectorate and exclusive Spanish control of their skin and hide trade. This last undercut the post-war economic recovery in Charleston and Savannah where merchants for twenty years had been the principal traders with the Indians. But Miró's success with the Indians cost the Spanish treasury dearly. Literally buying their friendship, he drew from quartermaster supplies enough rations for the members of each tribe to make the two-week return journey to their home villages. For example, the Chickasaws alone received 5,700 pounds of bread, 580 of fresh meat, 763 of bacon, 9,400 of rice, 2,500 of beans, plus 27 barrels of corn.

Despite these expensive commitments Miró was shrewd enough not to antagonize the United States openly with military threats through the Indians. Instead he tried to weaken the American position by strengthening the economic ties between the Indian tribes and Spain. But his system had a serious flaw. Spain did not manufacture enough of the trade goods demanded by the Indians; and besides the real market for the hides was in London and Paris, where young dandies set fashion trends by wearing tight-fitting doeskin britches. Miró was forced to license two English trading companies that had been established in the Floridas during the twenty-year British occupation. One of them, Panton, Leslie and Company, was already in partnership with Alexander McGillivray and therefore could easily get preferential treatment among the Creeks. This was a dangerous situation for Spain's position in the Southwest—and indirectly that of the United States—because the British never hid their own designs on the lower Mississippi valley.

For the next four years, nevertheless, this arrangement worked dramatically to Spain's advantage against the United States. In 1785 the State of Georgia sparked a bloody Indian war when it tried to create a county out of the Natchez district in an area extending from the 31st parallel to the Yazoo River. Although Miró outwardly kept Spain neutral in this war, he authorized secret aid to the Indians. He warned the Spanish commander at St. Louis "to observe the greatest secrecy in order not to give the slightest cause for suspicion to our neighbors, but you should not lose sight for one moment of the necessity of drawing the nations more and more to our friendship."

Miró's successes at New Orleans and Gardoqui's machinations in Philadelphia caused terror and then anger among the western American settlements. Fearing betrayal from easterners, trans-Appalachian settlers began looking elsewhere for help in defending themselves and their dreams for the future. In Kentucky frustration grew daily as appeals for statehood were ignored in Richmond. After 1785 separatism was discussed widely in pioneer villages, and a whole crop of local leaders sniffed personal opportunity in the air. Not unlike the Allen brothers simultaneously promoting Vermont nationalism, the Westerners encouraged thoughts of independence among their neighbors. Soon a whole parade of highly ambitious and colorful promoters complicated the politics of the Southwest. The most notorious were James Wilkinson, James Robertson, William Blount, John Sevier, and "Dr." James O'Fallon, whose schemes were discussed in New Orleans and Quebec, Madrid and London. Taking a lesson from the Founding Fathers of 1776, they turned to the Spanish or the British or both for aid, if not outright intervention, to promote their own personal ambitions.

These westerners played into Floridablanca's hands and set in motion the "Spanish Conspiracy," twenty years of secret bargaining between Spanish officials and American adventurers seeking advantages in one another's weaknesses. It began in 1787 when James Wilkinson boldly floated flatboats loaded with Kentucky produce downstream to New Orleans, bribing Spanish garrison commanders along the way. A surprised Miró listened attentively to Wilkinson's exaggerated reports of hostility building up in Kentucky and threats by the Kentuckians themselves (with British help?) to eject the Spanish forcibly from control of the Mississippi. He put down his observations and ideas in a memorial which Miró immediately dispatched to Madrid. In this Wilkinson proposed that Spain encourage a Spanish party in Kentucky, grant more liberal rules for commerce on the Mississippi through a special license to himself, offer generous terms to immigrants into Spanish-held territory, or give out-right support for the Kentucky secessionists. The Spaniard took full advantage of the American's offer. He sent Wilkinson back to Kentucky as his personal agent, authorized him to bring another flotilla of flatboats to New Orleans, and then awaited instructions from Madrid. In the meantime, other disgruntled entrepreneurs followed Wilkinson's lead and trekked to New Orleans to promote their own competitive schemes.

Floridablanca's response to Wilkinson's memorial came eighteen months later with a dramatic shift in Spanish policy. The Mississippi was opened to all Americans, but they had to pay duties on the goods they unloaded at New Orleans. Land grants in Spanish Louisiana were made available to American immigrants with promises of commercial privileges equal to those of Spanish subjects; these settlers would be granted religious toleration. But Miró was not to finance or promise military support for revolution among the frontier settlements. Only after the frontiersmen had actually established independence could he contact them.

This new policy was a frank admission that Spain could not defend the northeastern edge of her American empire. Her secret agents sent out from Philadelphia reported increasing British influence in Kentucky, especially among the followers of James O'Fallon. The Spanish feared a British thrust down the Mississippi to New Orleans. And they were partially aware that the dream of a French empire on the great river was still very much alive in Paris. France's minister to the United States, Eleanor F. Moustier, had revived this interest in early 1789 through a carefully detailed 300-page report of his investigations of the economic potential of the entire river valley. He had been instructed by his government to discourage the movement for a strong central government in the United States lest it be too powerful for the French to control. But his own observations concluded that one government would serve French purposes better than thirteen weak ones, especially in the West.

Spain's concern for British involvement in the Mississippi Question was based on hard evidence. Britain, too, saw disadvantages in stronger American government and tried to exploit the lull in leadership while Americans debated ratification of the Constitution. One of her agents in Kentucky proposed to Lord Dorchester that "it would be the interest of Spain to cede the Port of New Orleans to Great Britain, as well as the western side of the Mississippi for it would cut off all possible means of dispute between Spain and America." In April, 1789, the very moment when Washington was nervously awaiting the official call to the presidency, Dorchester reported to Lord Sydney that Kentucky separatists were suggesting to him that "Great Britain ought to prepare for the occassion, and she should employ the interval in forming confidential connections with men of enterprise, capacity and popular influence, resident on the western waters." In June he warned Sydney that Moustier's report recommending "France to take possession of New Orleans" was known in the United States and "discontented persons of consideration among [the Kentuckians] have caught the idea that Great Britain might be placed in the room of France, and have made me offers of their services to bring this about." In a secret dispatch the following October Grenville replied, "It appears extremely desirable that the turn of affairs in these settlements should lead to the establishment of a Government distinct from that of the Atlantic States." Dorchester was to prevent the Westerners from developing a close connection with the Spaniards and to "cultivate such an intercourse with the leading Men in the New Settlement as might give to this country a facility of acting if at any time a proper occassion should occur."

Thus exploiting the absence of a strong United States government, England and Spain squared off for control, if not outright ownership, of the southern half of the American backyard. Britain's already well-placed wedge north of the Ohio was being driven south of that river in an attempt to dislodge the entire trans-Appalachian region from the United States. And all the while the French waited, not timidly, for their own opportunities in the American weakness. If the fluid situation on the lower Mississippi was considered in Madrid a threat to one tiny corner of Spain's vast empire, how much more serious a danger was it to the fledgling United States?

Even before he became President, Washington worried about this power vacuum in the Southwest that invited European intrigue. It was this issue more than any other that convinced him of the need for the new federal government. While the Virginia Ratifying Convention argued over the Constitution, he wrote Henry Knox of his fears that the debates would cause a negative reaction among the Kentucky representatives "of unreal dangers respecting the navigation of the Mississippi and their organization into a separate State." Only slightly relieved by July of 1788, after ten states had ratified, he commented, "I flatter myself the interior Settlements will find their interest concur with their inclination in maintaining an intimate connection with the Atlantic States." Interestingly, however, he had no comment on the fact that the delegates from the West had voted against ratification!

As President, he wanted to show the flag of federal authority in the Southwest as quickly as possible. He tried, with little initial success, to exert that authority over the western settlements. But until North Carolina ratified the Constitution, Tennessee was not part of the Union. He would, however, open direct negotiations with the Indian tribes farther south. By doing so he indicated his own conviction that Georgia's sales of large tracts along the Mississippi and Yazoo were unconstitutional, violating previous treaties made in the name of the United States. And he kept alive his line of communication to Madrid. Before Gardoqui sailed for Spain Washington had Foreign Secretary John Jay brief the Spanish minister on the intentions of the new American government regarding the Southwest.

Washington sought solutions for these problems in the Southwest in his typical methodical fashion. Within a month of his inauguration he asked Jay for a brief written summary of the status of United States foreign relations, but, he pleaded, "without overburdening or confusing a mind which has very many objects to claim its attention." By July he had sorted out the major issues and began developing his strategies. He pushed Jay to remind the departing Gardoqui that the United States wanted to maintain friendship with Spain and to reopen negotiations on the entire Mississippi Question. He was troubled, too, about his own constitutional status regarding these negotiations, and asked Jay if he could do this "without previously advising the Senate." Jay encourged his right as president to initiate negotiations. So he accepted Gardoqui's private assurances of friendship, probably unaware that the Spaniard had left behind an effective network of secret contacts with Kentucky separatists whose control was in the hands of two young chargés d'affaires.

Also focusing his attention on Alexander McGillivray and the other Creek chiefs, Washington was convinced that stability in the Southwest could come only if "a due regard should be extended to those Indians whose happiness in the course of events so materially depends on the national justice and humanity of the United States." He asked Congress for permission and funds to send a negotiating team into the

Southwest to meet the Creek chieftains; but to overcome the embarrassing weakness in the American bargaining position he asked Congress to establish "some uniform and effective system for the Militia of the United States." The tight-fisted Congressmen created no proper military force but did approve and fund the peace commission. In a flattering gesture to McGillivray's stature, Washington selected a distinguished trio for the mission: Revolutionary War General Benjamin Lincoln, who had accepted Cornwallis' sword at Yorktown; Cyrus Griffin, the last president of the Continental Congress; and David Humphreys, former secretary to Franklin and Jefferson in Paris.

McGillivray was not impressed.

He regarded the commission's hat-in-hand attitude an acknowledgement of the weak American position. He was already armed with Miró's assurance that Spain's new king, Carlos IV, wanted to help "you to defend yourselves and to protect the lands that belong to you." So he refused to accept two articles in the proposed treaty which the Americans considered as non-negotiable. One called for the shifting of the limit of Georgia settlements westward beyond the St. Mary's River. The other was the commission's insistence that Creeks living within the boundaries of American territory accept the protection of the United States "and no other Sovereign whatsoever." This second point was the most crucial to the United States, for any challenge to American authority in the Southwest would endanger the Union itself. But if the Creeks agreed to it, they would terminate years of beneficial support from Spain with nothing better as a substitute. Convinced the Americans would not budge from either of these articles, McGillivray abruptly walked away from the bargaining campsite and silently disappeared into the wilderness, taking his followers with him. With no word of explanation, he had broken off the negotiations.

Yet with the cunning of a seasoned European diplomat, he

kept open the door to future negotiations. Shortly after abandoning General Lincoln's peace commission he "suddenly" remembered an unanswered letter he had received the previous August from Secretary of War Knox. In his new response to Knox he still dangled the prospects of peace by expressing a willingness to meet again with Americans the next spring. Sensing that time was on his side, he boasted to his partner, William Panton, that "the operation of the new Constitution is much dreaded by most of the better sort of the upper Gentry. In conversation with some of them, they asked me when & where I was going to settle my new State, for there are above 1500 families waiting my pleasure in Georgia." While McGillivary waited to develop his own plans, the winter of 1789–90 was filled with sporadic Indian forays against the western edges of Georgian settlement.

As 1789 came to an end the President agonized over the failure of his initiative in the West. He spent days sitting impatiently at his desk trying to sort out the Mississippi problems. Finally he produced a list of "Queries," each one raising a question or focusing concern on a specific problem. No strong majority appeared in the Senate to support his adamant nationalism. This by itself undermined his insistence that American claims to navigation of the Mississippi "ought not be weakened by any negotiation whatsoever." Senate debates reflected a growing East-South split that actually encouraged separatist talk in Kentucky. Recent letters from the West reported how much that sentiment was growing, for which he blamed Spain. Pessimistically he concluded, "Spain is playing a game which, if not counteracted, will depopulate that country and carry most of the future immigrants to her territory." The grayness of winter added to his despondency, but like most men he looked forward to the promise of spring. The new year itself might offer new opportunities.

It did, for despite Washington's pessimism the spirit of

nationalism was growing in the United States. In February North Carolina joined the Union and surrendered all of its western territory to the federal government. Now the entire great block of land south of Kentucky was officially a part of the American nation. In May, Congress organized it under presidential jurisdiction, thereby lessening the sting of Spanish-inspired charges that eastern states cared little for the future of the West. The President now removed the sting altogether, for instead of sending eastern carpetbaggers to run the new territorial government, he selected the most prominent Westerners for positions of authority. If he actually knew that any of them had intrigued with Spain, he ignored the fact. William Blount became Governor and Superintendent of Indian Affairs, while John Sevier and James Robertson were to organize the territorial militia as brigadier generals. By late summer, this injection of federal authority caused sentiment in Kentucky to shift from independence to statehood. And this time the Virginia legislature cooperated and encouraged the process.

Washington's nemesis was still Alexander McGillivray, for without his cooperation nothing could be accomplished. The Creek chieftain had left ajar the door to future negotiations in his letter to Knox, so the President tried a different approach. Instead of another formal peace commission, he sent Colonel Marinus Willet to the Creek country as his personal representative. Willet enjoyed an enviable reputation all along the frontier among Indians as well as whites. His woodsman's skill in New York's border wars during the Revolution had made him a hero, and he was also known for his honesty in dealing with the Indians. Now Washington gave him a new and almost impossible task. He was to convince McGillivray of Washington's sincerity by assuring him the President considered as illegal Georgia's land sales to the Yazoo companies. Of greater importance, he was to persuade the chief to travel to New York and negotiate directly with the federal government. This time

McGillivray was impressed; he found the Colonel "a Candid and Benevolent Character, possessing abilitys but without Show or parade." He agreed to go to New York.

Burning no bridges behind him, McGillivray began his own diplomatic balancing act. He viewed the American purpose as giving "Congress an opporutnity of Defeating the late Grants to those Companies & to restore to & secure to us our Rights of Territory." Yet he would not betray his commitments to Spain. He explained to Miró, "Independent of other considerations I think I can best serve our own & the King's Interests by the Journey. Tho I do not pretend to the ability of a Machiavel in Politics, yet I can find out from my Slender abilities pretty near the disposition of the American Politics so far as they respect the Spanish Nation, & Your Excellency may depend on receiving a faithful account of every matter whenever I may return." Perhaps his humble denial of Machiavellian abilities was meant only to convince himself, for he also quickly informed the British of his travel plans. He wrote Panton and Leslie, "all the eagerness which Washington shows to treat with me on such liberal terms is not based, I am persuaded, on principles of justice and humanity. . . . I think that it would be better for our interests and for those of our friends for me to go to New York. There is still time for Spain to protect her western possessions."

When McGillivray and twenty other Creek chiefs reached New York in mid-July it was a bad moment for both Indians and Americans. "Nootka" had grown into a full-blown crisis on both sides of the Atlantic, changing the setting as well as the purpose of negotiations for both sides. A jittery Washington became alarmed over rumors that the British intended to mount a joint Canada-Kentucky downriver attack on New Orleans. He was not comforted to learn that an equally anxious Miró was desperately strengthening the defense perimeter of New Orleans to repel the expected invasion. If war actually broke out between England and Spain, Indians and Americans once again would be caught in the middle. Both McGillivray and Washington were forced to reassess each other's positions and try to get the best out of a bad situation.

New York City outdid itself to support Washington's cause. Treating McGillivray with all the pomp necessary for a visiting head-of-state may have galled some of its citizens with lingering memories of past Indians wars, but the treatment fitted Washington's plans. The Sons of St. Tammany, in splendid regalia, met the Creek chiefs at the edge of the city and escorted them to Federal Hall where Congress waited to offer its greetings. The President himself extended his welcome at a formal reception. In the evening Governor George Clinton and Secretary of War Henry Knox hosted them for a dinner at City Tavern. By nightfall the chiefs refused further hospitality and set up their own camp about a half mile outside the city, but McGillivray, the object of most of the attention, agreed to be Knox's house guest. His frail, sickly appearance was a sharp and almost comic contrast to that of his hosts, for Knox weighed 280 pounds and his wife 240. Knox's hospitality, however, had a significant secondary purpose. Washington had warned him to keep McGillivray isolated from contact with European agents.

Such precautions were necessary. The British, French, and Spanish did little to hide the fact they had agents living in the city; some were outright spies whose activities were well known to the American government. McGillivray's presence in New York with all its attendant publicity would draw them out. What influence they could—or did—have could only be guessed. Washington would not risk it, for he knew that the governor of East Florida had sent a certain Don Carlos Howard to Philadelphia for "reasons of health," but with $50,000 to buy wheat. The President forewarned Willet, guiding the Creeks on their way to New York, to expect a contact as the party passed through Philadelphia. He expected another contact from Josef de Viar, the young Spanish chargé left behind in New York by Gardoqui. But Washington's warnings were unfortunately ineffective. The ubiquitous Briton, George Beckwith, somehow breached American security and met with McGillivray. Later he reported to Dorchester Hamilton's complaint that the Americans believed, but without proof, that the Spaniards had indeed met the Creeks and "gave them large presents in this city."

McGillivray regarded the clumsy American attempts to isolate him more with amusement than anger, but he exaggerated the importance of the Creeks to the foreign policy aims of all the other nations involved. As long as the war crisis boiled in Europe he could find his own advantages in it; if it ended he needed to have some new friends. He was willing, therefore, to bargain with the Americans to reach a satisfactory compromise.

Washington's summit meeting with the leadership of the Creek nation, therefore, paid some dividends after all. On August 13, 1790, the Indians and Americans signed the Treaty of New York, a compromise to be sure, but a workable and satisfactory arrangement for both. The Creeks accepted American sovereignty wherever they resided within the territorial limits of the United States, neatly sidestepping the question of the exact location of the American boundary with West Florida. For a price they formally ceded the partially settled lands between the Oconee and Ogeechee rivers, an area that had caused most of the dispute between the Creeks and the State of Georgia. This set the boundary of that state much farther east than the Georgians had hoped. On the other hand, the Creeks remained faithful to their commercial commitments with the British and refused to authorize Americans to trade among their villages. Surprisingly, on this point, Washington in a secret article made an unusual concession, perhaps as a future foot in the door. If a war should ever disturb the normal pattern of Creek trade, the United States would permit $50,000 worth of trade goods to pass duty-free through the country directly to the Creeks themselves. And in another secret agreement he commissioned McGillivray an American brigadier general, named him United States agent to the Creek nation, and gave him an annual salary of $1,200. This last was in part to compensate him for the loss of his father's property confiscated as Loyalist holdings by the State of Georgia during the Revolution.

Obviously McGillivray had won this first round in Creek-American negotiations. He had found his advantage in Washington's weakened military position, giving little and taking much. As he had promised, he dutifully summarized the treaty, including its secret provisions, in a series of letters to his Spanish allies. In defending his actions to Miró he concluded astutely that the American position proceeded "from their poverty & inability to Support & maintain a Vigorous Contest to reduce us by force. It is better to treat with an enemy under Such circumstances, than a more powerful one." Washington would have been even more humiliated had he read McGillivray's humorous recounting of the failure of the Americans to prevent him from meeting Beckwith, Viar, and Howard, especially that Howard "advised me in letters which they could not detect."

Washington, nonetheless, made good on his part of the bargain struck with the Creeks. In a presidential proclamation of August 26 he denounced any possible Kentucky-based armed attack on New Orleans. Americans could not become involved in either side of an Anglo-Spanish conflict, an action that could easily suck the United States into an unwanted war. More particularly, he had to stop irresponsible frontier action from upsetting the delicate peace he had just negotiated with the Creeks. He was forced into the difficult position of threatening to use American military forces against American settlers to protect the Creeks—and indirectly the Spanish. His best hope to take the pressure off his Southwest diplomacy was General Harmar's planned offensive against the Indians north of the Ohio. If Harmar were successful, British attention would be diverted from any designs they had afoot in Kentucky.

If McGillivray hoped to find some advantage in the "Nootka Crisis," so too did Washington. Perhaps Spain, confronting a war with England, might now be amenable to renewing the negotiations broken off when Gardoqui returned to Europe. Jefferson proposed trying again to the President, insisting, however, that negotiations take place in Madrid and not New York. The Secretary of State, shortly after assuming his duties, recognized immediately that Josef de Viar and Josef de Jaudenes could not possibly negotiate on behalf of the Spanish government. Gardoqui had left these two young men in charge of the Spanish mission in the United States, but for reasons of pique or snobbishness gave them no official diplomatic status, although they referred to themselves as "chargé d'affaires." And besides, they were untrustworthy. Jefferson learned quickly that they were actually running a small network of paid Spanish agents operating throughout the American West. In reality the young Spaniards were merely conduits for information to be funneled back to Spain. So Jefferson proposed, as early as March, that William Carmichael, the American chargé in Madrid, ought to reopen negotiations with the Spanish government for a commercial agreement and a relaxation of the Spanish hold on the Mississippi. Washington finally agreed, as the war crisis mounted in the late summer.

Having made his point, Jefferson, however, was soon having second thoughts. Carmichael was for the Secretary of State as much an enigma as he had been for former Foreign Secretary John Jay. Stationed in Madrid since 1779, he had served originally as secretary to the American minister when Jay came to seek Spanish aid during the Revolution. After Jay left for Paris in 1782 to participate in negotiations that ended the war, Carmichael was given responsibility for American affairs in Spain. By 1784 King Carlos had formally recognized him as chargé d'affaires. Since then little had been heard from him. So Jefferson complained about the paucity of Carmichael's reports and lost confidence in his abilities. Had Jefferson known how the Spanish were lavishing attention on Carmichael during the summer of 1790 he might have had a different opinion. Lord Fitzherbert, England's ambassador in Madrid, reported to London that "Mr. Carmichael is very much caressed at Court, and he has artfully availed himself . . . in procuring from the Spanish minister the liquidation of a Number of private claims."

Not knowing any of this, Jefferson decided to prod Carmichael and at the same time coordinate the rest of American diplomacy in Europe. In August he sent David Humphreys as a secret courier to carry letters to Carmichael in Madrid, to Gouverneur Morris in London, and to William Short, the American chargé in Paris. Seemingly Humphreys was a good choice, for he was considered intelligent, discreet, and reliable; he was, moreover, a close friend of the President and one of the three men Washington sent to meet with McGillivray the previous October. But Jefferson had not counted on interference from Alexander Hamilton, who worried that Jefferson's gambit toward Spain during the war crisis would disrupt Anglo-American friendship. Tragically, Humphreys was also a bit naive and too trustful of the Secretary of the Treasury. Before he sailed for Europe he let Hamilton induce him to meet George Beckwith and foolishly reveal the true nature of his mission. By the time he arrived in London the British government knew in detail his purposes. The real tragedy for American foreign affairs, of course, was that this would not be the only time Jefferson and Hamilton worked at cross-purposes, almost always without the President's knowledge.

Humphreys' letters arrived in Europe too late to do the American cause much good. Spain had capitulated to England on the Nootka issue, and with the evaporation of the war scare the bargaining position of the United States materially weakened. Spain, nevertheless, had learned a valuable lesson: the Family Compact was no longer valid and therefore she could no longer rely on France to come to her aid. She must treat with the United States or strengthen her position in the Mississippi Valley, or both. When Carmichael presented Washington's request to reopen negotiations, he found Floridablanca in a receptive mood.

Jefferson's instructions, however, forced Carmichael to take a stronger stand than the Spaniard had expected. The United States insisted not only that its citizens have the right to navigate the Mississippi but also the equally important right to pass through Spanish-held territory to trade their goods at a seaport, the "right of deposit." As Jefferson explained to Carmichael, "the right to use a thing comprehends a right to the means necessary to its use, and without which it would be useless." In the meantime, in order to help Carmichael, the Secretary of State tried to open another door to Madrid through Paris. In March, 1791 he authorized William Short to seek French backing of the American effort with the Spanish. Short complied in his own strongly worded memorial setting out American claims for full use of the Mississippi. With LaFayette's assistance he was able to get the French foreign minister, the Comte de Montmorin, to forward the memorial to Floridablanca. Montmorin offered no evaluation to the Spanish, but confided to Short if the Americans wanted the Mississippi Valley they should take it. In saying this he was probably agreeing with a recent report from his consul general in New York, who insisted if the United States held Louisiana and the Floridas, French influence could counterbalance the British in

North America for "American commerce must be sold at an advantage for France."

Although angered by this two-pronged approach to him, Floridablanca finally agreed to reopen negotiations with the United States. Through Jaudenes and Viar he informed Washington in November, 1791, that Spain was willing to send a special representative to America or accept a "suitable person" to carry on the discussions in Madrid. The President was satisfied that at last some progress was being made and turned over direction of the negotiations to his Secretary of State. But in the process he unwittingly allowed Jefferson to complete a triple *faux pas* that added to the irritability in Madrid. Instead of sending to Madrid a "suitable person"—which to the Spanish meant prominent—Jefferson used the two men he had in Europe, Carmichael and Short, even though Jaudenes had warned that Carmichael was no longer held in high esteem. And he tolerated Short's year-long delay in not getting to Madrid until February, 1793.

In part, Jefferson can be excused for his cumbersome handling of these highly significant negotiations. It took twelve to fourteen weeks before he could get answers to questions sent to American representatives in Europe, and the situation there was becoming more fluid with each passing day as the French Revolution grew in intensity, causing shifts in the international alliance structure. By the time he received news of a specific event, its impact was already outdated. The Secretary of State was merely playing for time to find the best American advantage in Europe's distresses. From month to month neither he nor the President ever fully understood what was happening in Europe.

And, too, Jefferson unnecessarily was forced to play musical chairs with his diplomatic personnel in Europe, with an extra chair in Portugal that he had not expected. After David

Humphreys finished delivering his mail to London, Paris, and Madrid he took up residence in Lisbon as chargé of the American mission, only to find that the Portuguese government had already decided to accredit its own minister to the United States. To save embarrassment and to follow protocol, Humphreys was raised to the status of minister, with an increase in salary and staff. A parsimonious Congress, still unwilling to fund an extensive foreign service, was not pleased with this development.

In Paris, meanwhile, Washington had created additional confusion. Without consulting Jefferson, the President directed Gouverneur Morris to take over as minister to France as soon as Thomas Pinckney arrived in London. This left an angry, disappointed William Short without a chair. Short had been Jefferson's secretary in Paris in the late '80s, had handled affairs rather well after the Virginian returned home to become Secretary of State, and honestly expected to be named the American minister in Paris. As a sop to Short's ego, Washington agreed he should be sent to the lesser post of minister to the Netherlands. He dragged his heels in establishing himself at the Hague, and either misunderstood or deliberately ignored the urgency of his special mission to Madrid.

By the time the music stopped a whole year had passed, and the entire diplomatic situation in Europe had changed so thoroughly that earlier American strategies were no longer valid. In Spain the new king, Carlos IV, gradually brought new personalities to positions of power and dramatic shifts in Spanish foreign policy. Floridablanca had been replaced by the Conde de Aranda, who in turn was replaced in November, 1792, by the Queen's handsome favorite, the twenty-five-year-old Manuel de Godoy. A court adventurer who benefited greatly from Queen Luisa's physical attraction for him, Godoy was created Duke of Alcudia and became the most powerful of the Spanish ministers. He made up for his lack of experience

and mature wisdom with prodigious energy, youthful enthusiasm, and a sense of personal loyalty that raised the spirits of his
underlings in the foreign office. It was Godoy's immaturity and
Spanish pride that Washington finally had to confront in finding a solution to the Mississippi Question.

In the meantime, a similar and equally significant change
occurred in Spain's administration of her Mississippi provinces.
At the end of 1791 Estevan Miró completed his ten years of
overseas service and returned to Spain. He was replaced as
governor by Hector, Baron de Carondolet, transferred from a
similar post at San Salvador. Carondolet was the wrong man in
the wrong position to improve Spanish-American relations,
for he was totally unfamiliar with Louisiana, knew no English,
yet was impulsive and at times dangerously aggressive. Whereas
Miró had carefully followed Floridablanca's cautious guidelines
not to offend the United States openly, Carondolet exercised
no such caution. With little restraint from the erratic Godoy he
invited disaster for the Spanish position on the Mississippi,
indirectly forcing the United States closer and closer to an
unwanted war.

Carondolet saw his purpose as two-fold: strengthen
Spain's physical defenses for its Mississippi provinces and restore Spain's prestige among the Indians. To undercut growing
American influence resulting from the Treaty of New York, he
sent his own officers as agents into the Indian villages rather
than rely on vague cooperation of individual Indians. He also
tried to wean McGillivray away from his commitments to the
United States. For this he found an ally in the ambitious and
outrageous William Augustus Bowles, a British trader with
strong contacts among the more southern of the Creek tribes.
Bowles had taken several Creek and Cherokee chiefs to London to get British backing for an independent Indian state in
the American Southwest. Bowles' timing was perfect, for the
delegation arrived in England at the height of the Nootka

crisis. Although the British, according to Lord Grenville, gave them "no kind of encouragement," Pitt's government used them as window dressing in its strong posture against Spain. Bowles' obvious ties with the British ministry strengthened his prestige with the chiefs, and he challenged McGillivray for leadership among the Creeks, who were becoming increasingly dissatisfied with concessions made to the Americans. Already his trading partners in New Providence, Bahamas, were competing successfully with Panton and Leslie.

To maintain his own prestige McGillivray was forced to mend his fences with Spain. With little persuasion from Carondolet, on July 6, 1792, he signed the Treaty of New Orleans. This new agreement went far beyond the cautious limitations of Miró. It promised in addition to a Spanish guarantee of "Lands belonging too and actually possessed by the Creek Nation" arms and ammunition to the Creeks "not only to defend their country, but even to regain their encroached Lands, should the Americans refuse willingly & peaceably to retire in the time pointed out." More importantly, the treaty bound the Creeks within two months to expel "all intruders" on their lands beyond the limits formerly granted to the British. In one bold stroke Carondolet completely reversed Spanish colonial policies in the Southwest and involved McGillivray in the process. For his part, McGillivray was rewarded with an increase of 1,500 pesos in his annual pension from the Spanish.

With the Treaty of New Orleans in his pocket, Carondolet now pushed Spain's position aggressively northward. He ordered the building of a fort at Nogales (Vicksburg), over one hundred miles north of the 31st parallel. He excused this act, as he explained to a few nervous Indian chiefs, as a counter to possible occupation of the Yazoo area by Georgia speculators. He also began the volatile process of welding all of the Indian nations south of Kentucky into an anti-American confederation. He even took advantage of St. Clair's disastrous defeat on the Maumee to offer friendship and cooperation with the tribes north of the Ohio. At the same time he reopened contact with James Wilkinson, hoping to revive the spirit of independence in Kentucky. As with McGillivray, he got Wilkinson's attention with Spanish cash. He sent the happy news to the American general that he would receive an annual pension of $2,000, retroactive to January 1, 1789. It had taken Carondolet less than six months to undo most of Washington's patient efforts to bring peace to the Southwest.

There was almost no limit to the President's fury over what he called McGillivray's duplicity. He was most incensed that the Creek leader completely ignored his honest attempts to implement the Treaty of New York with as much fairness as possible. He had deliberately selected the most qualified men available as American representatives to the Indian nations, and had directed them to be carefully sympathetic to Indian sensibilities. One of these, James Seagrove, young, well-informed, and loyal, was specifically sent to work with McGillivray. It was Seagrove's responsibility to arrange for a surveying team to run the boundary agreed upon in the treaty. Carondolet, however, successfully countered Seagrove's influence by sending his own agent, Pedro Oliver, into the Creek villages. Not only were the surveyors unwelcome to the Creeks, but Seagrove himself was in danger.

"The conduct of Spain in this business is so unprovoked, so misterious, and so hostile in appearance," snapped the angry President as he assessed Seagrove's report of McGillivray's betrayal. It made no sense to him that Spain would deliberately stir up an Indian war, so he was willing "to acquit the Spanish *government* of measures so unfriendly to the U. States." To be sure, he sent Seagrove's dispatches to Jefferson, admonishing the Secretary of State to confront Jaudenes and Viar with the evidence and demand an explanation of "these proceedings in some of [Spain's] Officers." Losing his patience, he let his suspicions get the best of him, for he could not shake the fear "that there is a very clear understanding between the courts of London and Madrid; and it is calculated to check, as far as they can, the rapid increase, extension and consequence of this country."

Washington's fears may have been justified. Jefferson got no satisfaction from Viar and Jaudenes in Philadelphia. Obviously answers had to come from Madrid. But what of news from Spain? A still angry President wrote his Secretary of State, "I believe we are never to hear *from* Mr. Carmichael; nor *of him* but through the medium of a third person. His _____ I really do not know what epithet to fill the blank, is, to me, amongst the most unaccountable of all unaccountable things!"

Frustration and isolation thus characterized United States relations with Spain all during 1792. Frustration came from what seemed a collapse of the southern Indian policy in the face of renewed Spanish determination. Isolation was a result of agonizing weeks of waiting for precise information to cross and recross the Atlantic, heightened, for the President at least, by the lack of news that William Short had actually arrived in Madrid to begin substantive talks with the Spanish. Until these talks were completed there would be no peace in the Southwest.

In the meantime all Washington and his government could do was hold off as long as possible the threatened Indian wars. Until General Wayne demonstrated American military strength north of the Ohio, the President could only continue his appeasement of the tribes to the south. It was a weak position and it galled him, but he was determined no American would upset the delicately balanced peace. Basing his views on Seagrove's advice, he directed Secretary of War Knox to warn Governor Edward Telfair of Georgia that settlers on the frontier of that state were interfering with the boundary survey agreed to in the Treaty of New York "that now has become a law of the

Land." He reinforced his unpopular instructions to Governor Blount and other southwestern leaders to restrain any aggressive action that might excite the Indians. And he ordered that no one without authority from the War Department meet with the Indians, "or Counteraction of the measures of Government, perplexity and confusion will inevitably ensue."

Governor Blount tried his best to implement these policies, but with little success. In June he personally visited 2,000 Cherokees and Chickamaugas in an attempt to convince their chiefs to confer with Washington in Philadelphia. They refused, and the only concession Blount could get was permission for an American agent, James Craig, to reside among the Cherokees. In fact the anti-American hostility was so great that just after the meeting broke up a band of disgruntled and uncontrolled Indians attacked a small stockade near Nashville, killing five, wounding five, and capturing twelve.

By September, 1792, peace in the Southwest had evaporated completely, and the Spanish-sponsored Indian confederation unleashed a major attack against frontier settlements. Had their chiefs been able to agree on a single offensive, as the Spanish wanted, it could have been devastating. As it was, they had no European-style discipline, preferring their traditional scatter-shot hit-and-run tactics that in reality were more easily resisted by frontier defenders. The situation worsened the following winter, however, when a delegation from the northern tribes urged the Creeks and Cherokees to join with them in a united Indian front against General Wayne's expected military operations in Ohio. This conference produced an inter-Indian war as the Creeks marched against the Chickasaws, the only southern nation friendly to the United States. In February, McGillivray, still young at thirty-two, died. His death was a significant blow to United States policy despite his vacillations between Americans and Spaniards. His was the only prominent influence among the southern Indians, and without him there was no longer a focus for future American diplomatic effort.

Falling federal prestige prompted James Seagrove to warn that frontiersmen "now consider the troops and servants of the United States nearly as great enemies as they do the Indians." By the summer of 1793 dissatisfaction and discontent with the ineffective resistance to Indian raids was prevalent throughout the Southwest, and Washington's call for caution was ignored. In June, Captain James Beard, with too much anger and too little common sense, deliberately ignored orders and attacked a delegation of chiefs preparing to go to Philadelphia. Governor Blount ordered a court-martial, but violent opposition from the settlers forced him to drop the charges. Beard, not Blount, was a hero in the West.

President Washington was, therefore, no more successful with Spain and her client Indian nations in the Southwest than he was with the British and their allies in the north. By the end of his first term, his patient diplomacy had earned only frustration, fear, and distrust. He had failed to prevent emboldened Indians on the northern and southern frontiers from still being used as pawns by the European great powers. His frontier problems seemed always to originate in Europe, and they could not be solved until the United States gathered the military strength to assert its authority in the West, or until the Europeans reevaluated the existence of the new American republic—or both. Washington had to confront Europe directly if the foreign policies of his second administration were to be more successful than those of his first. The key to the survival of the United States was in Europe. The only way to find that key was to discover American advantages in Europe's own distresses. For Washington and for his country, Europe's greatest distress was the French Revolution.

CHAPTER FIVE

"The French Albatross"

GATHERING CLOUDS from the French Revolution loomed ominously over Washington's entire administration. They were mere puffs of hope when the Estates General met for the first time since 1614 on May 1, 1789, the day after Washington first took the oath as President. The release of 175 years of pent-up frustration and anger quickly unleashed violent storms that destroyed the Old Regime, plunged Europe into twenty-two years of furious warfare, and drastically shifted the balance of power. The French Revolution was the most dynamic force to hit Europe since the Reformation, spilling beyond national boundaries and laying a challenge to traditional politics, economics, and society. For the leaders of the old ways it was a devious challenge that had to be contained and then destroyed, lest they and the world they represented be swept away. Such a clash of ideologies in Europe sent a threatening rumble across the Atlantic that could only endanger the new and fragile United States.

Most Americans were fascinated by the French Revolution and saw little danger to themselves in it. Almost from the beginning they felt a sense of continuity, a sympathy of kindred spirits, as though the torch of liberty was now being passed from the revolution in North America to that in France. They felt excitement and pride that their revolution was a model for their former war-time allies; the principles of the Declaration of Independence were echoed in the Declaration of the Rights of

Man. They could not avoid celebrating as they watched almost breathlessly the unfolding drama in Paris.

Perhaps at first Washington was even more excited than his fellow Americans. He waited anxiously for the detailed letters from his former protégé, the young Marquis de La Fayette. He, too, thrilled over the sense of continuity, as he recognized that this man, whom he loved almost as a son, was one of the guiding forces of the Revolution. He undoubtedly wept as he read and reread the Frenchman's exciting description of the storming of the old royal prison of the Bastille, the gloomy symbol of Old Regime repression. LaFayette, himself, confirmed the continuity between the two revolutions when he sent the American President the key to the Bastille with this dedication: "It is a tribute which I owe as a son to my adopted father, as an aide-de-camp to my general, as a missionary of liberty to its patriarch." Washington also recognized the great debt the United States owed France for her earlier assistance, and his enthusiasm for the new France grew. He wrote in early 1790 that "the renovation of the French constitution is indeed one of the most wonderful events in the history of mankind." Clearly there was much to expect and little to fear from revolutionary France.

Despite this enthusiasm, Washington was a realist. He saw clearly that relations between the two countries had not developed the way the French had expected when they committed themselves to the American cause in the alliance of 1778. Commerical interdependence had not brought mutual benefits. On the contrary, since the peace of 1783 Americans had reverted to their pre-war trade patterns with Great Britain. Even though French ministers to the Continental Congress protested, by the end of the 1780s Britain once again dominated the American economy as she had before independence. Frustrated in his inability to persuade Congress to remedy the situation, the Count de Moustier in 1788 appealed to Washington for help. Shrewdly he attempted to build a closer personal friendship, recognizing that the Virginia planter would soon be the most powerful official in the new republic. But the yet-to-be-elected President could only sympathize.

Washington did, however, point out to Moustier that part of the problem lay with France herself. Monopolistic control of the tobacco market in France was no different from the "English and Scottish who used to conduct it" and was unpopular in Virginia and Maryland. French merchants also demanded cash payment, rarely extending long-term credits as British merchants were willing to do. In a succinct statement Washington answered Moustier "that in proportion as France shall increase the facility of our making remittance, in the same ratio shall we increase the consumption of her produce and manufactures." Finally, if her government would open up trade to her West Indies islands the credits thus earned by American merchants would encourage an expansion of purchases from France. The only solutions he could really offer in 1788 were the pending changes in the government of the United States: "I will not undertake to predict, I hope and trust the ties which connect this Nation with France, will be strengthened and made durable by it."

Soon after his inauguration he expressed the same sentiments again to Moustier, but this time he gave the French diplomat a lesson in how American foreign relations would now be conducted. In a rather strong and detailed letter he coolly rejected Moustier's offer to discuss personally with the President all aspects of Franco-American affairs. Such discussions, as "in most polished nations," ought to follow traditional practices by going through the department of foreign affairs and its secretary. Moustier obviously was trying to take advantage of the friendship he had cultivated earlier between himself and the Virginia farmer. He probably hoped to install himself as a resident adviser at President Washington's court in somewhat the same way his predecessors had done with the Continental Congress. Moustier saw obvious advantages. The Spanish minister was about to return home; there was no official British representative, nor were there any ranking diplomats from the other European countries. The opening days of a new government would be a golden opportunity to establish French influence over the future of American policies. But Washington found the idea "not prudent for a young state." Despite his personal affection for France, the President would carry on his country's relations to all nations with equal circumspection.

Dissension in these relations with France became increasingly apparent as the Revolution grew in intensity and vigor. Although a royalist, Moustier reflected heightened French nationalism and complained bitterly to sympathetic Congressmen that American tariff policies gave no preferences to French trade. His complaints fueled the fire of anti-British sentiment, leading to efforts in each session of Congress to pass discriminatory legislation against the British. And each time, of course, the effort was defeated by the growing strength of a loosely organized coalition of Senators desiring closer commercial ties with England. By his refusal to interfere in the politics of the Congress, Washington, regardless of his personal sympathies toward France, imperceptibly but inadvertently permitted American policies to irritate the French.

He did not improve the situation by his decision to send Gouverneur Morris as first minister to France. After Congress appropriated funds for American legations in Europe, Washington still would not appoint a minister to Great Britain until he was assured the English would reciprocate. He felt, however, that Morris should be rewarded for services as the President's personal representative in London. Without consulting Jefferson, he submitted the New Yorker's name to the Senate for confirmation. It would prove to be a poor choice, for Morris was sent to the right place at the wrong time. Even though the

English considered him *persona non grata* for his seemingly pro-French indiscretions, he was not sympathetic to the Revolution. He was as indiscreet in Paris as he had been in London, often supporting the monarchy in both public and private comments even after the Republic had been proclaimed. For a brief time his home outside Paris was a refuge for escapees from the Revolution; and once he was falsely accused of being involved in a secret plot to effect the King's escape from prison.

Until it was almost too late Washington ignored unofficial reports concerning Morris' conduct in Paris. In the meantime, however, he did assist the hapless emigrés driven by a violent slave insurrection from the French island of San Domingo in the Caribbean. The Revolution's ideas of "Liberty, Equality and Fraternity" had inspired the island's exploited slave population into a desperate rebellion characterized by rape, pillage, and murder. During the opening phases of this rebellion, in the summer of 1791, the French minister appealed directly to Washington for financial and military aid so the island's colonial government could defend itself. The President agreed with Secretary Knox's observation that it was "a singular opportunity for the United States to repay in some degree the assistance afforded us during the perilous struggles of the late war," and authorized money for food purchases and supplies from the American military arsenal drawn as advance payments on the American Revolutionary War debt still owed to France. He also put to rest Moustier's fear that the United States might take over the potentially independent San Domingo, assuring him instead that Americans wanted "to render every aid in their power to our good friends and Allies the French to quell" the insurrection. Later, as the rebellion's violence reached an intensity that drove thousands of planters, merchants, colonial officials, and their families to seek refuge in the United States, he joined in a nationwide effort to provide them with monetary aid and opportunities for resettlement.

Washington's admiration for the French and respect for their Revolution were put under extreme strain when events in Paris began to run their true course. The storm that burst upon France swept away the Old Regime's tradition of monarchy, aristocracy, and church, and replaced them with a dizzying succession of increasingly radical and militantly nationalistic governments. A blundering plot to rescue the closely guarded Louis XVI and his queen aborted and resulted in violent over-throw of the monarchy. A republic was proclaimed; the ex-king was tried for treason, found guilty, and executed; aristocrats were driven into exile or murdered in their beds. Leadership of one republican government found itself too moderate for its political opposition and was driven to exile, prison, or death. Successor governments in turn were superseded by even more rabid groups of leaders. The Revolution fed upon itself until France was wracked by political instability, civil war, economic maladjustment, and critical food shortages. Despite these weak-nesses, virulent French national republicanism overflowed the country's geographic boundaries. With more enthusiasm than rationality the Revolution attacked the array of monarchies ringed along its periphery. By early 1793 the Republic of France was at war with Great Britain, Spain, Austria-Hungary, Prus-sia, and the Netherlands. It was a war that pitted the new spirit of democracy and republicanism against the old traditions of monarchy and aristocracy.

Washington could hardly keep up with these rapid changes in Europe's politics let alone determine their impact on his own problems. Because communications in the late eighteenth cen-tury were still frustratingly slow, there were weeks of often disastrous ignorance until he received official confirmation of a change in a belligerent's policies. While he tried to keep his government informed of the situation across the Atlantic his heart was heavy because of what he considered a personal loss. He had set high hopes on LaFayette's ability to guide the Revolution into a rational, liberal constitutional monarchy. Instead, LaFayette was as discredited as the monarchy he had tried to reform. Washington's beloved protégé languished in an Austrian prison despite the personal efforts of the American President to get him released.

Confusion in Paris created unique foreign policy debates for Washington's government. Were the successive administrations of the French Republic legitimate governments? Were American debt and treaty obligations to France only to the monarchy? If the United States were to accept the overthrow of the monarchy and recognize the Republic, what criteria for recognition should be followed? After recognition, to whom did the American minister present his credentials? Who within the French administration was responsible for acknowledging receipt of payments on the American debt to France? Of utmost importance, did the Franco-American military alliance of 1778 obligate the United States to come to the aid of its sister republic?

It was necessary to answer some of these questions shortly after Gouverneur Morris established his official residence in Paris. He had been instructed to arrange through Dutch bankers a substantial payment of the American debt still owed to France. This was the normal procedure for making regular payments of principal and accumulated interest established under Hamilton's refunding of the entire Revolutionary War debt. Morris made the arrangements, but before actual payment was delivered the monarchy was suspended and the king imprisoned. When pressed for the money by the new foreign minister Morris replied he had no instructions to treat with the new government. The baffled Frenchman could only wait until the American's status was clarified, and this could not come until Washington himself received clarification of what was going on in Paris.

The American people in their enthusiasm for the French

Revolution were not concerned over such official niceties. While their president carefully pondered every scrap of information filtering in from Europe, they snatched at bits and pieces of news brought in by almost every vessel touching at a local port. They badgered newly arrived passengers and ships' crews for everything known about the successive events in Paris. They were so caught up in emotional excitement they accepted rumor as well as fact; their enthusiasm reached a frenzy when they learned that a republic had been proclaimed. Truly now the "Torch of Liberty" had passed from the New World to the Old, and American republicans cheered the success of the new republic across the Atlantic. There was, of course, some disaffection caused by the execution of the King, but this was soon overcome by news that the Republic had declared war on its monarchical enemies. Sympathetic Americans—and there were a lot of them—publicly celebrated each victory of French Republican armies with huge bonfires, church bells, and the singing of French and American patriotic hymns.

This unabashed, broadly distributed excitement in favor of the French Republic caught Washington's foreign policy in an almost impossible dilemma, for it hit at several different but highly significant levels. The President had no great love for the English or the other European monarchies, yet he feared the embrace of an aggressive French Republic he neither understood nor trusted. More than that, the growing American enthusiasm for the new French government had ominous overtones for the stability of his own administration. The most vociferous pro-French sentiment came from already existing groups called Democratic-Republican societies, that had appeared in the West and South as early as 1789 and 1790. Initially organized to debate the policies—in some cases, the lack of policies—of Washington's administration, they were in part formed from the remnants of the opposition to ratification of the Constitution. Their original concern was over the centralizing tendencies of the new federal government. Symbolizing a revival of the "Spirit of '76" their very names—"The Political Club," "The Republican Society," "Society of Federal Republicans," "The Society of United Freemen"—indicated a defense of democracy and republicanism in the face of an unfair, but often accepted view that Washington's government was drifting toward monarchy. With the editorial support of many like-minded newspaper publishers, they provided a logical base for organizing opposition to federalist programs. Expanding in number and vociferousness by 1793, they became a significant outlet for popular dissidence as they looked with increasing suspicion on the intent and purpose of many of the government's policies.

These societies were a burr under the saddle of the Hero-President. He had always feared "political factions" and their potential danger to stable government. He simply had no understanding of the function of political parties in the processes of government. On the contrary, he rather naively tried to keep his administration above politics, hoping that maintaining a balance of representative opinion within his cabinet would help him find an acceptable middle ground. But growing vocal support for the revolution in France drove a wedge even into his own official family. From the very beginning Jefferson was strongly sympathetic to France, while the cautious Hamilton opposed almost any policy that he considered adverse to his plans for strengthening commercial ties with England. Of the other two cabinet members, Randolph usually, but not always, sided with Jefferson, and Knox habitually agreed with Hamilton; thus opinion from the president's advisers more often than not was split equally down the middle. The danger for Washington came from members of Congress who took advantage of this split in cabinet opinion. The anti-British faction, led by Madison in the House, looked to Jefferson for leadership, while pro-British strength, especially in the Senate, already had found its leader in Hamilton. The early attempts to have discriminatory tariffs against the British grew by 1793 to strong pressures for federal actions avowedly pro-French. Worse still, since the proclamation of a French Republic the democratic-republican societies began to chant that refusal to aid France indicated the *anti-republican* drift of the American government itself. It was unfortunate, but true, that foreign affairs issues easily became entwined in on-going debates over controversial domestic programs—such items as the Bank of the United States, the whiskey excise, import tariffs, and even the sale of federal lands. As a result the exaggerated enthusiasm on behalf of France focused unnecessary attention on domestic legislation that should have been considered on its own merits. The French Revolution indeed had spun off a separate storm across the Atlantic that was to vex Washington for the rest of his life.

At root was a fundamental problem for the first President. His country was so new, his government so untried, that ideas—any ideas—concerning federal legislation or administration attitudes on economics or foreign relations were frightening to someone someplace. Whether its citizens admitted it or not, the opening years of the American experiment in national self-determination were a frightful experience, with dangers, some real and some imagined, lurking in every direction. Even after shaking off the traditions of colonial subservience, the American people were still insecure about that future Washington so accurately had described "as a sea of uncertain difficulties." As a result, fear of the future caused passions to run high among groups as well as individuals. They felt their ideas—and only theirs—were the safest basis for government policies. They were intolerant, often to the point of violence, of those ideas, policies, and programs they were convinced could only destroy their country. The nation was about to plunge itself into its worst era of vituperative news reporting and character assassination. Even the god-like Washington was not immune.

He felt the first barbs of public criticism when he stopped temporarily the debt payments to France. By accepting Hamilton's irrefutable logic that there was too much uncertainty about the French government, the President angered Jefferson as well as the democratic-republican societies. But the Secretary of State carefully gathered documents convincing him that the French Republic was indeed legitimate. In the autumn of 1792 Gouverneur Morris was directed to complete his arrangements for making the installment on the debt as long as he received proper receipts from an officially designated agent. In effect, Washington had granted *de facto* recognition of the French Republic.

Similar confrontations over decision-making concerning France and its revolutionary governments made Washington's second administration far more stormy than his first. The new situations did, however, force him to establish policies and procedures that would be fundamental to carrying on the nation's foreign relations. The first issue presented itself in April, 1793, when official notices arrived that the French had executed their ex-king, had declared war on Great Britain, and were sending Citizen Edmund Genet as the Republic's first minister to the United States.

News of the startling events reached the President at Mount Vernon. He had returned to Virginia shortly after his second inauguration because of the untimely death of his nephew, Major John Washington. His period of mourning was cut short by Jefferson's urgent dispatch hastening him back to Philadelphia.

Five uncomfortable days of jostling carriage and bouncing

ferry added to the morose President's mounting irritability, but they gave him time to think about the perplexing problems requiring his immediate attention. Already he had received rumors that American vessels were being outfitted as privateers to prey on the shipping of both Britain and France. His first reaction was a deep fear that broad based popular enthusiasm for France, now inflamed over the war against England, might induce Americans to take irrational actions that could only draw the United States into the war. He was convinced, and rightly so, that a still weak, still divided America could not possibly survive involvement as a belligerent in another of Europe's wars. And he found the realities of American treaty relations with France even more frightening. Would the French, now engaged in yet another war with the English, invoke the Franco-American Alliance of 1778 and demand that the United States honor its promise to defend French possessons in the Western hemisphere? Before he could answer this enormous question, he had to decide whether or not to receive Citizen Genet, an act of formal recognition of the Republic of France. If he received Genet the United States would stand alone among nations in its legal acknowledgement of the new French government at the very moment the powers of Europe were trying to destroy it!

The need for haste did not deter Washington from his methodical approach to problem-solving. Before he left Mount Vernon he dispatched a post-rider with terse commands to Jefferson, Hamilton, and Knox to prepare for his return to the national capital with "mature consideration" on "precautionary measures." It was an immediate necessity, he reminded them, to enunciate a clear-cut government policy of maintaining a "strict neutrality." As soon as he arrived in Philadelphia he fired off a summons to the three of them to meet with him the next morning. To each he sent a list of thirteen questions, a breakdown of the broad problem into its logical and discussable parts. In a sense, the last question was the most significant. Should he call Congress into session and, if so, "what should be the particular object of such a call?"

Washington's cabinet members angered and frustrated him, for he was now painfully aware of their deep ideological division. Hamilton continued to insist that the French Republic was not viable. He argued strongly that the American commitments made in the Alliance of 1778 were made to the King of France; therefore with his death and the creation of a republic the treaty no longer existed. Jefferson surprisingly held his temper, and perhaps with less emotion but more logic argued that the United States should recognize the Republic of France by receiving its minister. With even greater care he reasoned convincingly that the Alliance of 1778 had been made with the French people, not exclusively with the administration of their government, and so the treaty was binding. But the United States could and should, of course, consult its own best interests if ever French demands under the treaty compromised American security or sovereignty.

Despite these vast differences of opinion the cabinet agreed that the United States had to preserve its neutrality at all costs. It also agreed, much to Washington's relief, that as President he possessed all the constitutional powers necessary to set forth policies to meet the current emergency. That question, he would find out later, was fundamental. There were many Americans, not only among members of Congress, who sincerely felt that Congress should determine basic directions in foreign relations, in particular the formalities of recognition and neutrality. Although the Constitution clearly stated the President "shall receive ambassadors and other public ministers," critics would argue this was merely a formal function of the chief of state. Because Congress alone had the power to declare war it also had exclusive power to declare peace. This was a convoluted argument that led to the conclusion that peace and neutrality were the same thing.

Washington was no usurper, but he was a pragmatist. Calling Congress into session would take weeks, and the pressing issues of Franco-American relations could not wait. Moreover, the widening split in public opinion probably would be reflected in Congress itself; debate would rage on for months before Congress could make a decision—if ever. So the President took the initiative, made his decisions, determined his policies, and stuck by them.

Accepting Jefferson's reasoning that the Treaty of 1778 was still in force, he would receive Citizen Genet. If the French later were to make demands under the treaty's terms, these would be decided on their merits. At the same time he agreed with Hamilton that American neutrality must be clear, strict, and impartial even if it compromised some of the treaty terms. This decision in itself was momentous, for the President was defining wholly new principles of neutrality. Traditionally European countries had followed neutrality practices based on self-interest, a "wait and see" attitude.

When Washington issued his now famous "Proclamation" on April 22, 1793, he truly meant that the United States "should with sincerity and good faith adopt and pursue a conduct friendly and impartial towards the belligerent powers." He also meant "to exhort and warn the citizens of the United States carefully to avoid all acts and proceedings whatsoever, which may in any manner tend to contravene such disposition." Despite public sentiment to the contrary, nothing nor no one was to compromise the American position. Interestingly, the word "neutrality" did not appear in the proclamation itself. The President agreed with Jefferson's fear that the overly nationalistic French might consider the word as indication of American antagonism toward France.

Unfortunately for Washington, defining neutrality and enforcing it were two different things. Almost immediately the Proclamation became unpopular with the democratic-republican societies who found it made illegal their activities on behalf of France. They opposed it, and many of their members openly resisted state militia and police authorities charged by the President to enforce it. They publicly denied his constitutional right to issue it. In fact, the neutrality proclamation marks the beginning of the decline in Washington's personal popularity. His self-conviction to the contrary, the partisan press, with some accuracy, was gradually identifying him with Hamilton's Federalism. At first, fortunately for his own sensibilities, he was merely accused of being an innocent dupe in the hands of Hamilton and the pro-British clique in the Senate.

Citizen Genet deliberately tried to prove this point. If ever there was a man with an exaggerated view of his own importance it was Edmund Charles Genet. Foppish in manner and somewhat overweight, he certainly was not cast in the mold of a heroic revolutionary. Yet he had talents; he was one of the best linguists in the Foreign Office, and through his diplomat-father's connections he already had extensive diplomatic experience of his own. He could be charming and witty, but more often than not he was arrogant, especially in his strident defense of the Republic. His arrogance, unrelieved by common sense, forced him to abandon a diplomatic assignment in St. Petersburg. Now armed with instructions that would seriously strain relations with the United States, he began a clash of wills with the American President.

Genet represented a French government dominated by the Gironde, a group of young, inexperienced, idealistic revolutionaries who viewed the world with the narrow vision of extreme nationalism and rabid republicanism. Their mass declarations of war in February, 1793 were really a crusade against monarchy everywhere; their goal was the establishment of republican governments wherever possible. The Gironde charged Genet with the responsibility of making republican United States a partner in their great struggle.

Genet threw himself into his task with all the zeal of a fanatic crusader storming the fortress of the infidel. Landing at Charleston instead of Philadelphia, he shrewdly exploited the strong pro-French sympathies existing throughout the deep South. William Moultrie, South Carolina's governor, was among the enthusiastic hundreds who gave him a hero's welcome upon his arrival. With so much popular approval and with the governor's blessing, Genet began to turn this important southern port into a base of operations for French activities. Using blank forms provided by his own government he issued letters of marque to American shipowners willing to risk their vessels as French privateers to prey on British shipping. He armed French vessels already in port and sent them out as commerce raiders. And, with more brashness than common sense, he ordered the French consul, Michael Ange Mangourit, to establish at Charleston a prize court to determine awards of ships and cargoes captured by the privateers as well as those taken by the French themselves. Finally, he turned his attention to the American Southwest, where he knew that a little encouragement could reap tremendous advantages for France. Here no less a person than Revolutionary war-hero George Rogers Clark awaited a signal from the French. Months earlier Clark had offered to lead from Kentucky a downriver offensive against Spanish Louisiana. All that was needed, Clark had boasted, were the blessings of the French government and a little of its money. Genet now provided both. He sent his own agents into Kentucky, and then giving Mangourit blank commissions in the French army and navy, he ordered the consul to coordinate the invasion.

His ego inflated by the early successes of his mission,

Genet decided to take the overland route to Philadelphia. This would give him new opportunities to gather support for the French cause. Each town and village gave him a hero's welcome with fireworks, bonfires, and clanging church bells. Gradually his progression northward took on the aspects of a triumphal procession. His reputation for charm as well as enthusiasm for France preceded him. By the time he reached Philadelphia he found the City of Brotherly Love had prepared the most lavish reception he had yet received. But it had taken him a month to get there!

In the meantime Genet learned that some of his schemes were already meeting success. The *Embuscade*, the French frigate that carried him to Charleston, had captured several British merchantmen and hauled them into American ports as prizes. All of these had been taken close off the coast, and one, the *Grange*, was actually seized within Delaware Bay. It was docked at Philadelphia, closely guarded by French-paid agents waiting Genet's instructions for its future use. He was now satisfied with the conduct of his mission, and, flattered by the tumultuous reception he had encountered everywhere, he was convinced the American people would support him.

By this time a furious Washington waited impatiently for Genet's formal presentation as the envoy of republican France. This was finally arranged for May 18, 1793, fifty days after the Frenchman had landed in the United States, an unconscionable delay even for eighteenth-century travel standards. With considerable forebearance the President kept his temper in check and offered Genet a dignified but cool reception with a brief speech that noticeably said little about the traditionally close ties between the United States and France. For his part Genet was surprised and angry. He was surprised because the President's coolness was in such sharp contrast to the ebullience he had already witnessed. And he was angered when he noticed a bust of Louis XVI in the President's office. He had expected far more officially from the United States, even within the framework of its declared neutrality. Instead he found an aloof, almost hostile President and a Neutrality Proclamation that hampered his mission.

Genet's anger increased when Secretary of State Jefferson presented Washington's demand that the *Grange* be returned to its rightful British owners. This was done at the insistence of George Hammond, the British minister, who protested all the seizures of British ships in American waters. It was obvious to Genet the American government had accepted the British position, and this was too much for him. Despite formal American statements of affection for France, United States neutrality was really pro-British. Genet now convinced himself that Washington's neutrality policies were really not what the American people themselves wanted. Washington was out of step with his own people.

Thus convinced, Genet set out to develop his own plans for Franco-American cooperation, but he made two fatal errors: he misjudged the temper of the American people and he challenged the leadership of their President. To promote his aims he took advantage of the friendliness of Jefferson, ultimately forcing the well-meaning Secretary of State into an embarrassing conflict of interests. Taking Jefferson into his confidence he convinced the Secretary that France did not intend to invoke the Treaty of 1778 and require the United States to defend French American possessions. At this point Jefferson undoubtedly sighed in relief. On the contrary, France wanted the United States to remain a non-belligerent. Then with convoluted logic, Genet insisted since the Alliance denied Britain the use of American ports to outfit privateers and repair naval vessels it did not preclude France from doing so. He interpreted the Alliance to give France wide latitude in its use of American neutrality. He also wanted advance payments on the American debt; secretly he planned to finance his invasion of Louisiana and Florida with these funds. Genet made these demands palatable by offering as bait a new commercial treaty which would open more French ports to American shipping. In his long rambling conversations with Jefferson, he continuously implied that Washington no longer understood the desires of his own people.

Jefferson was now trapped between his emotional preferences for France and the realities of preserving American neutrality. He personally liked Genet, initially at least, and spoke quite freely with him. But he totally rejected Genet's interpretation of the Alliance and pressed for the quick release of the *Grange*. He had already made the situation difficult for himself through his method of dealing with the British minister. By insisting on written memos between himself and Hammond, he forced the Englishman to seek the more sympathetic ear of Alexander Hamilton to push British views. Jefferson's stubbornness on this point permitted Hamilton to intrude more directly in foreign affairs than Jefferson would have wanted. As a result Jefferson's effectiveness as Secretary of State declined, while his frustrations grew with each new crisis with France.

Because Hamilton voiced Hammond's views and Jefferson those of Genet, it was difficult for Washington to get his Cabinet to determine an objective set of policies for preserving United States neutrality. Because it was precedent-setting the Proclamation itself caused problems and raised serious questions that had to be answered immediately. In the absence of statute and national precedent, what exactly was American neutrality? How could its broadly-stated terms be translated into legally accepted specifics? What agencies would enforce those specifics? What should be done to prevent the over-zealous democratic-republican societies from compromising neutrality and Genet from undermining it? With Congress not in session, how far dared the President go in the use of executive proclamations? And, of even greater importance, did the American people in general really want neutrality? It was obviously unpopular in the South and West, yet these areas were not the whole country. But could Genet be right?

Washington had deep personal misgivings about all of these questions. For the first time in his public career he was uncertain of his position; he desired to use power, not to abuse it. Yet he felt American neutrality had to be understood completely and preserved; anything less would tear his country apart. Already Genet's activities had poked holes in his Proclamation, while the British minister's protests daily piled up on Jefferson's desk. He did, however, receive some comfort from "The Merchants and Traders of the City of Philadelphia" who were not enamored of Citizen Genet. Their memorial to the President of May 16 strongly supported his policy. Gratefully he used the opportunity of his reply to publicize his own convictions: "I trust therefore, that the good citizens of the United States will show to the world, that they have as much wisdom in preserving peace at this critical juncture, as they have heretofore displayed valour in defending their just rights." His pride in the unique destiny of the United States made the preservation of peace the essential goal of his foreign policy. As he wrote David Humphreys, the American minister in Lisbon, "if we are permitted to improve without interruption, the great advantages which nature and circumstances have placed within our reach, many years will not revolve before we may be ranked not only among the most respectable, but among the happiest people on this Globe."

And so Washington and his Cabinet wrestled with these momentous questions all during the summer of 1793, one of the most significant moments in the development of American foreign policy. The President had tried to get unanimity on the decisions. Failing that, he more often than not accepted the strict neutrality positions proposed by Hamilton and seconded by Knox. Gradually a clear policy emerged. The American government would not permit vessels of war to be outfitted in its ports. It would issue orders to the various state governors to prevent the organization of any military forces on American territory for use against friendly nations. American citizens must be warned again through presidential proclamations to avoid any actions that violated the official policy of neutrality. And the government would make no additional advance payments on the debt to France lest these funds be used to compromise the United States through military activity against France's enemies.

Washington's most serious problem was the inability of his government to enforce these decisions. He had no navy (or coast guard) and his only authorized army was being gathered together along the Ohio for an Indian war. He could rely only on continuous protests to the French minister and assistance from state governments and their militias. This in itself was a weakness, for many of the southern and western governors were indifferent or openly hostile to the neutrality policy and therefore not always cooperative. This particular weakness in his position forced Washington to lead the country into a delicate balancing act between its inherent sympathy for republican France and the awful specter of involvement in the European war. While he worked to preserve neutrality he could not afford to offend France, for his own personal sympathies were for her success. Despite his dislike of Genet, only a week after his irritating introduction to that Frenchman, he took the opportunity of the return of the former minister, Jean Ternant, to write the Executive Council of France. He assured the council "with a sincere participation, of the great and constant friendship, which these U.S. bear to the French nation . . . hoping god to have them and you, very great and good friends and allies, in his holy keeping."

The deep division in public opinion and in the Cabinet

itself nevertheless undermined Washington's efforts to keep clear the definition of neutrality. Hamilton, too closely advised by Hammond, continued to propose specific acts that would benefit England. While Jefferson, so blinded by his admiration for Genet that he frequently lost his perspective, too often argued almost illogically in support of some of the less noxious of Genet's plans. Indeed, Jefferson's long, indiscreet conversations with Genet encouraged rather than prevented French violations, and they left Genet with a strong feeling that the real obstacle to a pro-French nonbelligerency was Washington himself. In the American confusion during those opening days of another great world war both Hamilton and Jefferson listened too closely to foreign advisers and allowed themselves to be maneuvered into positions which were not to their country's best interests. If Washington were aware of the sources of this division among his advisers, he gave no indication of it. Either he was terribly naive or his high personal affection for both Hamilton and Jefferson caused him to ignore it. Whatever his reasons, the North American policies of the English and French were being fought out to a great degree in his Cabinet.

In the midst of the President's struggle to keep these foreign influences to a minimum, personal problems intruded to divert his attention. The death of his nephew and then later, in early summer, the death of his plantation manager left the conduct of his affairs at Mount Vernon in a shambles. Always a good manager himself he could not tolerate, nor could he afford financially, poor management of his farms. Anxiously he dashed off long letters to Mount Vernon carefully detailing what he wanted done. To a great degree these letters were a diversion for him; their frequency and attention to specifics appear as therapy from the cares of state. But even their insistent detail could not get his problems solved. Out of desperation he made a flying trip to Virginia in midsummer at the very height of his government's crises with Genet.

These crises began with Genet's deliberate challenge of the Neutrality Proclamation itself, using the forum of a public jury trial to do so. Two American citizens had been arrested for violating the terms of the proclamation after they enlisted for service aboard a French privateer. Genet decided to finance the defense of one of these men, Gideon Henfield, and make his trial a test case. Genet's argument, and it had validity, was that actually there were no laws prohibiting Americans from serving on French armed vessels. But Attorney General Edmund Randolph convincingly presented the government's position before the Federal Circuit Court in Philadelphia. The judges instructed the jury that Henfield's offense was indeed punishable under existing laws. The jury, however, thought differently; caught up in the wave of popular enthusiasm for France, it acquitted Henfield. The verdict was a personal triumph for Genet, and he squeezed from it every possible bit of anti-administration propaganda.

Emboldened by the Henfield verdict Genet created the next crisis in the *Little Sarah* affair. This small but fast English brigantine, armed with four cannon, was captured by the *Embuscade* and taken as a prize to Philadelphia. Here, with Genet's approval, it was outfitted with fourteen cannon, prepared for sea as a French privateer, and renamed *La Petite Democrat*. Jefferson, prodded by Hammond and uncertain of his own authority in the absence of the President, tried to prevent a confrontation. He turned to Pennsylvania's Governor Thomas Mifflin for help, requesting an investigation. Genet fumed at the governor's agent that he had every right to arm the vessel and, if necessary, he would go over the head of the President and appeal directly to the people themselves. Jefferson, alarmed by this boldness, tried to reason with Genet, but all he got for his trouble was a warning that any attempt to capture the vessel would be resisted by its armed crew. Once again the Secretary of State was trapped between his official responsibilities and his personal sympathies; he found appalling the idea of a clash between armed forces of the world's only two republics.

A see-saw battle of words and of action by competing security forces now elevated the *Little Sarah* affair to the status of a major international crisis. Genet's contempt for the American government was obvious. Hammond was equally contemptuous; his reports to London berated the ineffectiveness of Washington's authority. Both the British and the French were prepared to take advantage of this national weakness. Already there were at least four French privateers and one British in American ports waiting the outcome. In the meantime Governor Mifflin attempted to minimize the problem by sending a squad of militia to guard the *Little Sarah* and prevent it from slipping out to sea. A desperate and timid Jefferson sent a hurried request for the President to return to Philadelphia as soon as possible. Mollified by Genet's promise that the ship would not sail until after the President could deal with the matter personally, he convinced Mifflin to withdraw the militia.

Back in Virginia an angry Washington prepared for a hurried return to the capital, his personal business still incomplete. Once again he dashed off terse orders for an emergency cabinet meeting. In his brief absence he had been defied, insulted, threatened, and made to appear a fool. Worse still, the authority of the federal government had been flaunted successfully, its weaknesses glaringly apparent to the warring powers. "What," he cried "must the world think of such conduct, and of the Government of the U. States in submitting to it?" By the time he reached Philadelphia the days in the jostling carriage had brought his temper to a boiling point. For the first time he lost control, and in a tirade that left the Cabinet members speechless he demanded "What is to be done in the case of the Little Sarah?"

The Cabinet had no answers. Instead, its wrangling over the issue showed all too obviously the deep division in sentiment. While the Cabinet debated, the *Little Sarah*, now *La Petite Democrat*, left unguarded, slipped down the Delaware and out to sea. Once again American authority had been flouted. Finally, out of sheer desperation Jefferson, with the support of the other Cabinet members, convinced the President to lay the entire matter before the Supreme Court for its interpretation. On July 18, 1783, Washington submitted to the Court twenty-nine questions concerning specific aspects of neutrality enforcement. His first question struck at the core of the problem as he began "Do the treaties between the United States and France give to France or her Citizens a right . . ." After two weeks of deliberation, and prodded frequently by the President for quick action, the reluctant justices found a suitable excuse for evading an unpopular issue. In a highly significant decision, they claimed that under the separation of powers the Court had no jurisdiction over strictly executive matters. The President received no help from them, but the startling assertion "that your judgment will discern what is right."

Surprisingly, Washington had not called Congress into session. There had been sufficient time, for three months had elapsed between news of the war in Europe and his appeal to the Supreme Court. Now he questioned his Cabinet as to the advisability of consulting Congress. Only Jefferson supported the idea; the others agreed with the Court that the problem belonged to the Executive. But the President still needed answers and the means to enforce the answers. Because he could not dump the responsibility he turned again to the Cabinet for ideas, reminding it "to fix rules on substantial and impartial ground, conformably to treaties, and the Laws of Nations, is extremely desireable." Together they hammered out eight "Rules Governing Belligerents" with the most important prohibiting the outfitting of privateers in American ports, the recruiting for foreign military service on American soil, and all foreign consular prize courts in American ports. Because the President no longer had confidence in the assistance of state governments he accepted an idea proposed by Hamilton the previous May. Much to the chagrin of Jefferson, he authorized Hamilton to use customs officials of the Treasury department to enforce the neutrality laws. The matter now was entirely in the hands of the federal government.

Genet represented yet another problem. The storm he had generated led to newspaper assaults on the President. Genet had added dangerously to the divisiveness in public opinion regarding republican France. By helping organize at Philadelphia the "Society of Friends of Liberty and Equality," a group decidedly opposed to administration policy, he had directly intruded himself into domestic American politics. By defying the American government he had blundered badly, driving a wedge between the United States and France and thereby destroying his effectiveness as the representative of his government. Genet had to go. There was no division in Washington's cabinet on this point. Even Jefferson agreed. The only question was on the method of getting rid of Genet. Some feared he might cause even more trouble if he knew the administration was considering his recall. After considerable discussion the Cabinet advised the President to follow the only viable option open to him. He ordered Gouverneur Morris in Paris to demand Genet's recall and sent as evidence a thick file of documented complaints to lay before the French government. Genet was not told of this decision.

At the very moment of these discussions, unknown to Washington's administration or to Genet, his sponsors in the Gironde had been driven from power, some to exile, some to prison or death. The new French government of the radical Jacobins, led by the volatile Robespierre, unleashed a bloody purge of its political opponents that kept the guillotine busy for weeks. It was even more nationalistic than its predecessor but saw the role of American neutrality in a different light. The United States should not be alienated; its friendship and cooperation were too highly prized. As a result, the new foreign minister, aware of Genet's insulting indiscretions, sent him fiery reprimands, demanding he make amends. Either through stupidity or stubbornness, however, he did little to heed these instructions or Jefferson's complaints. By the time the American request for his recall reached Paris in October, his fate was already being debated. He was recalled in November, and a new minister appointed to take his place.

In his brief encounter during the historic moment of the formation of the emerging nation's foreign policy Genet left an indelible mark. In truth, he had not caused the divisiveness in American public opinion; on the contrary, his activities had only given focus to a division that already existed. The Neutrality Proclamation was from the beginning damned by some citizens who saw it as a leap into the outstretched arms of the hated British. Others saw it as the only refuge in an engulfing republican storm that would undermine the world's political and economic stability. In part, the issue reflected public favor for France or for England in the new European war; in part the issue was even more fundamental, involving debate on economic and political systems essential to the future development of the country. As a form of government, republicanism was still very, very new to the eighteenth century. There were those who honestly preferred to see President George Washington become King George I, while others lived in constant fear the President's policies were drifting in such a way that he would soon be king. For the first time in its brief history, the federal republic confronted its citizens with a true political issue which involved the determination of foreign policy. From then on, with only rare exceptions, American foreign policy would be inextricably entwined with American politics. What Washington had hoped to prevent was now occurring—the American system of political parties was taking form in the debate on neutrality. The issue was not Genet himself, but the policies of the Washington administration as they concerned the war in Europe.

Also for the first time, Washington suffered "the slings and arrows" of American political debate. His hero's image was becoming tarnished, and the process made him uncomfortable. The existence of a free press in the United States made possible the appearance of editorial columns in the nation's newspapers. Although the practice of editors expressing their own opinions was not yet prevalent, they willingly published the writings of others. The results, too often, were vitriolic attacks on persons and policies, rarely tempered by decency or courtesy. Even staid members of the administration and of Congress, masquerading under pseudonyms, joined the fray. Washington himself was frequently the target, for it was his administration and his policies that were under attack. His confrontation with the popular Genet identified him, fairly or not, with the Hamiltonian drift toward Britain, and the democratic-republican societies would not forgive him for it. Genet's blundering threat "to appeal to the people," however, brought the President support from another direction. In the time-honored practice of his day he received dozens of memorials or addresses from groups willing to go on record in favor of his policies. He heard from such citizen associations as "The Inhabitants of Trenton," "The Landholders and Other Citizens of Dorchester," "The Citizens of Anapolis," "The Inhabitants of Morris County," and "The Mechanical Society of Baltimore." In acknowledging their memorials he seized the opportunity to defend his position. To the Baltimore Society, for example, he wrote, "the happiness and true interests of a people are best secured by observing such a line of conduct as will preserve to their country peace with other Nations." And to the "Freeholders and Other Inhabitants of Salem, in Massachusetts," he wrote simply, "in making this declaration, I was persuaded that I spoke the wishes of my countrymen without violating any political or moral obligation."

Washington may have rid himself of Genet through his request for the recall of the French minister, but he certainly had not eliminated his problems with France. On the contrary, its government put such increasing strains on American neutrality that eventually Washington would leave to his successor, John Adams, the beginnings of an undeclared naval war. France, involved in a desperate struggle with England, found the British navy to be its nemesis. As in previous Anglo-French wars Britannia "ruled the waves," easily sweeping French commerce from the high seas. The British fleet cut off the French West Indies from maritime contact with the mother country, thereby denying them both the vital home market for their molasses and the source of necessary supplies of food grains, livestock, barrels, and building timbers.

While the islands suffered loss of trade, the French economy was disrupted by internal civil disorders and the heavy demands for men and material by the huge armies fighting its combined enemies. Critical food shortages appeared in the crowded cities of the country that once had been the most prosperous and bountiful agricultural producer in Europe. In desperation the French National Convention, during the late spring and summer of 1793, issued a series of "provisioning" decrees that in effect set aside France's old mercantilist traditions. French home and colonial ports were thrown open to United States shippers on the same footing as French citizens. These decrees were far more generous to American commerce than any of the previous special privileges granted by Louis XVI in the Treaty of Amity and Commerce of 1778. Through its provisioning decrees Republican France invited American shippers to replace its own merchant marine as a vital link to its

American colonies and as its principal supplier of food and raw materials.

Americans eagerly accepted the invitation. By late summer of 1793, hundreds of ships flying the Stars and Stripes flitted between American ports, the French Caribbean islands, and the ports of France. Prosperity returned to the American shipping industry, while commodity prices increased as much as fifty per cent at Charleston, Baltimore, Philadelphia, and New York. By November neutral American commerce had almost entirely replaced the French merchant marine as supplier of provisions and carrier of French inter-colonial commerce. This was exactly the role the government in Paris had visualized for its ally—a benevolent neutral used to support its war for the promotion of republicanism.

The government in London viewed with alarm this American success as carrier for French commerce. In effect British naval superiority was nullified; the French had merely replaced their own merchant marine with the American. Britain's Foreign Secretary, Lord Grenville, had already warned his minister in Philadelphia that this would happen. He exhorted Hammond to protest to the American government any attempt by Genet to use the United States as a source of provisions for France. As early as March he wrote, "It is indeed necessary to state on this occasion that the Principle of free Ships making free Goods, is one which never has been recognized by this Country and that it undoubtedly will not be allowed in the present case." More ominously he ordered Hammond that if "any Corn or Provisions shall have been actually purchased for the Use of the French and should have been shipped on board of any vessels, in the Ports of America, for the purpose of their being transported to France, You will not fail of giving Notice of this Circumstance to the Commanders of any of His Majesty's Ships who may be Cruizing in those Seas." In a later instruction to Hammond in July, Grenville stated the basis of the British position: "You will not fail to remark to the American government by the law of Nations as laid down by the most modern Writers, particularly by Vattel, it is expressly stated that all provisions are to be considered as Articles of contraband, and as such liable for confiscation, in the case where the depriving an Enemy of these Supplies is one of the means intended to be employed for reducing him to reasonable terms of peace."

As Grenville clearly indicated, the character of warfare was changing. It was the beginning of a new era in which war was something more than the clash of armies or navies. New strategies called for economic warfare, people-to-people conflicts. The French themselves had changed the rules, as Grenville noted, by "the unusual mode of war employed by the Enemy himself in having armed almost the whole labouring class of the French Nation for the purpose of commencing and supporting hostilities against all the governments of Europe." As a result, anything that contributed to the strength of the enemy had to be eliminated even if it meant reducing the enemy's population to starvation. Britain's reaction to French use of American neutral commerce was merely the beginning of new definitions for the conduct of wars that presaged the horrors of twentieth-century warfare. Because of their naval superiority the British could redefine international maritime law to their advantage without serious challenges. To counter the French provisioning decrees, therefore, they reached back into their experiences during the Seven Years War and dusted off the "Rule of 1756," that what was illegal in peacetime was illegal in wartime. Applying it to the situation in 1793, the British insisted that since the French normally prohibited non-French shipping between France and her colonies it was still prohibited even though the French themselves had suspended the policy. In essence, Britain now claimed the right to enforce French peacetime policies whether or not the French wanted them.

Pitt's government broadly defined contraband and declared that neutral shipping—that is, "free ships"—did not make legal or "free" their cargoes of French produce. Both ship and cargo were subject to confiscation. In an Order-in-Council of November 6, 1793, Pitt unleashed his ship captains to clear the Caribbean of this commerce. Within months British warships seized over 260 American vessels, condemned their cargoes in Admiralty courts, and in some cases interned their crews. They extended the practice by condemning cargoes of other American ships in the trans-Atlantic crossing, leaving frustrated captains confronted with financial losses. It was at this time, too, the British navy began its nefarious practice of impressing seamen from American merchant ships, men they claimed were runaway British sailors.

In the late autumn of 1793 Washington had not yet learned of these British depredations on American shipping. True, rumors began to trickle in from the West Indies, although the President himself had received no official notice of British naval activity or change in policy. He did, however, recognize that American neutral shipping was being squeezed between the Tricolor and the Union Jack. Communications from Gouverneur Morris finally arrived informing him that the French would resist attempts to divert American provisioning ships to English ports by seizing American cargoes themselves. And the same long delay in trans-Atlantic mail left him impatiently waiting for Genet's recall, while that erratic Frenchman continued to stir up trouble.

For the moment at least, the President's greatest frustrations still came from the British. Their heavy-handed actions in the Northwest deliberately undercut his plans for reaching an accommodation with the Indian tribes of the region. As

Secretary of War Knox had promised the chiefs the previous year, the President sent a commission of distinguished Americans to meet with them at Sandusky in June. The commissioners—General Benjamin Lincoln, Timothy Pickering, and Beverly Randolph—were selected as much for their political acceptability within the United States as for their reputable characters in the eyes of the Indians. To reach Sandusky they had to travel through British occupied territory, forcing them to seek help from Colonel John Simcoe at Fort Niagara. Simcoe, recently appointed Lieutenant Governor of the newly created province of Upper Canada, had never hidden his dislike for the United States. Yet with much fuss and flattery he extended the "hospitality" of his residence to the Americans, deliberately delaying them six weeks. The most humiliating experience of their journey was having to ask Simcoe for a "protective" guard and a passport to travel through what was technically a part of the United States. When they finally reached the western end of Lake Erie the British troops encamped them on the Canadian shore, still a considerable distance by water from the meeting place; they were even politely prevented from taking a boat to make the crossing themselves. In the meantime, Simcoe, through his underling, Alexander McKee, the American-baiting commander of the British garrison at Detroit, convinced the Indians at Sandusky that the Americans would never arrive and that they should continue to insist on the Ohio River as the southern boundary of their territories. Only after the Indians left the conference site were the Americans able to return home, a return clouded with failure, humiliation, and considerable anger.

With the British irreconcilable, the French erratic, and the Indians intractable, Washington could do little but continue his juggling act, trying to protect both American sovereignty and American neutrality.

Still uncertain of his constitutional prerogatives, he

turned to the Congress for its opinions and support as well as to legalize much that he had done previously to define American neutrality. He approached it with considerable trepidation, for this new Congress, elected in 1792 before Genet had made his appearance, already reflected much more divisiveness than its two predecessors. Opponents of Hamilton's fiscal policies who were also pro-French coalesced about the leadership of James Madison, who was privately encouraged and supported by Jefferson. Reflecting their fears that the government was drifting toward monarchy, they labeled themselves "Republicans." Hamilton's supporters, a few admittedly monarchists, favored the centralizing tendencies of the government and his friendship for England and were generally known as "Federalists." Hamilton's influence had declined, for the Republicans held a slight majority in the House and had a stronger, more vocal minority in the Senate. The pro-French frenzy and debate over neutrality of the previous summer merely hardened attitudes held at the time of the members' elections. By December 1793 when Congress convened, for good or ill, a two-party system of politics had emerged.

Despite this development the President needed the support and cooperation of Congress. The increasingly partisan press was mauling him badly, misinterpreting his intentions. The more assertive Republican sheets, especially Benjamin Franklin Bache's *Aurora* and Philip Freneau's *National Gazette*, openly challenged his sincerity and competency. Washington's approach to Congress, therefore, was conciliatory and cooperative. Commenting on his re-election and "renewed testimony of public approbation," he defined his actions of the past months as "influenced by the belief, that my conduct would be estimated according to its real motives; and the people, and the authorities derived from them, would support exertions, having nothing personal for this object." This was as far as the dignified President would go to defend the sincerity of his purpose against what he felt were the calumnies of the press. Then he turned to the controversy arising from his Neutrality Proclamation. Explaining his reasons for this policy, he appealed for "the wisdom of Congress to correct, improve or enforce this plan of procedure." He thus shrewdly broadened the basis of his own support by focusing the nationwide argument over neutrality into a Congressional debate. It was now up to Congress to legalize by statute what had been created by executive decree.

He was shrewd, too, in flooding Congress with copies of a wide range of diplomatic correspondence, knowing that most of it would quickly find its way to the major newspapers. He did this with a series of messages summarizing the problems with France caused by Genet and the status of negotiations with Great Britain and Spain, each accompanied by the pertinent diplomatic exchanges. It was a well-balanced sop to all political factions. Federalists could find in the Genet papers solid proof of the French minister's machinations. Republicans gleefully discovered confirmation for their suspicions of British intentions, especially in the Northwest, and rationalized a new call for anti-British tariff discrimination. Naturally George Hammond, England's minister, was furious and embarrassed. His complaint to London that his letters had been made public elicited from Foreign Secretary Grenville the caustic comment that "no Government, however feebly constituted, can be under a necessity of thus prematurely appealing to the public." Grenville should not have been so patronizing, for Washington knew exactly what he was doing.

One of his messages to Congress, involving a dispatch of David Humphreys from Lisbon, enhanced the wave of anti-British anger in both political factions. Perfidious England, reported Humphreys, had arranged a truce between the Dey of Algiers and Portugal, Britain's ally in its war against France. For decades Algiers and the other Barbary states scattered along the northwest coast of Africa had made a national business of preying on commerce entering the Mediterranean through the Straits of Gibraltar. Their corsairs, nothing more than pirates, easily seized unprotected merchant vessels, selling ship and cargo and holding the crews for ransom. Nations that wanted to ply the Mediterranean trade had to come to terms with these Barbary pirates either through a show of force or by painfully negotiated treaties in which the ransom was the key ingredient. Washington's administration had already confronted their outrageous demands with not much success. The recent truce diverted attention from the Portuguese and exposed American shipping even more to the African marauders, free now to sail into the Atlantic. Within weeks fifteen American ships had been captured. No wonder sentiment within the United States found Britain's involvement in the "Algerine Business" one more indication of her total disdain for American rights on the high seas.

Jefferson deliberately fanned these flames of anger in his valedictory to Congress. Using the occasion of his retirement as Secretary of State, he took advantage of the momentary discomfort of the Federalists. In a thoughtful and documented report he presented to Congress his analysis of the state of American foreign relations at the end of 1793. Drawing out the causes of the friction between the United States and Great Britain, he urged a safer future for the country by closer relations with France. Considered by later generations as among the best of Jefferson's state papers, the report was really a political position paper and a call for action. Its meaning was not wasted on Madison and his Republican followers.

In the meantime, however, Jefferson's resignation was a personal blow for the President. Long dissatisfied with his own effectiveness as Secretary of State, Jefferson had wanted to leave the office earlier. Washington had prevailed upon him to stay at least until the opening of the first session of the new

Congress. Washington would miss the balance of opinion he offered in Cabinet discussions, if not the heat of some of his arguments with Hamilton. The President's respect for him remained high, nevertheless, and he wrote the departing Secretary "the opinion, which I had formed, of your intergrity and talents, and which dictated your original nomination, has been confirmed by the fullest experience."

Jefferson himself was to blame for much of his dissatisfaction. From the very beginning he had resented Hamilton's interference in the management of foreign affairs, yet more often than not he handed Hamilton the opportunity. A clear example occurred at the time Washington first learned of the new war in Europe the previous April. When the President hastily returned to the capital from Mount Vernon, Jefferson had no plan for his consideration. Yet Hamilton hurried along to his chief his own set of questions that needed answers, basically the same questions Washington would introduce for Cabinet discussion. In the reprise of July when Washington again rushed back to Philadelphia as a result of the *Little Sarah* incident, Jefferson, claiming illness, was not even in the city when the President needed him—a slight Washington had difficulty forgiving. Again it was Hamilton who presented specific proposals. Thus Jefferson let himself be outmaneuvered in the Cabinet and frustrated over what he felt was a gradual drift of the President's views toward favoritism for Britain and hostility toward France. His evaluation was unfair and probably far from the mark, but because he confided his views to his personal memoirs, most historians have concluded that Washington's foreign policy was rapidly becoming really Hamilton's. Since Jefferson was no longer in the Cabinet after January 1, 1794, there was no strong voice to represent a contrary view. Edmund Randolph, the former Attorney General and his successor as Secretary of State, could not offer Washington the same high quality of advice as had Jefferson.

Madison now attempted to fill the void, but through strong Congressional action. Armed with Jefferson's report and the Anglo-American correspondence Washington had laid before Congress, he tried to revive in the House his long dormant anti-British tariff discrimination. This time, because the Republican majority was joined by a small group of Federalists disaffected by British attacks on American shipping, his chances of success were greater. And Senate Republicans, at the risk of embarrassing the President, maneuvered to have Gouverneur Morris recalled from Paris. They blamed his indiscretions on behalf of French royalists for the breakdown in Franco-American relations. If the French government was expected to recall Genet, they reasoned, the Americans should recall Morris. To find evidence to support this conclusion the Senate requested the President to submit copies of all of Morris' diplomatic correspondence since he had taken up his duties as minister to France. This request was a senatorial challenge to presidential prerogative in the conduct of foreign relations.

Washington recognized it for what it was. Not wanting to offend Congress and needing its support, he sought counsel from his Cabinet. Only Randolph felt the President was obligated to supply the requested papers; the others considered it an invasion of his responsibilities. As a compromise, he directed the Secretary of State to review the papers and to remove any that it might be imprudent to publish. Of the forty Morris dispatches, he sent thirty-nine to the Senate. In a sense, however, the issue was moot. He had already decided to recall Morris, for he had known a year earlier of the unhappiness caused by Morris among French officials. The more important question was whom to name as a successor.

While Washington mulled over this question another of his problems with France was solved beautifully. The almost providential arrival of the new French minister melted away much of the remnants of hostility for France at the very mo-

ment anger toward Britain grew in every direction. Jean An-
toine Fauchet, heading a four-man delegation, arrived in time
to present his credentials as part of the President's birthday
celebration, February 22. And it proved to be a delightful
birthday present. Fauchet's attitude and approach to Franco-
American relations was in such contrast to Genet's that Washington was forced to comment they "appear to have been cast
in very different moulds."

Fauchet had been instructed to placate the American
government and in particular to smooth the President's ruffled
feathers. Almost immediately he issued a proclamation condemning Genet's proposed Kentucky-based invasion of Spanish Louisiana. At the same time he checked the French consuls
whose activities flagrantly abused American neutrality. The
President grew to like him and found his declarations of "the
friendly dispositions of his Nation to this country are strong and
apparently sincere."

Fauchet went further than Washington wanted, however,
with an order from his government for Genet's arrest and return to France as a political prisoner. Genet was accused of
treason, and the mood of the new French leadership meant his
execution was certain. This Washington had not wanted nor
would tolerate; he refused to permit the arrest and granted
Genet political asylum. Wisely Fauchet let the matter drop.
Genet, the French glamour-boy of 1793, an accused traitor in
1794, quickly disappeared into the obscurity of a happy marriage to one of Governor Clinton's daughters and the quiet life
of a New York gentleman farmer. With Genet gone and a more
cooperative Fauchet in his place, Washington could relax and
hope that friction between the United States and France had
been minimized—for the present at least.

But the wave of public sentiment against Great Britain
was almost frightening to Washington's government. The arrival at Philadelphia of each new ship that had eluded British

warships in the Caribbean touched off riots in the city's streets. Along the frontiers of New York, Pennsylvania, and Kentucky settlements girded themselves for renewed Indian war, all clamoring for more federal troops. The democratic-republican societies, at last relieved of embarrassment over Genet's insults, demanded through the press and in public addresses to Congress and the President a hard line against anything British. In South Carolina and in Kentucky the societies ignored Fauchet's withdrawal of French support and continued their own plans to harass Britain's Spanish ally in both Louisiana and Florida. In Kentucky and Tennessee George Rogers Clark still sent out recruiting broadsides for his invasion force. In Vermont the societies planned an attack on Canada and secretly encouraged rebellion among French-Canadian farmers.

Congress could not ignore this growing public outcry against Britain, nor did it want to. The new friendly disposition of France represented by Fauchet weakened the unity of the Federalists, and many joined with Republicans clamoring for war. In March the Congress put aside consideration of Madison's mild tariff discrimination proposals, and majorities in both houses voted a thirty day embargo of all American trade with foreign countries. Then Congress vented its anger with an unusual disregard for finances by appropriating funds for the building and arming of six frigates to protect American shipping against the Algerine pirates, the creation of a 25,000 man army, coastal fortifications to defend American port cities, and 80,000 effective militia ready "to march at a moment's warning." As if this were not enough both houses seriously considered even more stringent anti-British measures, in particular sequestration of all private debts Americans owed to British creditors (by 1794 this amounted to almost £4 million) and total non-intercourse with any part of the British empire. But non-intercourse was dangerous, for it almost certainly would invite British retaliation. Surprisingly, nevertheless, it almost became law. It passed the House easily on April 25, and enough Senate Federalists, caught up in the war hysteria, broke ranks to cause an equal division in the Senate's vote. Only Vice President John Adams' tie-breaking "nay" saved the administration from an unwanted foreign policy blunder. In the meantime Congress had already voted a thirty-day extension of the general embargo and looked to the President to lead the country out of the engulfing crisis.

Cause for all this war hysteria came from the British themselves. Week after week news of a startling series of British activities dramatically shifted the attention of country and Congress away from such minor issues as the peccadilloes of Gouverneur Morris to the far more significant arrogance of Great Britain. It began in February when United States consuls in the West Indies finally confirmed the rumors of the Royal Navy's violation of neutral shipping. They reported dozens, perhaps hundreds (the actual total was 263), of captive American merchantmen waiting idly at Caribbean wharves while slow moving admiralty courts decided their fate and the ownership of their cargoes. Their half-starved crews, thrown on the beach without resources or interned in rotting prison hulks, suffered unnecessarily.

While anger grew over this insult to American national pride, in March another set of rumors trickled into Philadelphia—this time from Canada. They were quickly confirmed in a letter from New York's Governor George Clinton to the President. At Quebec Lord Dorchester had warned a delegation of Indian chiefs from the Great Lakes region that war was imminent between Great Britain and the United States. Apparently reacting to unconfirmed rumors of an invasion from Vermont and of the growing strength of Anthony Wayne's force on the Ohio, Dorchester urged the tribes to prepare to enforce their claim to the Ohio River boundary line. A week later (this was not known in Philadelphia until May), as if to underscore the importance of his own war preparations, he authorized the rebuilding of an abandoned fortified trading post at the rapids of the Maumee, a threatening new British thrust fifty miles south of Detroit. Obviously the Canadian Governor General was willing to unleash the horrors of an Indian War to protect the southern flanks of his province.

Washington seethed with anger when he learned of Dorchester's speech. He was convinced, he wrote Clinton, the speech was authentic and Dorchester "has spoken the Sentimts of the British Cabinet." This last point reflected his turn of mind by the spring of 1794. Although he did not want war and privately feared that it would be a national disaster, he increasingly moved to acceptance of the view that England was deliberately forcing war on the United States. He took what steps he could to prepare for a conflict. He asked Governor Clinton to investigate the relative military strength of the settlements on both sides of the New York-Lake Ontario frontier in case "a rupture between this Country and G. Britain should take place." To be certain "British spies & agents" did not undermine the precarious diplomacy he had developed with friendly Indian tribes, he authorized Secretary of War Knox to bribe their chiefs, including an offer of a $1500 annuity to Joseph Brant, leader of the still cooperative Iroquois. He hovered over Knox's preparations for coastal defenses, giving advice on the locations of fortifications and the distribution of garrisons of recruits.

Then in April came a set of angry dispatches from Thomas Pinckney in London. Each one confirmed the President's suspicions of British intentions, and he wasted no time in sending them on to the Congress. Pinckney informed his government of the Order-in-Council of November 6, 1793 that had caused all the misery for American shipping in the West Indies. His anger stemmed from Pitt's deliberate delay in making public—or known to him—this Order-in-Council until late December, thus allowing ample time for the Royal Navy to swoop down on unsuspecting neutral ships. He was angry, too, because Lord Grenville categorically refused to discuss any possible arrangements for turning over the frontier posts to American forces; negotiations on this sore point were broken off completely. Even though in a later dispatch Pinckney reported that the British ministry had modified the November Order with a moderate one in January, the damage was done. Britain's intentions were clear!

Grenville naively had underestimated the reaction in the United States to the November Order-in-Council. He had not impressed Pinckney by his explanation of the unique purpose of that order nor with his promise to the American minister that the new January order indicated a moderation in British policies. He was forced to warn Hammond in January "it is possible with respect to the former of these orders a considerable degree of dissatisfaction may have arisen in America." He advised Hammond "confine Yourself to observing that this order no longer subsists," explaining the workings of new practices which in actuality merely drew a fine line between adjudication and outright confiscation of neutral shipping. He also directed his representative in Philadelphia to be certain that Britain's role in the Portuguese-Algiers treaty not "become a matter of clamour and misrepresentation in America."

By the time Hammond received these warnings it was already too late to prevent a "clamour" in America. Much of the populace, even the government itself, had already decided the meaning of British intentions and had bluntly let him know its sentiments. For weeks he was a social outcast, ignored even by those Federalists who at first had voiced support for Britain in her war with France. He and three British consuls had been physically threatened, although no harm had actually befallen them, but four of His Majesty's ship-captains were mobbed in Philadelphia. Frightened, Hammond sought the counsel of

Alexander Hamilton, the one American he thought understood Britain's purposes.

Hamilton, however, shocked the unsuspecting Briton by unloading on him his own frustration and embarrassment. The Secretary of the Treasury blamed the current popular hostility on England's indifference to the wrongs she inflicted on American commerce. He was angry too that these narrow war-time policies had so quickly undermined his own attempts to build close relationships between their two countries. He considered Dorchester's remarks to the Indians as the final insult. Hamilton warned Hammond that war was not merely a remote possibility, but he could do little to prevent it. This vehemence so surprised the British minister that he described Hamilton to Grenville as sounding like "the demagogues of the house of representatives." Later Hamilton would calm down enough to listen to an explanation of British rationale. He gradually implied an acceptance of the basic principles of the Rule of 1756. The United States could, he felt, tolerate confiscation of actual French-owned goods carried in American bottoms. At this point Hamilton's moderation was the result of his own last minute efforts to keep slightly ajar the door to restoring Anglo-American friendship.

Other Federalists were trying to open that door even wider. A good many of them felt that war was almost inevitable simply because misunderstanding and misapprehension had arisen as a result of the delays in communication between London and Philadelphia. If war was to be avoided a more direct contact between the two capitals would have to be established, and the United States would have to take the initiative in establishing it. In March an idea was born from the conversations of four eastern Federalist senators—Cabot, Ellsworth, King, and Strong—and they hurried Ellsworth to the President to suggest an extraordinary mission to London.

This was an idea whose time had come, but it was not new. The previous November several senators had proposed a special emissary to London to negotiate British withdrawal from the frontier posts. They had become totally dissatisfied with Hammond's narrow perspective when he refused to inform his government of the importance of this issue to the United States. At the time, however, the thought of sending such an envoy rankled the President, for it offended his sense of national pride to go hat-in-hand to the Court of St. James's for anything. It also bothered his sense of decency to send a special representative whose presence in London most certainly would embarrass the American minister already in place. He was being forced to recall a loyal representative in Gouverneur Morris, and now he was asked to undercut Thomas Pinckney. In November he had rejected the idea.

Washington's common sense, however, eventually convinced him that he must not let his pride stand in the way of peace. He would make one last effort, yet the burden for maintaining peace must fall on Great Britain. He listened to Ellsworth's arguments and later to those of the other three Federalist senators as well as the views of his Cabinet. Once convinced, he turned to the vital question of whom to send as an appropriately strong spokesman for American interests. In the face of a wide range of almost violent press opinion in opposition to the mission almost any individual selected would make his own political enemies and unleash new attacks on the administration itself. Federalist advice quite naturally suggested Hamilton. The Secretary of the Treasury, however, stood at the lowest ebb of his popularity, having barely survived a congressional investigation into alleged mishandling of Treasury funds. Hamilton was, furthermore, so obviously pro-British he could not be objective. This point was stressed in the unsolicited advice in a letter from Senator James Monroe, one of the Republicans' new critics of administration foreign policy. To this the angry President snapped, "I *alone* am responsible for a proper nomination."

Monroe was correct, of course, and the President knew it. Finally with more advice than he wanted Washington chose Chief Justice John Jay, a compromise nominee among Federalist opinion. Republican newspapers now challenged his right to ignore the constitutional separation of powers by using the head of the federal judiciary in a purely executive manner. One editor reached a new low by insisting the Chief Justice was being sent from the country to prevent him from presiding over a trial in case impeachment proceedings were instituted against Washington for his misdeeds as president. Ignoring this insult to his integrity, the President did, however, recognize some validity in the argument about violation of the Constitution. In it, however, he saw the opportunity to solve two of his major problems with one stroke. He proposed to Jay that he resign as Chief Justice and accept a permanent appointment as minister to Great Britain. This would free Pinckney to replace Morris in Paris. Jay refused to resign, but he was willing to take on the extraordinary mission abroad. With some misgivings over the long-term results, Washington submitted Jay's name as minister extraordinary to Great Britain, and the Senate quickly affirmed it.

It proved to be an unwise appointment. Yet it was the best the President could do, for no one would have been wholly acceptable. An experienced diplomat, Jay had been Secretary of Foreign Affairs, and he understood as well as anyone the government's problems with Great Britain. He was, however, especially unpopular among Republicans. Several of his decisions as Chief Justice had annoyed Southerners who also resented his willingness to stop temporarily American settlement on the Mississippi in the aborted negotiations with Diego de Gardoqui in 1786. His nomination drew scorn from House

Republicans as well as their newspaper spokesmen. In Kentucky and Tennessee he was hung in effigy. Such opposition jeopardized the effectiveness of his mission.

Washington thoughtfully tried to placate the opposition to Jay's appointment by sending a prominent Republican to Paris to replace Morris. The idea was easier to conceive than to implement, for again he wrestled with the chronic problem of finding a qualified individual willing to accept a federal appointment. What competent Republican would be willing to identify himself with administration policies already discredited in the Republican press? Washington finally settled on James Monroe and in the process solved another problem. Monroe, although not yet heir to the Jefferson-Madison leadership of the Republicans, was already the Senate's most outspoken critic of the administration. He could do some good in Paris and his absence from Philadelphia might reduce opposition in the Senate. Monroe, dissatisfied with his role in the Senate, surprisingly accepted the assignment. Washington hated being so devious and despised playing politics in this way, for it ran counter to his concepts of using the best men available in the service of their country regardless of their position on the political spectrum. The experiences of five and a half years in office, however, had taught him that, if nothing else, the presidency is truly a political office.

Having selected his two newest diplomats, Washington left the business of writing their instructions to others. Secretary Randolph worked out the details for Monroe. By now Randolph had become so disgusted with Hammond's studied indifference to legitimate American claims that he became more pro-French with each passing day. As Jefferson had confided in Genet, Randolph more and more confided in Fauchet (a development which later would turn out to be his undoing). As a result Monroe's instructions were strongly worded to encourage a return to close friendship between the two republics.

In particular he was to overcome French suspicions arising from Jay's special mission to London and to assure them "that, in case of war with any nation on earth, we shall consider France as our first and natural ally." Given his own predilections Monroe would be a willing worker for the cause of Franco-American relations.

Jay's instructions were a different matter. Randolph had little to do with their content, although as Secretary of State he would officially write them. But the delicacy of relations with England was now so important they could not be entrusted to his unsympathetic hands. The responsibility fell, with the President's blessing, to the over-willing Hamilton. Jay's main purpose was, of course, to find avenues for maintaining peace, and he was free to use his own discretion with little specific guidance. No final agreement could be made that violated already existing obligations to France. There were, however, specific points still unsettled from the peace treaty of 1783 that must be resolved. Most important of these were withdrawal of British troops from the frontier posts and indemnification for Negro slaves carried away during the Revolution. Jay was also expected to try again for a commercial treaty that would reopen American trade to the British West Indies. The American positions on the thorny questions of the impact of the Rule of 1756 and impressment of American sailors were not clearly spelled out. In short, Jay was given one of the most open-ended sets of instructions ever written for an American diplomat.

Had Hamilton gone no farther than this in the conduct of relations with Great Britain, Jay's mission might have been a resounding success. He had, however, become paranoid over the fear that growing anti-British hysteria, coupled with traditional affection for France, would push the country into an unnecessary war. As he saw it, this war fever resulted from a popular exaggeration of the value to the United States of the Franco-American Alliance. To him the validity of the Alliance had ended the previous year when war broke out in Europe. And now problems with Britain had arisen over the commerce that Alliance made possible, a commerce benefitting France. When peace was restored the trade again would be prohibited, so the United States had little to gain from it while risking loss of long-term British markets and British credit. Popular support for the Alliance was thus forcing a misreading of true American national priorities. For Hamilton the Alliance was a French albatross around the neck of the United States.

To prevent what he feared was an impending national disaster, therefore, Hamilton made himself a willing dupe for the British. Unknown even to Washington—or to any other American—he met secretly with George Hammond at least twice, each time at the British minister's request. At their first meeting he vented his justifiable anger over Britain's demeaning attitude toward American commerce, but his temper quickly cooled. During the second meeting, in answer to the Englishman's questions he explained the real purpose of Jay's mission. In the process, unintentionally perhaps, he undermined Jay's bargaining position. He assured Hammond that Anthony Wayne's planned spring offensive in the Ohio country was in no way intended as a challenge to the British garrison at Detroit. And he surprisingly acquiesced in the Rule of 1756 and Britain's right to enforce it. He found fault only with the most flagrant admiralty court interpretations of the November Order-in-Council, while acknowledging as legitimate the confiscation of cargoes of American vessels proven to be of French origin. He never mentioned the popular anger over impressment of American sailors nor the requested commercial treaty to reopen trade to the West Indies. Taken all together, Hamilton's conversations with Hammond minimized privately what Jay would propose publicly as the areas of compromise necessary to restore amicable relations between the two countries. He had in effect betrayed Jay's mission even before it started.

Naturally Hammond rushed summaries of these conversations to Lord Grenville. His dispatches left Philadelphia simultaneously with Jay's departure. By the time the American envoy presented his credentials in London, Pitt's cabinet knew better than Jay himself the limitations of his negotiations. Pitt and Grenville could, and would, ignore some of the American's stronger demands and threats of reprisal. As a result, too often during the negotiations Jay was forced to shadow-box rather than confront his opponent in a fair match.

In the meantime throughout the United States the very existence of the Jay mission removed much of the heat from the bubbling cauldron of war hysteria. Most of the protagonists on either side of the war issue appeared willing to await the outcome of Jay's efforts. Even Congress seemed to have spent its wrath. The placid last month of its session was in sharp contrast to the virulence of March. Its quiet adjournment was such an anticlimax that the nation in general relaxed in relief that congressional hotheads had not actually forced a war.

An unwary Washington also relaxed. Immediately after Congress adjourned he fled the dusty streets of Philadelphia and hurried home to the freshly sown fields of Mount Vernon. After seven hectic months of the congressional session he needed a vacation and was unashamed to take it. By June of 1794 his country's foreign relations were in much better shape than he had any hope of expecting the previous December. By sending Jay to London he had, at least for the moment, averted a war with Britain. Monroe was on his way to replace Morris in Paris; Franco-American tensions would therefore be reduced. Short was already in Madrid laying the groundwork for new negotiations with Spain over the Mississippi Question. And Wayne's careful buildup of military force ought soon to minimize the Indian menace in the Northwest.

Washington could do little else but relax in the early summer of 1794, waiting for news from the agents he sent to safeguard the peace and tranquility of the United States. As for any citizen the wait would be frustrating. He had done all that he could under the circumstances, and the fate of his policies was now in the hands of others. The results of their endeavors would determine whether his administration would be considered a success or a failure.

"....to preserve the country in peace if I can"

WASHINGTON MUST HAVE FELT almost helpless as he waited out the summer of 1794 for news of the successes—or failures—of his foreign policy directives. John Jay could not possibly arrive in London before mid-June, and it would be several more weeks before a preliminary report from him reached Philadelphia. Nothing had been heard from Madrid for so long that he again wondered if Carmichael would ever send a report. And only rumors, most of them false, trickled in from the northwestern frontier where Anthony Wayne's agonizingly slow preparations for an offensive against the Indians frustrated even the President's over-extended patience. As the summer wore on he explained, perhaps as much to himself as to Gouverneur Morris, the purposes of his policies when he wrote, "My primary objects, and to which I steadily adhered, have been to preserve the country in peace if I can, and to be prepared for war if I cannot." Then, in reference to the multitude of self-appointed advisers, he added wryly, "the affairs of this country *cannot go amiss.* There are *so many watchful guardians of them,* and such *infallible guides,* that one is at no loss for a director at every turn."

Despite the sarcasm, Washington still held a deep conviction of the unique destiny of the United States. But it placed him well ahead of contemporaries in his belief that "providence" would indeed guide and protect his country. As a result he honestly expected successes at such diverse and scattered sites as London, Paris, Madrid, and the banks of the Maumee. Over the next eighteen months the dramas unfolding at each of these locations would represent the culmination of six years of his efforts to create an American foreign policy and would demonstrate convincingly whether or not his faith had been well-placed. Each in its own way affected the outcome of the others, for the extensive interlocking of British and Spanish self-interest would not easily be disentangled. But he still had many months of tortuous negotiations and a whole series of frustrating issues to face before he could be certain that his unshaken faith was indeed justified.

Even though Washington preferred to preserve the country in peace, it was war that broke the deadlock on his diplomacy. In the Northwest Anthony Wayne at last struck a major military blow that was a disaster to the Indian confederations and forced a quick end to the dragging negotiations in both London and Madrid. The dreams of either British or Spanish dominion over the eastern half of the Mississippi valley were shattered by "Mad Anthony."

Despite widely circulated rumors to the contrary General Wayne was neither inactive nor incompetent. These rumors were spread by Wayne's second in command, James Wilkinson, to promote his own ambitions as a western leader. Washington and Knox, understanding their source and probably their purpose, gave Wayne their complete confidence. With such support the general cajoled military contractors to provide needed supplies and drilled his recruits unmercifully. Ignoring growing hostility from frontiersmen who saw his delays as proof of Wilkinson's accusations, Wayne waited until he knew his army was an effective fighting unit. With still fresh memories of the disasters of Harmar and St. Clair hanging over his men, he refused to advance against the Indians until he knew they were ready for combat.

His careful preparations had begun the previous October

when he led 3000 troops, including 600 mounted Kentucky riflemen, northward from Fort Washington (Cincinnati). To avoid the surprise attacks that had routed the earlier expeditions of Harmar and St. Clair, he ordered temporary fortifications for each night's encampment and sent out continuous roving patrols. He strengthened each of the forts St. Clair had built in 1791, leaving them with well-disciplined garrisons under seasoned, reliable commanders. By Christmas, 1793, he finally reached the site of St. Clair's defeat and here erected Fort Recovery. Luckily, search parties discovered St. Clair's artillery abandoned in the hasty American withdrawal of 1791 and buried by the victorious Indians. With these pieces mounted within its walls, Fort Recovery became an almost impregnable American bastion and safe winter quarters for the army. From here Wayne sent out emissaries in a final attempt to arrange peace conferences with the individual tribes, but with little success.

By late spring of 1794 Indian strength had grown for a final confrontation with American forces. Almost 2000 warriors had gathered at Au Glaize, the center of Miami towns and cornfields. Some had come from as far away as the northern lakes of Canada, while others were from the Cherokee country well south of the Ohio. Altogether it was an impressive confederation of Indian tribes drawn from an area almost a thousand miles long and over six hundred miles wide. Encouraged by Lord Dorchester's war-baiting speech and materially supported by supplies from the British garrison at Detroit, they were ready to crush the American invader once and for all. And they had a pre-taste of victory with successful harassing attacks on Wayne's supply lines. To make the victory complete they had to meet Wayne head on and destroy him as they had Harmar and St. Clair.

General Wayne had other plans. Unable to move until a supporting column reached him, he waited and waited.

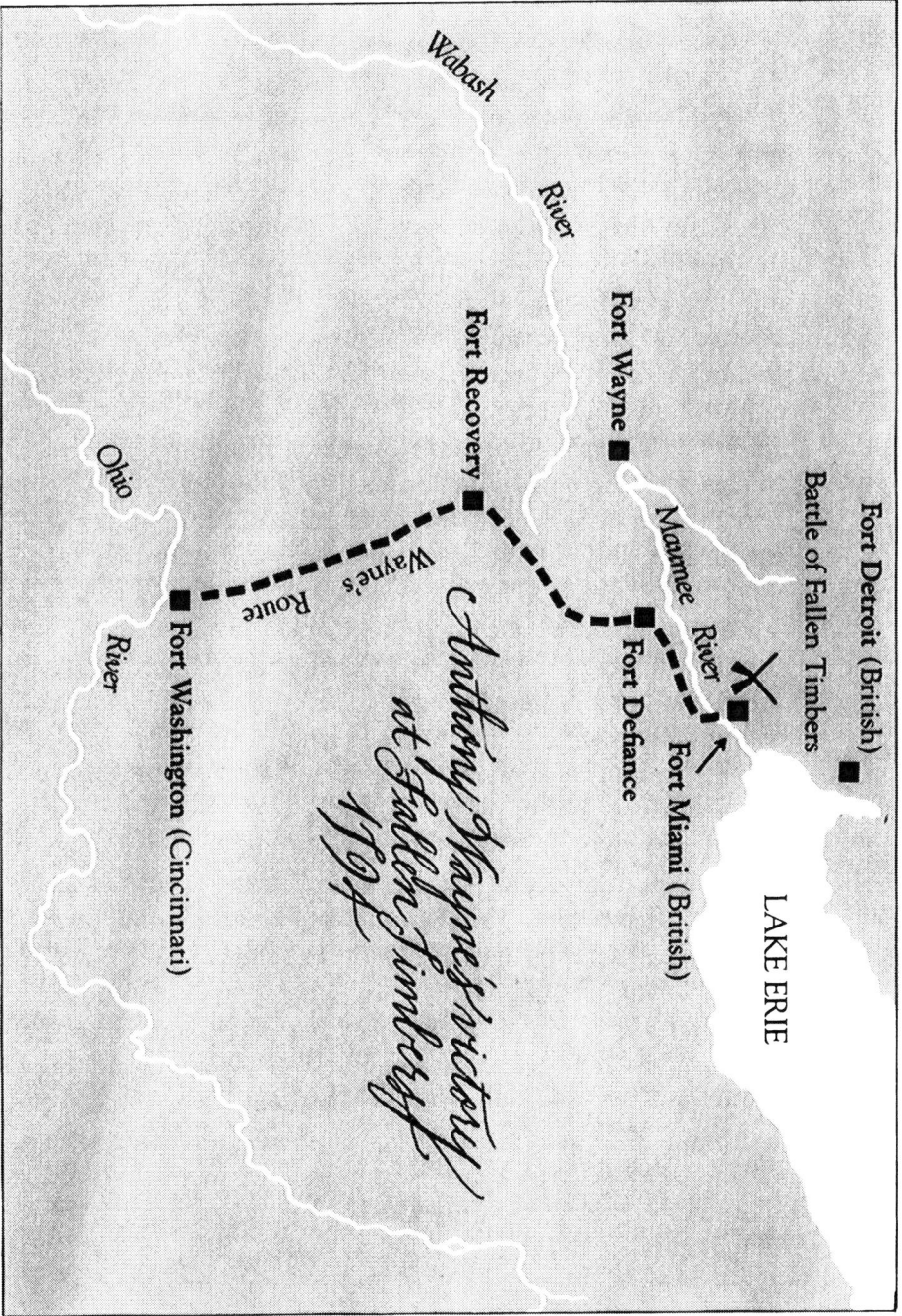

Anthony Wayne's victory at Fallen Timbers 1794

Wabash River

Ohio River

Maumee River

LAKE ERIE

Fort Wayne

Fort Recovery

Fort Washington (Cincinnati)

Wayne's Route

Fort Defiance

Fort Miami (British)

Battle of Fallen Timbers

Fort Detroit (British)

Whether or not his delays were a deliberate part of his strategy, they worked to his advantage. Hundreds of emotionally-charged Indians from different tribes could not maintain discipline and quarrelled over their own strategy. Worse still, they exhausted their food supplies. Forced to send out hunting parties, the warriors broke up into roving bands, thereby destroying the effectiveness of a unified command. In July Wayne marched into the now weakly defended Au Glaize, destroying villages and supply caches along the way. In the very heart of the Miami nation he erected a new fort. To make his intentions clear to Briton and Indian alike, he named it Fort Defiance. He was barely five miles from the British garrison at the rebuilt Fort Miami whose nervous commander hastily begged Detroit for reinforcements. Then Wayne turned downriver toward the British fort, and an Anglo-American war seemed imminent.

The Indians, however, were prepared to stop Wayne's advance. Nature had provided them with a seemingly perfect defensive position. Years earlier a tornado had uprooted a two-mile-wide swath of trees laying at an angle to the Miami river, an excellent site for an attack on Wayne's flanks. Here Little Turtle, the Indian commander, positioned among the tangle of fallen timbers 1500 of his best warriors, ready to surprise the American army. But Wayne hesitated again. While his men were safe in their fortified encampment, hunger distracted the Indians. Traditionally Indian warriors fasted before a battle, and Wayne's delaying tactics weakened them physically as well as emotionally. Finally, after two days of waiting, on the morning of August 20, 1794, as the rising sun ended a rainstorm, Wayne advanced his troops along the river's shore toward the waiting Indian trap. To the Indians' surprise, their first flanking attack was allowed to pass through the disciplined militia to be quickly destroyed by the American rear. Then Wayne ordered a bayonet charge in the center and an encircling move of the mounted riflemen along the Indians' flanks. Dismayed by the steady march of the infantrymen, who ignored their fallen comrades, the first lines of warriors broke from the safety of the entangled trees, causing confusion deep within the mass of Indian defenders. Quickly abandoning the fight, many of the Indians fled to the expected security of Fort Miami, only to find its gates shut against them. The British refused to aid the terror-stricken Indians as the American advance came within rifle range of the fort's walls.

On that hot, muggy morning an astute American might have seen in the Union Jack that hung so listlessly over Fort Miami a symbol of the bankruptcy of British Indian policy. When the fort's garrison refused to succor its allies, the British admitted the failure of their position by abandoning the natives to whatever terms they could get from the American commander.

As military encounters go, the Battle of Fallen Timbers was relatively insignificant. Casualties were light on both sides—the Americans had 44 killed, 87 wounded, while the Indians had only about 50 killed. In terms of American prestige, however, the battle was tremendously important. Wayne's victory not only broke the Indian confederation, it also proved the effectiveness of well-trained militia against undisciplined, shifting Indian alliances, a lesson that would be repeated throughout the history of the American West. And of greatest importance, it ended once and for all Britain's bold-faced attempt to erect an Indian buffer zone out of the American Northwest.

War between the United States and Great Britain was still an immediate possibility. While the Americans carried out mopping up operations within shouting distance of Fort Miami, the fort's nervous garrison remained poised over its guns. Any trigger-happy subaltern on either side could have caused a disastrous exchange of fire. Neither Wayne nor British commander Major William Campbell wanted the onus of commencing a war that each had been ordered to prevent, and both carefully restrained their men. After the tension of the first hours passed, the two commanders exchanged acrimonious notes. Wayne bluntly told Campbell that he and his men were trespassing on American soil, and then withdrew his troops.

General Wayne was now free to establish United States sovereignty over the territory granted to it in the peace treaty of 1783. He built Fort Wayne on the upper curve of the Maumee, assuring American control of the vital portage between that river and the Wabash. Returning to north central Ohio, he established permanent quarters at Fort Greenville, and from here sent emissaries to all the Indian tribes demanding that they meet with him in a general peace conference early in the summer of 1795. With a conclusive military victory and a string of well established garrisons between the Ohio river and Lake Erie, Anthony Wayne was able to dictate peace terms favorable to the purposes of Washington's policies.

When the President finally learned of Fallen Timbers he could not fully savor the sweet taste of victory. Wayne's hard-spent courier caught up with him on the thirtieth of September at Morristown, Pennsylvania, where he was involved in suppressing an uprising of western farmers. He was so engrossed with this Whiskey Rebellion that he received the news from Ohio with a mixture of elation, vindication, and characteristic caution. From the reports, the military victory seemed complete, and it certainly justified his stubborn trust in Anthony Wayne. But there were too many unanswered questions to torment him. Would there be a true general peace in the Northwest? And what of British reactions in Quebec and in London? He would have to wait yet another summer to see the fruit of Wayne's negotiations at Greenville and get answers to his questions.

In the meantime, the Whiskey Rebellion overshadowed

every other consideration. Even though the battle at Fallen Timbers was a vital culmination of his years of planning and deep concern for the Northwest, he made no reference to it in otherwise detailed diary entries recounting his journey into western Pennsylvania to confront the rebellion. The insurrection—if truly it could be called that—was the first domestic challenge to the authority of his administration. It had little direct connection to foreign affairs, yet the President thought it did. And it had to be suppressed if the authority of the federal government was to be respected at home as well as abroad. For Washington it was natural to put all other considerations aside until this issue was resolved.

Like so many of the problems Washington had inherited, those on the western frontier were characterized by dissension and dissatisfaction. Harassed by Indians, stimulated to separatism by agents of Britain and Spain, and ignored by politicians on the Atlantic Coast, westerners traditionally took matters into their own hands, operating under a primitive democracy in semi-independent settlements. They viewed Washington's appeasement of the southern Indians as a betrayal, and they had only scorn for his seemingly inept military commanders. Yet they were Americans wanting desperately to share in the benefits of American national independence. When, therefore, Congress levied an excise on whiskey to overcome a dangerous gap in federal revenues, they rebelled.

The revolt centered in western Pennsylvania where farmers considered the excise an unwarranted blow to their livelihood. Too far from eastern markets to profit by shipping heavy sacks of flour over difficult mountain trails, they made whiskey instead. A pack animal could carry in distilled spirits the equivalent of six times the value in grains to a ready market of thirsty easterners. A cash crop was vital to the economic survival of the western farmers and a tax on their only marketable product was more than they could tolerate. Banding together, these farmers resisted the tax collectors and disrupted the agencies of federal authority. Worse still, from Washington's viewpoint at least, public meetings openly denounced his foreign policies, especially the Neutrality Proclamation, and praised such defiant attempts at independent action as George Rogers Clark's still-planned invasion of New Orleans.

For Washington the Whiskey Rebellion was more than just a tax revolt. It was a direct threat to his foreign policies. How could he earn the respect of nations if he could not preserve tranquility at home? If the challenge to federal authority went unchecked in the West, could not dissidents in other parts of the country defy the law over different issues? Would not such obvious weakening of the Union invite increased foreign meddling in American domestic affairs? Would not the British now be more intransigent in their negotiations with John Jay over the frontier posts? And too, how much of western dissatisfaction was still French-inspired, even though Edmund Genet had been discredited by his own government for sowing the seeds of discord?

There was no hard evidence to provide answers to the President's questions, for the paucity of official dispatches from the frontier and from Europe created an aura of uncertainty. Instead, rumor fed his suspicions and caused him to exaggerate the significance of the rebellion itself and the role the democratic-republican societies had in sustaining it.

He agreed with the Cabinet that a show of force was necessary. After the Pennsylvania farmers ignored two presidential proclamations, he reluctantly ordered up state militias to be used in suppressing the rebellion. To underscore his determination he set out in late September for western Pennsylvania to supervise personally the government's action. It was a difficult decision, for he could not accept the fact that honest American farmers would, of their own volition, rise up against their own government. He was not surprised, therefore, by the outpouring of popular support and public deference that greeted him all along his route, and gradually his black mood dissipated. By the time he reached Carlisle, Pennsylvania, 12,000 troops under the command of Virginia's governor, Revolutionary General Henry ("Light Horse Harry") Lee, were assembled ready to show the determination of federal authority. At the sight of this imposing force the revolt collapsed without a shot being fired. Events once again vindicated Washington's policies.

Contemporary critics accused the President of using an elephant to stomp a gnat. In the long run they were proven correct, for the violence of the outbreak—if not the general dissatisfaction with the tax—was the work of only a few hotheads who sought their own advantage from the turmoil of western politics. But to Washington the risk of doing too little too late was great. The uncertain success of the diplomatic maneuvers he had set in motion during the previous six months forced him into strong action. To defend himself he delivered to Congress in November the most detailed report of his administration, outlining the development of the uprising and his reasons for the steps taken to suppress it. In a rare moment of vehemence, uncharacteristic of his public addresses, he blamed the rebellion on "combinations of men, who careless of consequences, and disregarding the unerring truth, that those who rouse, cannot always appease a civil convulsion, have disseminated, from an ignorance or perversion of the facts, suspicions, jealousies, and accusations of the whole government." This obvious slap at the democratic-republican societies was quickly seen as an indirect accusation of disloyalty by the Jeffersonian Republicans. During the previous months, moreover, Washington had been expressing the same sentiments in his private letters, bitterly accusing the societies of deliberately fomenting discord to discredit his policies for their own political advantage. By identifying the Whiskey Rebellion with the growing

Republican opposition in Congress, the President committed a major political blunder he would later regret. Although he did not foresee the possibility at the time, Washington would reap a bitter harvest from these ill-chosen comments. The Republicans would retaliate by opposing the most significant of his recent initiatives, John Jay's mission to London.

Jay was no fool, however, having grown up with the now-maturing American political party structure, and he knew his selection for the assignment to England was not universally approved. He reached London on June 12 and was welcomed by a friendly and seemingly accommodating Foreign Secretary. Grenville apologized for Dorchester's aggressive speech to the Lakes Indians, promising to reprimand the Canadian Governor (it was one of the major reasons for Dorchester's later resignation) and explained in detail the reasons for the change in British maritime policy indicated in the January 1794 Order-in-Council. Grenville was even apologetic for some of the judicial misinterpretations arising from the Order-in-Council of the previous November that had so infuriated Americans. But beyond these polite introductory concessions Jay had gained little during his first three months at the English capital.

Unknown to Jay of course, on June 10 Grenville had received a long delayed packet of Hammond's reports from Philadelphia. Until then he had not been aware of the extent of anti-British hostility in the United States nor of the embargo on American commerce. The last thing he wanted for England was a war in the American wilderness at the very moment he was struggling to hold together the coalition of powers arrayed against the French Republic. Nor could he afford to risk losing important trade with the United States. He recognized in Jay's mission that Washington's government truly wanted to maintain peace, so he would accommodate the Americans. By midsummer, regardless of what Wayne was doing in Ohio, he and Pitt decided to relinquish the frontier posts. If not, they feared the United States in its anger would join the reborn League of Armed Neutrality recently created by Denmark and Sweden.

Later in the summer, however, he began to procrastinate, confusing Jay with a shift in tactics. By then, later dispatches from Hammond had revealed Alexander Hamilton's startling remarks that Britain need not worry about American hostility. Jay was to discuss nothing with the Danes or Swedes concerning membership in their association of neutrals. More important, Grenville also learned that Wayne had been ordered not to attack the British-held posts. Just two weeks earlier he had reprimanded Dorchester for actions that "may not rather provoke Hostilities than prevent them." Now he told the Governor-General to do all in his power to maintain the "status quo" on the frontier. Thus had Hamilton's indiscreet private conversations with Hammond gone so far to allay British fears that Grenville knew he need only make the minimum of concessions to Jay in order to placate the American government.

Washington knew nothing of Hamilton's revelations to Hammond nor of Grenville's earlier decision to yield the frontier posts. Although he had agreed with Hamilton that peace was necessary, he was rapidly losing patience with British intentions. In an angry, hastily-written letter of August 30, 1794, he complained bitterly to Jay of British duplicity of saying one thing in London and allowing their agents in North America to do the opposite. This time his anger was directed against Upper Canada's Governor, John Simcoe, who had ordered military interference with a new American settlement in upstate New York not far from British-held Fort Oswego "and far within the known, *and until now*, acknowledged limits of the United States." He warned Jay "it will be impossible to keep this Country in a state of amity with G. Britain long if the Posts are not surrendered."

Amid rumors that an Anglo-American wilderness war had already begun, a confused Jay formally protested Simcoe's

high-handed action on October 13. It was a disturbing situation, for his talks with Grenville had been gaining substance.
Some Londoners believed that General Wayne had precipi-
tated the hostilities. Grenville knew better, assured in his private knowledge of the limits in Wayne's instructions and his
own directive to Dorchester to avoid "anything like Hostilities
in consequence of the dispute concerning the Treaty Line." Jay
was also embarrassed by the lack of news concerning the course
of the Whiskey Rebellion. He was convinced the initiative was
slipping from the Americans and was only slightly relieved
when official dispatches reached London in mid-November
reporting the victory of General Wayne's forces at Fallen
Timbers.

By November Jay was willing to accept almost anything
Grenville offered, and the Englishman offered very little. But it
was enough to make the negotiations worth the effort and
assure peace between the two countries. On November 19,
1794, the two men signed the 7,500 word Treaty of Amity,
Commerce and Navigation, known subsequently and deri-
sively in the United States as "Jay's Treaty." In it the British
granted the minimum of concessions required to satisfy the
extremes of American nationalism, thereby removing the
threat of an unwanted war in the wrong place and yet not
weakening themselves in their war against republican France.

The treaty's terms were grouped into three parts. The first
settled most of the problems still unresolved from the Peace
Treaty of 1783 and were the major British concessions. Their
garrisons would withdraw from the frontier posts by June 1,
1796. They accepted the idea of a joint commission to determine which of the rivers in Maine's northeastern wilderness
was correctly the St. Croix, in order to define the boundary
between Maine and New Brunswick peacefully. They agreed to
a joint survey of the upper Mississippi to close the "northwestern gap," a two hundred mile wide error resulting from the

belief the Mississippi flowed from the Lake of the Woods. On their side, the Americans made concessions too. A mixed commission was to decide compensation to British creditors for pre-Revolutionary War debts not yet received "in the ordinary course of justice." But the treaty offered no counter-balancing mention of payments to southern slave-owners for their property taken or freed by the British army during the war.

The second group of articles dealt with more recent difficulties arising out of Britain's current war with France. They set procedures for settling American claims for illegal seizures of ships and cargoes and wrestled with Britain's vague but extensive definition of contraband. The remainder of the treaty was as close to a commercial agreement as the British would go. The British East Indies were open to American shipping (at the time an unrecognized boon for the development of an American Oriental trade). Trade to the British West Indies was legalized but limited to ships under United States registry of only 70 tons. Each nation extended to the other most-favored-nation status on tonnage and tariff duties, accepted a consular agreement, and promised in case of war between them not to sequester assets or otherwise disturb the legitimate personal or business properties of the other's nationals. Significantly, for the Americans at least, Jay's Treaty was silent on the causes for many serious American grievances: the "Rule of 1756," impressment of American sailors and the longheld American doctrine that "free ships make free goods."

It was now Washington's turn to be tantalized by rumors. By the end of the year he knew that a treaty had been signed, but nothing of its contents. Two hastily dispatched copies accidentally sent on the same British vessel were destroyed at sea when that ship was captured by the French. Finally, on March 7, 1795, a third copy was delivered personally to Secretary Randolph by an exhausted, harassed courier who was clever enough to hide it successfully when his own ship was searched by French officers. This delay in the arrival of the official text of the treaty was a disaster in itself, causing the President unavoidable difficulties. Originally he had intended to submit the treaty immediately for Senate consideration, but Congress had adjourned on March 4. Under the circumstances of the long delay he had no choice but to warn the Senate he would call it into special session in June. Three days less of waiting would have prevented three months of frustration and misunderstanding. In the meantime, he and the Cabinet agreed to keep the treaty's terms secret.

At first reading Washington was disappointed in the treaty. It was to have been the climax of his efforts to stabilize Anglo-American relations; instead, it left unresolved too many areas of friction between the two countries. Although he found it "unfavorable," he could do little else but submit it to the Senate rather than "suffer matters to remain as they are, unsettled." Yet by keeping it secret he implied the treaty was worse than it really was, and permitted rumor and misinformation to get out of hand. Political battle lines were already drawn by the time the Senate convened in June. Washington himself was in part responsible for this divisiveness, for his public and private remarks blaming the Whiskey Rebellion on the "self-created" democratic-republican societies implied a connection with the Jeffersonian Republicans. Resentful of this presidential slur, whether honestly intended or not, Senate Republicans were encouraged by colleagues in the House and in state organizations to defeat the treaty regardless of its contents. The Jay Treaty became the most volatile political issue of Washington's second term.

Although the Senate had agreed to deliberate in secret, copies of the treaty were leaked to the press. Benjamin Franklin Bache, editor of the administration-hating *Aurora*, printed over a thousand copies which he distributed throughout the country. The resulting public dissension provided a backdrop of confusion and anger for two weeks of Senate debate. On only one point did the Senators agree unanimously. With a deep sense of national pride that cut across party lines they voted to strike Article 12, the section that limited American trade in the British West Indies to small vessels and simultaneously prohibited re-exportation of West Indian produce. The Senators correctly saw this as Grenville's patronizing attempt to minimize American competition in the European market. Then by the closest vote possible, twenty to ten, the Senate "consented" to the treaty. The President could now ratify it— or could he?

Certainly he wanted to. But the groundswell of opposition erupted into invective and violence. Urged on by the *Aurora*, Republican newspapers denounced the treaty and attacked the President for even submitting it to the Senate. Anti-treaty riots broke out in Boston, New York, Philadelphia, and Charleston. Alexander Hamilton was stoned while defending the treaty at a public meeting of New York City's citizens. In Philadelphia a copy was burned on George Hammond's doorstep and the windows of his house were smashed. John Jay's effigy was hung, burned, and trampled on in dozens of town squares. Washington, himself, was deluged with anti-treaty resolutions, some "so rude" he refused to acknowledge them. The Republican press prayed that the President would overcome "the British party" and not ratify it. Deeply concerned over the impact of the public outcry, the President had yet another problem concerning ratification. Once the Senate had struck Article 12 could he indeed ratify the revised treaty or must he now renegotiate with the British?

Two events added to the President's confusion. In early July he learned that the British were again seizing provisioning cargoes bound for France. It angered him "that the domineering spirit of G. Britain should revive again," especially at the very moment anti-British sentiment was so inflamed in his country. The other event was as much personal as political and could not avoid affecting his judgment. His long-time friend, confidant and adviser, Secretary of State Edmund Randolph, was accused of treason.

The accusation came from Randolph's Cabinet colleagues, Thomas Pickering and Oliver Wolcott. How much of it was based in solid truth or how much was motivated by the developing controversy over the Jay Treaty will never be known. The Cabinet had changed considerably since the beginning of the year when Pickering replaced Knox as Secretary of War and Wolcott succeeded Hamilton at Treasury, both disciples of Hamilton, avid Federalists, and strongly pro-British. Randolph, though more objective than his predecessor, continued to voice Jefferson's Francophilia. Washington had changed his approach to the Cabinet, relying on Randolph for foreign policy matters rather than continuing his former practice of seeking opinions from the full Cabinet. At the critical moment in Washington's self-debate over ratification Pickering and Wolcott gave the President information received from George Hammond that shattered his confidence in Randolph.

This was the work of Lord Grenville. Months earlier, when he signed the treaty with Jay, his remaining concern was that Randolph would resist its ratification. To counteract the Secretary of State's influence he sent Hammond instructions, dated November 20, 1794, "to converse confidentially on this Subject with those Persons in America who are Friends to a System of amicable Intercourse between the two Countries . . . either to convince Mr. Randolph of the necessity of his adopting a different Language and Conduct, or at least, to place him in a Situation where his personal Sentiments may not endanger the Peace of Two Countries between whom I trust a permanent Union is now established." There is little evidence that Pickering or Wolcott were the willing dupes of

Hammond, yet their accusation had the exact effect Grenville desired.

An angered and humiliated President ratified the Jay Treaty. Temporarily ignoring the accusation and saying nothing about it to Randolph, Washington rushed the ratification process in time for the departure of George Hammond, who had been recalled by his government. He sent with Hammond the ratified treaty, a request that the British government accept it as amended, and a strong protest calling for the British navy to stop its illegal seizures of American cargoes. They did. Only then did he turn his attention to Randolph.

Perhaps the most sordid episode of Washington's entire administration, the Randolph affair attacked the tired, beleaguered president at the time he was most vulnerable to the criticisms of the opposition press. And it illustrated again how deep the hand of foreign intrigue dipped into his government. The affair had begun the previous March when a packet of Fauchet's dispatches fell to the British after the capture of the French corvette carrying them to Paris. Hurried on to the Foreign Office in London, the dispatches provided Grenville with the precise tool needed to discredit Randolph's resistance to Jay's Treaty. Grenville sent them to Hammond in Philadelphia with the admonition to use them as he saw fit "in the King's service." Hammond saw their immediate value and passed the most damning, No. 10, on to Oliver Wolcott, his closest contact in the American cabinet. In this particular dispatch Fauchet had written glowingly of Randolph's friendship for France, an innocent enough comment, but he implied the Secretary of State had accepted a bribe and would distribute funds to strengthen the pro-French faction in the United States. Then he boasted to his superiors that with but a few thousand dollars France could decide whether or not there would be a civil war in the United States.

Much of this made sense to Wolcott. Like most Federalists, he already believed that the French were behind the disturbances in western Pennsylvania. More directly, Randolph's well known unsteady personal finances gave credence to the idea of a bribe. Convinced that Randolph indeed was a traitor, Wolcott hastened to share his knowledge with Pickering. Neither Wolcott nor Pickering knew French well, and Pickering's amateurish translation of Fauchet's subtle phrases appeared even more damaging to Randolph. It was this translation the two men gave to the President.

Disturbed by a deep sense of betrayal, Washington accepted the evidence at face value. He was convinced that Randolph had to be removed from office but gave no hint of his feelings until the ratified Jay Treaty was safely on its way to London. In the meantime he sought the advice of Wolcott and Pickering on the best method of ridding himself of the untrustworthy Secretary of State, reminding them "for if he is guilty of what is charged, he merits no favor; and if he is not, he will accept none. And it is not difficult to perceive what turn *he* and his friends will give the act, namely that his friendship for the French nation, and his opposition to a compleat ratification have been the causes."

The opportunity came at a special Cabinet meeting when the President asked Randolph to read the lengthy original French document while he and the other secretaries watched in silence to observe the accused man's reactions. Randolph quickly perceived that he had already been tried and found guilty by his colleagues and, more importantly, by his chief. In an angry outburst that offered no defense he declared his unwillingness to continue as Secretary of State and resigned immediately. Over the next few months he frantically sought evidence to publish in a *Vindication*, never forgiving Washington for the shabbiness of his treatment.

The tragedy for the President and for his country lay in the easy success of Grenville's well-orchestrated control of events that could destroy the career of a well-respected American public servant. And of equal significance, Randolph's resignation removed the last of Washington's advisers to challenge the pro-British drift in his foreign policy, a situation that would have its own disastrous consequences. The experience caused Washington to abandon his traditional practice of seeking a wide range of representative opinion. After considerable and embarrassing delays he appointed Pickering as Secretary of State and his former Revolutionary War aide, Dr. James McHenry, as Secretary of War.

Washington was humiliated by the problems Randolph caused and was not well satisfied with his bittersweet settlement with Great Britain in the Jay Treaty. His anger and frustration during that difficult summer of 1795 were only partially relieved by news in late September that Anthony Wayne had at last concluded a treaty with the Indian tribes of the Northwest.

He should have been more elated, for Wayne had achieved practically everything the President had hoped to accomplish north of the Ohio. Wayne's Treaty of Greenville, bearing the signatures of every major Indian leader in the region, set a new boundary with the Indian nations. It opened to immediate American settlement most of the modern state of Ohio and gave to the United States control of the vital interior lines of communication as far west as the site of the future Chicago. The treaty was a major diplomatic triumph and a credit to the President's years of patience and persistence.

But the sobering experiences of the previous summer and the lack of news from Spain dampened his enthusiasm for Wayne's success in the Northwest. Indeed, he became increasingly angry because so little had been heard from Carmichael and Short in Madrid. Despite all his efforts to treat with the Indians south of the Ohio nothing could be done to extend federal sovereignty in the Southwest until a conclusive settlement of the Mississippi Question had been made with Spain. Much of the dissatisfaction among western settlers was caused by this chronic instability in Spanish-American relations.

Washington would have been even more angry had he understood the effect on his foreign policy of the developing tragicomedy of Spanish errors in judgment, deliberate procrastination, and outright misrepresentation. When he had dispatched John Jay on his special mission to London in May of 1794, he had honestly expected that the parallel negotiations of his two special commissioners in Madrid were about to bear fruit. They had been there almost a year and something positive should have developed. Unfortunately, by the time Short had made his way from the Hague to the Spanish capital, Carmichael had fallen dangerously ill, leaving much unattended business for his colleague. Spain, allied with Great Britain in the war against France, had followed British leadership and interfered with the American provision trade to French ports, violating the neutral rights of the United States. The results were an increasing number of spoliation claims by American ship captains against the Spanish government, claims more often than not ignored by officials in Madrid. Of necessity Short had to push hard to get recognition of American maritime rights.

In the meantime, Manuel de Godoy, Spain's principal minister, paid little attention to the Americans. Feeling himself safe in the new and strange embrace of the alliance with England, his only fears regarding America came from the inability of Washington's government to quiet pro-French threats to Louisiana and Florida from the western settlements. To avoid potential disaster he directed his agents in North America to turn western dissatisfaction to Spain's advantage.

From Philadelphia Jaudenes and Viar expanded their contacts in Kentucky and actually developed a secret liaison with a handful of the leaders of the Whiskey Rebellion. Jaudenes became blinded by the prospects for the creation of an independent western state covering a huge area, extending from the Tennessee River northwest to the Illinois and northeast as far as the headwaters of the Ohio. He reported to Madrid that he was already negotiating a defensive-offensive alliance with the future leaders of the new state, an action neither Godoy nor Spain's Council of State opposed. At the same time Baron de Carondolet in New Orleans strengthened his alliances with the southern Indians and sent $16,000 in silver to American General James Wilkinson to bribe Kentucky separatists. Carondolet, too, was blinded by his own ambitions. Ever watchful of Anthony Wayne's activities north of the Ohio, he sent his own representatives with the promise of aid to the Miamis months before the confrontation at Fallen Timbers. Even after that Indian debacle he let himself be convinced by information from those same agents that the battle was not a decisive American victory. In preparation for the day when he would strike an alliance with an independent Kentucky, he established a Spanish garrison at Chickasaw Bluffs (the site of Memphis, Tennessee), 355 miles north of the boundary with West Florida claimed by the United States.

In Madrid the two-faced Godoy continued to express a willingness to settle outstanding differences with the United States while at the same time deliberately permitting an undermining of American authority west of the mountains. He was encouraged by Jaudenes' exaggerations that the split between pro-French and pro-British factions within the United States had the country on the verge of a civil war—a war Godoy believed could only benefit Spain. Time for it to develop was necessary, however, and Godoy bought that time with a policy of procrastination in his negotiations with the United States. To justify this delay he found fault with the personality and competence of both Carmichael and Short. He ordered Jaudenes to inform President Washington that he required a "more splendid person" to treat with his king.

Quite naturally Washington was furious. He considered this latest gambit of the Spaniards undignified for them and insulting to the United States. He had already tried to mollify previous Spanish criticisms of the ineffective Carmichael and named Short the sole American representative in Madrid (the luckless Carmichael was too ill for the journey home and died a few months later). Despite having made this change the President had little choice but to accede to Godoy's wishes and send a special emissary to Madrid clothed with the same dignity and rank as Jay held in London. After both Thomas Jefferson and Patrick Henry declined this honor, he finally decided on Thomas Pinckney, his minister to England. Pinckney was a logical choice, close at hand and privy to all aspects of Jay's recent negotiations with the British.

Pinckney inadvertently aided Godoy's delaying tactics. Both he and Jay agreed to wait in London for the exchanges of the ratified Jay Treaty. As resident United States Minister to the Court of St. James's it would be his responsibility to arrange for its formal implementation. But when the two Americans learned that the official copy of the treaty had not reached Philadelphia until March and the Senate could not consider it until June, Jay decided to return home and Pinckney departed for Spain. He arrived in Madrid on June 28, 1795, well over a year after Godoy had demanded a more prestigious representative from the United States.

Time and the rapid change of events in Europe now played tricks on Godoy and turned his American diplomacy into a comedy of errors, trapping him in his own duplicity. Within weeks of his original instructions for Jaudenes to begin the policy of procrastination he was having second thoughts about the whole relationship to the United States. The embrace of the Anglo-Spanish alliance against France was becoming akin to the squeeze of a python. It became increasingly obvious to the rapidly-maturing Godoy that England's purpose in fighting France was not to protect Europe from republicanism but to extend the influence of the British Empire, especially after the English set fire to a captured French fleet at Toulon, a fleet the Spanish had wanted to incorporate into their own navy. By the summer of 1794 the Spanish government had found little, if anything, to gain from the unnatural alliance which pitted its country against its traditional French ally—republican or not. To make matters worse, the Prussians and the Dutch were about to abandon the coalition against France, leaving Spain alone on the continent to confront exuberant French republicanism.

As French troops poured across the Pyrenees a frightened Godoy sought an escape from impending disaster. He must make peace with France and withdraw from the English alliance. It was not as easy as it might appear, however. True, he could save his country from a French invasion, but he was haunted by the fear of British retribution against Spain and her empire. He had to create a new as well as secret foreign policy before he abandoned the old one. In July he completely reversed Spain's position regarding both France and the United States. He sent out peace feelers to the French and new instructions to Jaudenes.

Godoy abruptly shifted the entire negotiations for the resolution of Spanish-American differences back to Philadelphia. Even though Jaudenes did not hold "suitable" diplomatic rank as minister, Godoy authorized him to offer President Washington an almost complete concession to American claims for navigation of the Mississippi and an acceptance of the 31st parallel as the United States boundary with West Florida. And Jaudenes was to propose a commercial treaty in return for a defensive alliance in which each country guaranteed the other's North American possessions. Godoy admonished the chargé to minimize the activities of Spanish agents in Kentucky and to apologize for the excesses of Carondolet's Indian allies in the Southwest. Godoy hoped that while these negotiations were going on his secret contacts with France would produce peace and an alliance with that country as well. If negotiations with both countries were successful he would have a fait accompli before he withdrew Spain from the unwanted ties with England. A joint Spanish-French-American defensive alliance would protect Spain's interests in Europe and North America from a wrathful Great Britain. His July, 1794, instructions to Jaudenes were, therefore, vitally important to his overall policy.

When Pinckney finally arrived in Madrid eleven months later Godoy had every reason to believe the long-delayed appearance of the American was because President Washington had taken time to consider the new Spanish proposals and had sent a special emissary to negotiate an alliance. Nothing could have been farther from the truth. At the time Pinckney was ordered to Spain, neither he nor Washington and Randolph knew anything about the shift in Spanish policy. Instead, Jaudenes had deliberately ignored his instructions, trapping Godoy in his own duplicity. The wily Spanish chargé, blinded by the prospects for his intrigues in Kentucky and encouraged by the Whiskey uprising in western Pennsylvania, did not inform Secretary of State Randolph of his government's offer of concessions and an alliance. Pinckney, therefore, came to Madrid unprepared to react to the coming changes in the European power structure.

Only William Short among the Americans had an inkling of what was happening. Both Godoy and Gardoqui had hinted that he should expect new instructions from Philadelphia, but neither explained why. At first he considered these remarks as nothing more than the Spaniards' way of putting off substantive discussions of the issues. Suspicious, however, he sent enquiries to Randolph. By March, 1795, an angry American Secretary of State called in Jaudenes and demanded an explanation. Sheepishly, the irresponsible young Spaniard offered implausible explanations and finally produced a copy of the proposals sent to him the previous July. In the resulting confusion and embarrassment for Spain, Pinckney found his advantage.

Pinckney also found another advantage in the recent American settlement with Great Britain. Godoy knew, of course, that Jay had signed a treaty in London but there is considerable uncertainty whether he knew its contents. It would seem improbable, however, that with his deep concern for British reaction to his shift in policy he would not make every effort to find out. From Spain's perspective the Jay Treaty was at worst an Anglo-American alliance directed against Spanish Louisiana and at best a mere settlement of maritime difficulties between the two countries. Either way the British certainly would have agreed to withdraw from the frontier posts, for their occupation had caused most of American hostility toward Britain, and this meant the collapse of the whole idea for an Anglo-Spanish protectorate over the trans-Appalachian west. Realistically Godoy would have to reach a satisfactory accommodation with the Americans on the Mississippi Question as soon as he settled with the French.

Pinckney was forced to wait another month until Franco-Spanish bargaining reached a climax in the Peace of Basle, signed on July 22, 1795. Only then did Godoy offer him terms, and these along the lines of the proposals intended for President Washington in July, 1794. The American, however, made it quite clear that the United States would enter into no military alliance, and so the *quid pro quo* of a defensive alliance was abandoned immediately. Surprisingly Godoy seemed not to care and quickly accepted the American demand to navigate the entire Mississippi and claim to the 31st parallel boundary line. He agreed to withdraw Spanish garrisons north of that line and to assume responsibility for the actions of Indian tribes residing in remaining Spanish-held territory. But these detailed negotiations broke down over Spanish refusal to concede the "right of deposit," as essential to American internal commerce as travel on the Mississippi itself. Without the ability to barter or sell duty-free the produce of farm and forest at the mouths of rivers flowing into the Gulf of Mexico—all still to be held by Spain—the freedom of river travel would be an empty concession.

Pinckney recognized this tactic as nothing more than a Spanish diplomatic rear-guard action. After a long discussion with Short on the subtleties of Spanish thought processes, he called Godoy's bluff and demanded his passports—in effect breaking off negotiations. Godoy's resistance collapsed, and he agreed that his King would "permit" Americans to trade at New Orleans for three years, renewable in three year periods either there or at some equally suitable site. With this concession and Spain's acceptance of the "small-navy" definitions of neutral rights and contraband embodied in John Adams' Model Treaty of 1776, Pinckney had gained much for the future of American commerce. He had also drawn from Godoy a consular convention and an acceptable method of adjusting American claims arising over the violation of their neutral rights based on those definitions. Satisfied, he signed with Godoy the finalized treaty at the Spanish resort village of San Lorenzo on October 27, 1795.

Popularly known as Pinckney's Treaty, the Treaty of San Lorenzo was immediately accepted in the United States as the greatest diplomatic achievement of Washington's administration. It swept away at last Spanish resistance to American sovereignty in the Southwest. By prohibiting either nation from maintaining treaties with the tribes residing in the other's

territory it caused the collapse of the southern Indian confederations and their eventual removal west across the Mississippi. This plus the end of restrictions on river commerce
opened the rich soil of that river's east bank to a flood of
agricultural settlers. Despite Spain's last minute haggling over
implementation of the treaty, within five years the Americans
were poised and waiting for the next step in their inexorable
march westward—Jefferson's brilliant purchase of New Orleans
and its hinterland, Louisiana. Pinckney's Treaty finally placed
the gateway to the riches of the entire Mississippi Valley in the
grasp of the United States.

In sharp contrast to Jay's Treaty, Pinckney's settlement
with Spain was accompanied by portents of future blessings.
Auspiciously, the official copy arrived in Philadelphia on
Washington's birthday. For the President it was a most suitable
present, giving substance of genuine celebration to the fireworks displays and pealing church bells. Delighted with the
terms, he rushed it to the Senate where members of both
parties easily saw the vast potential and voted unanimous approval on March 3, 1796. Having this time no reason to hesitate, he ratified it immediately. And then, providentially, the
almost simultaneous appearance of yet another treaty brought
news of the end to the vexatious problems with one of the
Barbary pirate states.

This treaty, negotiated the previous September with the
Dey of Algiers, promised release of captive American sailors
after a ransom of $800,000 and no interference with American
commerce in the Mediterranean for an annual payment of
$24,000. On the surface it appeared to set humiliating condi-
tions for the United States, but most other maritime nations
accepted similar terms, finding it cheaper to pay tribute than
launch an expensive naval war in defense of national pride. For
the United States with no naval forces of consequence, patrol-
ling the Mediterranean sea-lanes almost 4000 miles away was

an obvious impossibility. It was a temporary solution at best, yet American commerce could benefit from it. With no comments on its terms, Washington accepted the treaty's realities and promulgated it on the same day as he did Pinckney's Treaty.

With these two diplomatic achievements to his credit, Washington began the final year of his presidency reasonably satisfied that the long-term goals he had established were now being reached. The nation was at peace; its sovereignty was recognized in both Northwest and Southwest; its people seemed contented. Even the furor over Jay's Treaty had apparently subsided. Expressing a rare sense of confidence, he wrote Gouverneur Morris, "a great change has been wrought in the public mind, with respect to this treaty within the last two months." He felt he had every reason to be confident of the future.

But when he attempted to implement the Jay Treaty a constitutional storm broke over his head. By mistake Britain's formal ratification was sent not to Philadelphia but to Charleston, where it was quickly published in a local newspaper. Angered and embarrassed, fearing another wave of anti-British demonstrations, Washington hastily proclaimed the treaty in effect and sent to the House of Representatives his request for the necessary appropriations to fund the mixed arbitration commissions and the army's occupation of the frontier posts. Immediately long-seething Republican hostility pounced on the treaty with the obvious intention of nullifying the entire settlement. For more than two weeks the House hotly debated a resolution calling for the President to submit to it all of the documents and correspondence relating to Jay's entire negotiation with the British. Although much of Republican sentiment came from dissatisfaction with the treaty itself, the debate really turned on a more fundamental constitutional question. House Republicans argued their own philosophy of government by insisting that because the House was the only direct representative of the American people it should share equally with the Senate and the executive in the formulation of treaties that affected the entire nation. The point finally carried, and on March 24, the House approved the resolution sixty-two to thirty-seven.

Washington understood clearly the significance of the issue. Unwilling to open a tear in the still-fragile fabric of the Constitution, he sought the advice of his Cabinet. He also asked the Attorney General to review the journal of the Constitutional Convention for references to the treaty-making power. And, as might be expected, he indirectly sought the opinion of Alexander Hamilton. All agreed with his own belief that the Constitution was quite clear: a treaty approved by the Senate and ratified by the President was the law of the land.

In a long response to the House on March 30, he refused its request. Defending his own conduct as "my constant endeavor to harmonize with the other branches," he reminded its members that "the nature of foreign negotiations requires caution; and their success must often depend on secrecy . . . [and] the necessity for such caution and secrecy was one cogent reason for vesting the power of making Treaties in the President, with the advice and consent of the Senate." Exposing such negotiations to the perusal of the House would make them too public, he argued, and therefore submitting the documents requested "would be to establish a dangerous precedent." Once again the President had interpreted the Constitution in a way that strengthened the Executive's role in the conduct of foreign affairs.

Believing he had answered the constitutional question as carefully and logically as possible, Washington hoped the House would soon vote the necessary appropriations for implementing the treaty with Great Britain. To placate its members, however, he had sent them on the twenty-ninth a copy of Pinckney's Treaty, which he knew they could support, and on the thirty-first announced his nominees for the mixed arbitration commissions. Instead, he got another month of acrimonious debate that could easily nullify the entire treaty by a mere refusal to vote the funds.

The business of government almost came to a stop during April of 1796 while the entire country watched the debate. Individuals as well as mercantile groups feared the worst and took steps to protect their special interests. In the port cities, for example, worried merchants expected British reprisals and refused to send their ships to sea. Federalists around the country, especially from New England, organized a write-in campaign to convince their representatives that it was absolutely essential for the nation to carry out the treaty's terms. Despite such efforts, in the end it was the eloquence of Fisher Ames that ended the debate. Massachusetts' most famous Federalist, frail and seriously ill, Ames delivered an impassioned ninety-minute argument that weakened Republican opposition by raising the specter of British retaliation. Finally, on April 30, the House voted fifty-one to forty-eight in favor of the appropriations.

Washington had won his battle with Congress, but at a price. Although he had deliberately avoided any attempt to influence the vote in the House, his position on the treaty clearly identified him with Federalist interests. Both houses of Congress were now so sharply divided along partisan lines that Republicans more than ever considered him a Federalist. Republican newspapers, in particular Bache's *Aurora*, attacked him as viciously as they did any Federalist. If he had seriously believed the country could avoid partisan politics during his presidency, the continuous controversy over Jay's Treaty made that impossible. And his anxious desire to get it implemented quickly branded him—unfairly or not—as a Federalist.

If he could have counterbalanced the obvious pro-British thrust of the Jay Treaty by a dramatic improvement in relations with France, he might still have been able to avoid the political split and remain a friend to the Republicans. When he sent James Monroe to Paris in the early summer of 1794, he had hoped his fellow Virginian could use his well-known friendship for France to advantage and overcome French misunderstandings concerning American neutrality. Events in Paris, however, were well beyond control by the President of the United States.

By the time Monroe reached the French capital on August 2, 1794, the Republic was in the throes of another violent change. Robespierre had been executed, a Committee of Public Safety formed the executive, and the National Convention constituted only a semblance of government. It was an inauspicious setting for a mission intended to restore Franco-American friendship. Monroe recognized immediately that indeed the relationship needed restoration, commenting, months later, "I found our affairs in the worst possible situation." The French were harassing American commerce almost as badly as were the British. French officials still considered the Neutrality Proclamation a breach of faith, a betrayal of the Alliance of 1778. And fed by the exaggerations of Pierre Auguste Adet, Fauchet's replacement as minister to the United States, they were suspicious of the purposes of Jay's mission to England.

Under the circumstances Monroe moved brilliantly, if not discreetly, to re-establish friendly discourse. He was able to capitalize on his reputation as one of the most severe critics in the United States Senate of the pro-British drift of American policy. To his delight, he was presented formally as American minister to France at a public ceremony of the National Convention rather than by the traditional practice of offering his credentials privately to the Committee of Public Safety. Here, before an excited audience, he delivered letters of greeting from both houses of Congress and from the President, and then followed with a rather dramatic speech of his own pledging continuous harmony between the two countries. Amid cheers from the delegates, he accepted the fraternal kiss and embrace from the Convention's president. In its enthusiasm the Convention voted to publish the day's proceedings and a resolution that the flags of both nations be displayed together in its meeting hall as a symbol of their unity. Two weeks later Monroe donated an American flag of his own for the purpose. It was altogether a good beginning.

Monroe had, however, overstepped the bounds of propriety for a representative of a neutral country to a nation at war. Protests of his performance came from both sides of the Atlantic. In the United States Federalists questioned his sincerity as spokesman of the American position; even the President began to have gnawing doubts. From London Jay, in the midst of his delicate discussions with Grenville, fired off an angry letter to the Secretary of State. Of necessity Randolph had to reprimand Monroe, although he was privately pleased with what had been accomplished thus far in Paris. Washington, on the other hand, was more confused than angry. Trying to placate Jay, he admitted Monroe's action "does not appear to have been well devised," yet he understood the importance of overcoming French misconceptions "by strong assurances of the good disposition of the people of the U: States towards that Nation."

Despite the respect the French held for him, Monroe was constantly frustrated by an inability to bring their leaders to an accommodation with the United States. Their suspicions of Jay's negotiations continuously thwarted his efforts, even though he explained numerous times that Jay's instructions forbade him from violating existing American commitments to France. Desperately Monroe appealed to Jay for information on the negotiations and if an agreement had been made to send him a copy. In the meantime, in an effort to get discussion on other matters started, he rashly promised the Committee of

Public Safety to reveal the treaty's contents as soon as he learned them himself. By now Jay distrusted Monroe and offered to send a copy but only in confidence between themselves. Monroe rejected these conditions. As a compromise Jay had his secretary memorize the entire treaty and then travel to Paris to recite it privately to his fellow minister. This too Monroe refused, fearing that such a mode of communication would violate his commitment to the Committee.

When the French did finally learn of the contents of Jay's Treaty in the summer of 1795, Monroe's influence in Paris diminished and Franco-American relations deteriorated even further. Once again the French had changed their government, replacing as executive the Committee of Public Safety with the Directory. This new French leadership was convinced that American neutrality was now a fiction and demanded that Monroe explain why the United States had not defended its own doctrine of "free ships, free goods" in the treaty with Great Britain. To the French, Jay's Treaty justified an open break with the United States.

Monroe's role was complicated by the vacillation of French officials in formulating a response to American policy. Over a period of seven months their plans, often announced but rarely carried out, confused him as well as his government. Jay's Treaty nullified the Alliance of 1778. To demonstrate French displeasure, Adet would be replaced by a minister plenipotentiary sent to Philadelphia specifically to abrogate the Alliance. Reprisals were threatened on American ships sailing to English ports. Enemy goods carried in American vessels were to be confiscated without compensation. Formal diplomatic relations between the two countries would be broken by recalling Adet and sending no replacement. Perhaps a chargé d'affaires might be appointed to maintain relations. Adet was to remain in Philadelphia but given new instructions.

During all this confusion Monroe argued continuously

that a complete break in relations could lead easily to war. His desperate diplomacy succeeded in holding off the most violent French reaction, at least until the summer of 1796. To do so, however, he unfortunately too often compromised his position by overplaying his personal sympathy for the French cause. And while the French listened with decreasing attention to Monroe's arguments, they tried to influence American policy at its source, especially to prevent ratification of Jay's Treaty. Undoubtedly Adet supplied much of the venom published in American newspaper attacks on the treaty and on Washington's policies in general. The double blow of the abrupt ratification of the treaty and Randolph's simultaneous fall from power only added to their hostility. In a final gamble they relied on French sympathizers among House Republicans to prevent the treaty's implementation. When this failed, they were convinced that American policy was being controlled by London. Monroe's mission had failed.

Yet Monroe had left a nagging promise of better future relations with the United States. Isolated from recent events at home, he had exaggerated the strength of the Republican opposition in American national politics. Convinced that Washington would not accept a third term, he privately encouraged the French to believe that the up-coming elections would produce as the next president a pro-French Republican, most probably Thomas Jefferson. If the French government would be patient and not force a formal rupture, a new American administration would reverse the direction of American foreign policy.

Monroe's mission had failed, too, in the eyes of the President and his advisers. His position in the United States had been undermined by Federalists who simply did not trust him. In part, he contributed to his own undoing. Never in strong support of the administration, he expressed critical sentiments in too many private letters to friends in the United States.

Often these circulated beyond their intended recipients, and parts of some were published in Republican newspapers where a *nom de plume* did not conceal the identity of the author. For months Washington had considered his recall and in July finally requested the Cabinet's opinion. Accompanying their response with one such letter from Monroe that had found its way to the Secretary of State, Cabinet members recommended recall because Monroe "had been amply furnished with documents to explain the views and conduct of the United States, yet his own letters authorize us to say, that he had omitted to use them, and thereby exposed the U. States to all the mischiefs which could flow from jealousies and erroneous conceptions of their views and conduct." Unwilling to condemn him out of hand, they concluded his conduct was the result either, of "such an attachment for the cause of France" or of being "too little mindful of the interests of his own Country." In either case, the Cabinet agreed, "the evil is the same." This opinion coincided with the President's own, and in August he directed that Monroe be recalled. Having learned another valuable lesson about appointing people who did not always share his views, Washington sought a replacement "who will promote, not thwart the neutral policy of the Government; and at the same time will not be obnoxious to the people among whom he is sent."

Charles Cotesworth Pinckney aptly fitted the President's job description and accepted the appointment. As in previous searches for a diplomat, he was not the first choice, but Washington found him quite suitable. He was active among Federalists in South Carolina, although not as outspoken nor as ambitious as his younger brother, the former minister to Great Britain. Thomas Pinckney had returned to the United States to pursue personal political opportunities generated by the fame earned from his successful negotiations with Spain; the first of many such successful diplomats to succumb to "White

House fever," he became the candidate of a Federalist faction that found him more palatable than John Adams and certainly preferable to Thomas Jefferson as the next president. C. C. Pinckney, on the other hand, was more popular among Southerners in general and yet enough of a Federalist to assure continued support in South Carolina for Washington's policies.

Unlike his brother, this Pinckney unfortunately did not score a diplomatic success. Instead, acrimony and embarrassment clouded his entire mission. When he reached Paris in late January 1797, the French were so angry over Monroe's recall and Adams' election as President, they refused to accept him. As an obvious affront to the retiring Washington they held an elaborate farewell for Monroe and totally ignored Pinckney. Bluntly, the new American minister was told he was unwelcome in France and for his own safety should leave the country. Pinckney hastily traveled to Amsterdam to wait out events in Paris or instructions from the new administration to return home.

In another gesture of defiance, the Directory ordered Adet to abandon the mission in Philadelphia and return to France. Formal diplomatic contact between France and the United States, continuous since 1778, was now broken. For all practical purposes, the Alliance of 1778 and its parallel Treaty of Amity and Commerce were ended. The French navy and French privateers openly attacked American shipping, and the Americans began arming themselves in defense. Tragically, the allies of the American Revolution became enemies during the Revolution of the French as ill will and misunderstanding ignited an undeclared naval war between the two nations.

These last indignities were spared Washington. News of the degrading treatment Pinckney had received in Paris did not reach Philadelphia until after the inauguration of the new President. Back home at Mount Vernon there was little he could do but mutter about the perfidy of the French. He had so hoped to deliver to his successor a country at peace, a country enjoying the prosperity of its farms and seas. But at the very end of his presidency America's earliest and greatest friend had become temporarily her enemy. American prosperity and quite possibly American security were now threatened by the legacy of one failure in his foreign policy—an unwanted, unofficial war he had tried to prevent. Searching for an explanation, he could only remark sadly to Secretary Pickering that the French government was "beyond calculation and unaccountable upon any principle of justice." Although his sincere efforts to convince the French of his government's goodwill had been spurned, it was not because he had bungled or misunderstood what steps were necessary. He learned, as his successors would discover, even for a United States no longer militarily weak, there is no way to make certain that any foreign policy will be wholly successful.

Washington should not have been so pessimistic about the break in formal diplomatic relations with France. True, it was a bitter postscript to his patient efforts to find understanding and accommodations with successive French governments. But it was also a clear illustration of the enormity of the task he had assumed in 1789. He had struggled for eight years to create a viable foreign policy for his country, a foreign policy that recognized both the inherent weaknesses of the United States and the harsh realities of European power politics. Time was necessary to overcome these weaknesses; only with sufficient time could the nation develop the strength to meet the challenges of the Europeans.

It was obvious to him from the beginning that the experiment in federalism could survive only in an era of domestic peace and economic stability. Yet each internal problem that arose was exacerbated by external forces. Relatively minor domestic issues became dangerously significant when they were magnified by European self-interest. Assuring "domestic tranquility" and earning "the respect of nations" were so closely intertwined that in practice they were but two sides of the same coin of the nation-building process. For the President, creating a foreign policy was as essential as organizing the structure of government.

As he predicted, the process of organizing a national government with all its attendant ramifications, including foreign policy issues, had been "an Ocean of difficulties." During the eight years of his presidency he had charted that ocean, plumbed its depths, avoided its shoals, found its directional points. And he had learned some hard lessons. The experience, especially during the last two years, made him apprehensive of the future. For this reason he decided in early 1796 to offer his people a valedictory—a farewell address that would focus their attention on the importance of what he had learned as their President.

He had planned such a statement as early as the spring of 1792, still believing he would serve only one term as president. At this time he turned for advice in preparing a forceful draft to James Madison whom he regarded as sharing his views on future directions for the Federal Union more than anyone else. He set aside this collaboration, however, when he reluctantly agreed to accept another term. By 1796, after the dynamics of the intervening four years had convinced him that two terms were enough, he had developed wholly new perspectives. The manifesto he and Madison had prepared no longer appeared applicable to the lessons of his more recent experiences. He was now even more determined that his people have an explanation of his conduct of their affairs. This time he sought the assistance of Alexander Hamilton, a choice that significantly indicated the depth of the ideological split among those on whom he had most relied for advice. It indicated, too, how he himself had developed policies that Hamilton had previously articulated. But Washington had not become a Hamiltonian. Even though many expressions in the "Farewell Address" are obviously Hamilton's, the fundamental concepts are Washington's, long held and often stated.

Washington's basic common sense is obvious throughout the entire address. Yet the newness of the experiment in democratic republicanism left him still so distrustful of developing political parties that he misjudged their role in a successful democracy. Seeing them as divisive rather than cohesive, he reminded his fellow citizens that "your Union ought to be considered as a main prop of your liberty" and then warned of the "baneful effects of the Spirit of Party" which he believed "opens the door to foreign influence and corruption." To avoid this corrupting influence "permanent, inveterate antipathies against particular Nations and passionate attachments for others should be excluded," for "an attachment of a small or weak, towards a great and powerful Nation, dooms the former to be a satellite of the latter." Such an attachment could easily weaken, if not destroy, the Union itself. To prove his point, he cited the Pinckney Treaty as an example of how an objective approach toward other nations could promote national unity. With justifiable pride he claimed the treaty was "a decisive proof" to the inhabitants of the West "how unfounded were the suspicions propagated among them of a policy in the General Government and the Atlantic States unfriendly in their Interests in regard to the Mississippi."

Because Washington's foreign policy concerns underlay so much of the "Farewell Address," posterity has given his pronouncements a greater permanence than he had intended. This has been especially true in the twentieth century as ardent nationalists, misunderstanding his purpose and misreading his words, have attempted to depict him as the first great American isolationist; on the contrary, he was a pragmatic chief of state willing to adapt to the realities in international politics of his own time. Actually, the four general directives he set forth for the future conduct of United States foreign relations were meant only to fit the needs of a weak, economically undeveloped, still emerging nation. They have a permanent significance only when properly applied.

In the first of these, the most famous and most quoted, he stated flatly "the Great rule of conduct for us, in regard to foreign Nations is in extending our commercial relations to have with them as little *political* connection as possible." He underscored "political" and then added "'tis our true policy to steer clear of permanent Alliances, with any portion of the foreign world." But he was too much of a realist not to recognize the occasional need to play balance of power politics and added this qualification: "Taking care always to keep ourselves, by suitable establishments, on a respectably defensive posture, we may safely trust to temporary alliances for extraordinary emergencies." Even in these situations, as he astutely observed, "'tis folly in one Nation to look for disinterested favors from another." Having thus suggested guidelines for the future drawn from his own experiences, Washington then summarized the purpose of his administration by writing simply, "with me, a predominant motive has been to endeavour to gain time to our country to settle and mature its yet recent institutions."

Indeed, the first President's great legacy in foreign affairs was that he had gained sufficient time for his country to establish its government, strengthen its unity, secure its borders, and promote its commerce. He had gained this time through patient diplomacy that neutralized the threats from England and Spain in the Northwest and the Southwest, pacified the Indians, and minimized regionalism by opening the West for protected and prosperous settlement. Of greatest significance, his firm neutrality policy regarding the war in Europe gained enough time to cool internal passions for a war which most certainly would have destroyed the nation's frail unity.

In all of this Washington not only determined foreign policy for the United States but he also established lasting precedents for the executive's control over American external affairs. Vague references in the Constitution to a handful of presidential responsibilities for official contacts with foreign nations became, after his eight years in office, a solid block of accepted procedures for presidential initiatives. Most important of these were selection and placement of American representatives abroad, recognition of foreign governments, negotiation and ratification of treaties, direction of a consular service, management of foreign debts. In addition, he secured clear presidential prerogatives in the use of the war-making power during frontier clashes with the Indians and the Whiskey Rebellion, in the right of executive privilege by refusing to share with the House documents pertaining to the Jay Treaty, and in reliance on personal representatives through Morris' mission to London. By the end of his term Washington's foreign policy was more than just a beginning direction for United States' relations with the rest of the world. It was a body of precedents and procedures that not only influenced and guided his successors but enabled them to direct foreign affairs effectively.

Essay on Sources

WHEN AMERICAN SCHOLARS sought to interpret the changed position of the United States in international affairs after the Second World War, they were forced to test long-held assumptions about the traditions of American foreign policy. New interpretations and new perspectives were required for a clearer understanding of the new and unfamiliar role the United States had assumed as a leader of the free world. Half-forgotten events and obscure diplomatic contacts were given new importance. Such frequently ignored internal forces as labor unrest, agrarian revolts, and religious attitudes were re-evaluated as influences on foreign policy decision-making. The activities of presidents, diplomats, military officers, and even private citizens took on new meaning. These fresh approaches to the past broadened the scope of diplomatic history and gave it new significance. In particular this applies to the history of the age of the Founding Fathers, an era in many respects not unlike our own. Aided by easier access to public and private archives, both foreign and domestic, and stimulated by the Bicentennial Celebration, scholarship on the founding of the Republic has opened totally new vistas for better understanding and further interpretation.

George Washington's role, of course, has been studied continuously since the first days of national independence, and the volume of literature on Washington is enormous. In general, the most recent is the best, giving accuracy of detail and correct evaluation of his activities while eliminating the often misleading hero-worship of more traditional biographies. Douglas Southall Freeman has provided a thorough, almost day-by-day account in his seven-volume *George Washington* (New York: Scribners, 1947–1958), with the final volume, subtitled *First in Peace*, completed after his death by John A. Carroll and Mary W. Ashworth. But Freeman's biography is often frustrating with its maze of detail and its even-handed chronology that considers parallel developments of significant issues simultaneously. This is not the problem in the four-volume *George Washington* (Boston: Little, Brown, 1965–1972) by cultural historian James T. Flexner who humanizes his subject by tempering his careful scholarship with a flair for the dramatic. The best overview of the first presidential administration is Forrest McDonald's concise but important monograph, *The Presidency of George Washington* (Lawrence: University of Kansas Press, 1972), the first in the University of Kansas American Presidency series. English historian Marcus Cunliffe, bringing much needed objectivity in his studies of American society and politics, offers a fascinating and provocative analysis in his *Washington: Man and Monument* (Boston: Collins, 1959).

Washington's vast range of interests and responsibilities can best be seen through his correspondence, although his letters too often are so formal and stilted they rarely reveal his inner feelings. The standard collection, edited by James C. Fitzpatrick, is the 39 volumes of *The Writings of George Washington from the Original Manuscript Sources* (Washington: G.P.O., 1931–1944). More revealing are many of his diary entries in Fitzpatrick's four-volume *The Diaries of George Washington* (Boston: Houghton Mifflin, 1925). Unfortunately the diaries are missing for the period February 3 to September 30, 1789, perhaps the most dramatic weeks of Washington's life—his election, his inauguration, the opening months of his administration. The University Press of Virginia is producing a more thoroughly annotated edition of the *Diaries* (Charlottesville,

1976–) under the editorship of Donald Jackson and Dorothy Twohig; several entries have been found to fill some gaps. This new series through its extensive footnotes provides valuable information about individuals and places mentioned by Washington.

The importance of the international setting to the development of Washington's foreign policies is apparent as early as the Seven Years War. The best on this topic is Lawrence H. Gipson, *The Great War for the Empire: The Culmination* (New York: Knopf, 1953), volume eight in his extensive *The British Empire Before the American Revolution*. Several older studies are quite valuable as introduction. Frederic A. Ogg, *The Opening of the Mississippi: A Struggle for Supremacy in the American Frontier* (New York: Cooper Square reissue, 1968) first focused attention on European interests in the Mississippi Valley. Edwin S. Corwin presented a still sound interpretation of French thinking in his 1916 study, *French Policy and the American Alliance of 1778* (Hamden, Conn.: Archon Books reedition, 1962), as did Clarence W. Alvord in *The Mississippi Valley in British Politics* (New York: Russell & Russell reissue, 1959). Equally important among these early works was Paul C. Phillips' 1913 *The West in the Diplomacy of the American Revolution* (New York: Russell & Russell reissue, 1967).

European manipulation of the fledgling United States can be seen most clearly in the negotiations that ended the Revolutionary War. The premier study is Samuel Flagg Bemis, *The Diplomacy of the American Revolution*, originally published in 1935 and revised slightly in 1957 (Bloomington: Indiana University Press, 1957). With more archival material available, Richard B. Morris has updated Bemis, providing additional information and a broader interpretation in his *The Peacemakers: The Great Powers and American Independence* (New York: Harper & Row, 1965). Interesting and important is John J. Meng, *The Comte De Vergennes: European Phases of His*

American Diplomacy (Washington: Catholic University Press, 1932). Spain's reaction to the peace treaty is well detailed in Arthur P. Whitaker, *The Spanish-American Frontier, 1783–1795* (Gloucester: Peter Smith reprint, 1962). England's concern with its American problems is described in J. Leitch Wright, Jr., *Anglo-Spanish Rivalry in North America* (Athens: University of Georgia Press, 1971) and its sequel, *Britain and the American Frontier, 1783–1815* (Athens: University of Georgia Press, 1975). A broad overview of continuous European interest in western development is in James A. Robertson, *Louisiana Under the Rule of Spain, France and the United States, 1785–1807* (Cleveland: Arthur Clark, 1911).

Another important part of the background to Washington's administration was the struggle within the United States to develop a consensus for nationhood during the Confederation era. John Fiske set forth the now traditional view that the Articles of Confederation were too weak to overcome centrifugal forces destroying the Union in his *Critical Period in American History* (Boston: Houghton Mifflin, 1888). His interpretation was challenged as uncritical and unscholarly by Andrew C. McLaughlin in *Confederation and Constitution* (New York: Harper, 1905). Charles A. Beard in *Economic Interpretation of the Constitution* (New York: Macmillan, 1921) proposed that, although the Articles were working as an instrument of government, a clique of conservatives pushed acceptance of the Constitution to protect their own economic interests. This "conspiracy theory" has been under attack by several scholars in recent years. Merrill Jensen refuted some of Beard's scholarship and offered a more positive interpretation of the Articles in *The New Nation: A History of the United States During the Confederation, 1781–1789* (New York: Knopf, 1950); some of his conclusions, however, also have been challenged. Forrest McDonald took a more realistic view of active political and economic factors in his *E Pluribus Unum: The Formation of the American*

Republic, 1776–1790 (Boston: Houghton Mifflin, 1965). In the excellent *The Creation of the American Republic, 1776–1787* (Chapel Hill: University of North Carolina Press, 1969), Gordon S. Wood discussed important philosophical and intellectual influences. An interesting if subtle factor is described by Louise B. Dunbar in *A Study of "Monarchical" Tendencies in the United States, 1776–1801* (Urbana: University of Illinois Press, 1923).

The best survey of the processes in the establishment of the new federal government is John C. Miller's *The Federalist Era, 1789–1801* (New York: Harper, 1960), even though he overstates Hamilton's role at the expense of those of Madison, Jefferson, and Washington himself. This is corrected to a degree in the previously mentioned McDonald, *The Presidency of George Washington.* Nathan Schachner offers an even more detailed overview with strong emphasis on the interplay of politics and foreign relations in *The Founding Fathers* (New York: Putnam, 1959). The actual structuring of the federal bureaucracy is thoroughly described in Leonard D. White, *The Federalists: A Study in Administrative History, 1789–1801* (Toronto: Collier-Macmillan, 1948). Curtis P. Nettels explores the importance of economic factors to national growth and international affairs in his *Emergence of a National Economy, 1778–1815* (New York: Holt, Rinehart & Winston, 1962). The tremendous impact of foreign policy issues on developing American politics can best be seen in William N. Chambers, *Political Parties in a New Nation, 1776–1809* (New York: Oxford, 1963) and in *Making of the American Party System, 1789 to 1809*, edited by Noble E. Cunningham, Jr. (Englewood Cliffs: Prentice Hall 1965). Three posthumously published essays of Joseph Charles, *The Origin of the American Party System* (Williamsburg: Institute of Early American History and Culture, 1956), offer some important interpretations, especially the third essay which treats the Jay Treaty. Eugene P. Link, *Demo-*

cratic-Republican Societies, 1790–1800 (New York: Columbia University Press, 1942) presents a careful analysis of the relationship of the societies to the growth of political parties as well as to foreign policy decisions. The significance of the agrarian revolt in western Pennsylvania is clearly shown in Leland Baldwin, *Whiskey Rebels* (Pittsburgh: University of Pittsburgh Press, 1939).

With these solid secondary works as background, good primary sources on the Washington presidency are available in published collections of official documents and personal correspondence. Most important are the *American State Papers: Documents, Legislative and Executive* (Washington: Gales & Seaton, 1832), especially in the numbered series volumes 1, 8, and 16 on Foreign Affairs, Indian Relations, and Military Affairs respectively. Important collections of the papers of other influential participants in the Washington presidency are: the Andrew Lipscomb edition of *The Writings of Thomas Jefferson* (Washington: Thomas Jefferson Memorial Association, 1904) plus the more carefully annotated but still incomplete series, *The Papers of Thomas Jefferson*, edited by Julian Boyd (Princeton: Princeton University Press, 1950–); *The Papers of Alexander Hamilton*, edited by Harold C. Syrett and Jacob Cooke (New York: Columbia University Press, 1961–); Henry Johnston, editor, *The Correspondence and Public Papers of John Jay* (New York: Burt Franklin re-edition, 1970); and Ann Cary Morris, editor, *Diary and Letters of Gouverneur Morris* (New York: Scribners, 1888). George Gibbs, editor, *Memoirs of the Administrations of Washington and John Adams* (New York: Van Norden, 1846) provides a Federalist bias of events seen through the correspondence of Alexander Hamilton's protege Oliver Wolcott.

Although none focus specifically on foreign affairs, several good biographies add significantly to an understanding of prevailing attitudes during the period. Robert Ketcham's *James*

Madison (New York: Macmillan, 1971) is excellent. So too is Merrill D. Peterson's *Thomas Jefferson and the New Nation* (New York: Oxford, 1970). The latter is best supplemented for greater detail and deeper insights into Jefferson's personality by Dumas Malone's monumental six-volume *Jefferson and His Times*, in particular volume two, *Jefferson and the Rights of Man* (Boston: Little, Brown, 1951) and volume three, *Jefferson and the Ordeal of Liberty* (1962); each volume includes a helpful chronology. Vice President Adams' experiences in foreign policy are well examined in volume two of Page Smith's important *John Adams* (Garden City: Doubleday, 1962). The two best approaches to Hamilton are John C. Miller, *Alexander Hamilton: Portrait in Paradox* (New York: Harper, 1959) and Broadus Mitchell's careful two-volume *Alexander Hamilton* (New York; Macmillan, 1957 and 1962). Brief sketches of the early secretaries of state and how they confronted their problems can be found in volume two of the very helpful *The American Secretaries of State and Their Diplomacy*, Samuel Flagg Bemis, general editor (New York: Cooper Square reprint, 1963). Bemis' own "Thomas Jefferson" is a dispassionate overview of the first secretary's tenure, while "Edmund Randolph" by Dice Robbins Anderson offers no defense for his subject in the Randolph-Fauchet crisis.

A good general background to Anglo-American relations during the early years of the Republic is Vincent Harlow's *The Founding of the Second British Empire*, 2 volumes (London: Longmans Green, 1964) which describes the younger Pitt's global vision for Britain's commercial empire. Closer to specific American issues is A. L. Burt's older but valuable *The United States, Great Britain and British North America, from the Revolution to the Establishment of Peace After the War of 1812* (New Haven: Yale University Press, 1940). Charles R. Ritcheson, extensively using official British documents and English newspapers, deliberately provides a corrective to traditionally held

American views of detrimental British intentions in his fascinating *Aftermath of Revolution: British Policy Toward the United States, 1783–1795* (Dallas: S.M.U. Press, 1969). The questions in the Nootka crisis are thoroughly detailed by William R. Manning in "The Nootka Sound Controversy," part of the *Annual Report* of the American Historical Association for 1904 (Washington: G.P.O., 1905), pages 281–478. Samuel Flagg Bemis, *Jay's Treaty: A Study in Commerce and Diplomacy* (New Haven: Yale University Press, 2nd. edition, 1962) is still the standard work on that significant topic. But the more recent *The Jay Treaty: Political Background of the Founding Fathers* (Los Angeles: University of California Press, 1970), by Jerald A. Combs, discusses in more detail the treaty's ramifications on domestic politics and offers some slight revision to Bemis. More intriguing is Julian Boyd's indictment of Hamilton's betrayal of Jay's mission in his *Number 7: Alexander Hamilton's Secret Attempts to Control American Foreign Policy* (Princeton: Princeton University Press, 1964) which uses as supporting evidence an extensive appendix containing George Beckwith's reports to Lord Grenville found in the Public Record Office of London. Bemis also has two important and interesting articles: "The Vermont Separatists and Great Britain, 1789–1791," *American Historical Review*, XXI (1916), pages 547–560, and "The London Mission of Thomas Pinckney, 1792–1796," *American Historical Review*, XXVIII (1923), pages 228 to 247.

Most helpful of British government documents located at the Public Record Office in London is the correspondence of the Colonial Office and the Foreign Office. Particularly revealing are Lord Dorchester's worried observations on frontier conditions found in Colonial Office-Canada. Over half of Beckwith's reports are mixed in with Dorchester's dispatches, although those sent after July 1790 are in Foreign Office-America. The Treasury Series also yields some important information on West Indies commerce and the North American fur trade and includes several interesting recommendations from the Board of Trade. Of equal importance are the personal papers of Lord Leeds (Carmarthen), Lord Liverpool (Hawkesbury), and Lord Auckland (William Eden) classified under "Additional Manuscripts" in the British Museum. The letters of Foreign Secretary George Grenville are printed in the first three volumes of Historical Manuscripts Commission, *The Manuscripts of J. B. Fortescue preserved at Dropmore*, 10 volumes, (London: H.M.S.O., 1892–1894). Most valuable for concise explanation of British attitudes toward the United States are Grenville's directions to George Hammond which are conveniently published in Bernard Mayo, editor, *Instructions to the British Ministers to the United States, 1791–1812* (Washington: G.P.O., 1941), volume III of the Annual Report of the American Historical Association, 1936.

Spain's concern for the American Southwest can be seen as part of a larger set of issues in Richard Herr, *The Eighteenth Century Revolution in Spain* (Princeton: Princeton University Press, 1958). An overview of imperial rivalries is in J. H. Parry, *Trade and Dominion: The European Overseas Empires in the Eighteenth Century* (London: Weidenfeld and Nicolson, 1971). Jack D. L. Holmes analyzes the difficulties for Spanish colonial administration in *Gayoso: The Life of a Spanish Governor in the Mississippi, 1789–1799* (Baton Rouge: Louisiana University Press, 1965). A similar approach is offered in Janice Borton Miller, *Juan Nepomuceno De Quesada: Governor of Spanish East Florida, 1790–1795* (Washington: University Presses of America, 1981). Charles E. Bennett focuses on a potentially dangerous issue for Spanish-American affairs in his *Florida's "French" Revolution, 1793–1795* (Gainesville: University Presses of Florida, 1981). Spain's overall policy to contain American expansion can be seen in its working detail from a well-annotated selection of documents from Spanish archives edited by Lawrence Kinnaird in *Spain in the Mississippi Valley, 1765–1794* (Washington: G.P.O., 1946), volumes II–IV of the Annual Report of the American Historical Association, 1945. More specific Spanish attempts to influence the Creek Indians are well illustrated by the letters and biography of Alexander McGillivray in John W. Caughey's valuable *McGillivray of the Creeks* (Norman: University of Oklahoma Press, 1938).

For American interaction with Spain the basic studies are still Whitaker's previously cited *The Spanish-American Frontier* and Samuel Flagg Bemis, *Pinckney's Treaty* (Baltimore: Johns Hopkins Press, 1926). Although both trace Spanish-American relations from the origins of the Mississippi Question to the Treaty of San Lorenzo, Whitaker concentrates on frontier developments while Bemis details negotiations in Philadelphia and Madrid. They differ, however, on the important question of whether or not Godoy knew the terms of the Jay Treaty before he signed the treaty with Pinckney. Whitaker claims Godoy did and later supports his conclusion in "Godoy's Knowledge of Jay's Treaty," *American Historical Review*, XXXV (July, 1930), pages 804–810. Bemis acknowledges Whitaker's research but rejects this conclusion in a long explanatory footnote added to the 1941 second printing of his *Pinckney's Treaty*. Some earlier aspects of American diplomacy with Spain are found in Samuel Grayson Coe, *Mission of William Carmichael to Spain* (Baltimore: Johns Hopkins University Studies XLVI, 1928).

Westward expansion caused most of American difficulties with Great Britain and Spain. The importance of the interaction of settlement, Indian relations, and military activity to diplomacy is quite clear in Arthur B. Darling, *Our Rising Empire, 1763–1803* (New Haven: Yale University Press, 1940) and Dale Van Every, *Ark of Empire: The American Frontier, 1784–1803* (New York: William Morrow, 1963). The latter is most helpful with individual chapters on the personal ambitions of prominent Westerners who often worked at cross-purposes to national policy. A collection of General Josiah Harmar's letters clearly indicates the problems for the Army in carrying out its responsibilities against Indians aided by either or both European governments; these are published in Gayle Thornbrough, editor, *Outpost on the Wabash, 1787–1791* (Indianapolis: Indiana Historical Society, 1957). Reginald Horsman provides a short interesting account of how the British offered that aid to the Indians in "The British Indian Department and the Resistance to General Anthony Wayne, 1793–1795," *Mississippi Valley Historical Review*, XLIX (September, 1962), pages 269 to 290.

American relations with France during Washington's administration are well described in Alexander De Conde, *Entangling Alliance: Politics and Diplomacy under George Washington* (Durham, N.C.: Duke University Press, 1958). De Conde uses as his central theme the Franco-American Alliance and continues the narrative begun in Corwin's *French Policy and the American Alliance of 1778.* Writing as much from a French as an American viewpoint, Albert H. Bowman uses French archives extensively for his informative *The Struggle for Neutrality: Franco-American Diplomacy During the Federalist Era* (Knoxville: University of Tennessee Press, 1974). Louis M. Sears offers far more about American attitudes than implied by the title of his book in *George Washington and The French Revolution* (Westport, Conn.: Greenwood Press reprint, 1973). Still of value is Beverly W. Bond, *The Monroe Mission to France, 1794–1796* (Baltimore: Johns Hopkins Press, 1907).

Several important journal articles focus on specific friction points in Franco-American affairs. The sensitive issue of American debt repayments is covered by Samuel Flagg Bemis, "Payment of French Loans to the United States, 1778–1795," and by Henri L. Bourdin, "How French Envoys Sought Payment of America," both in the same issue of *Current History*, XXIII (March, 1926), pages 824–831 and 832–836. Frederick Jackson Turner explored the importance of long-held French interests in the American West in "Policy of France toward the Mississippi Valley in the Period of Washington and Adams," *American Historical Review*, X (1904–1905), pages 249–279. Citizen Genet's impact is described by Harry Ammon in "The Genet Mission and the Development of American Political Parties," *Journal of American History*, LII (March, 1966), pages 725–741.

Official French diplomatic documents are in the Archives des Affaires Etrangeres located at the Ministry of Foreign Affairs in Paris. Those pertaining to the United States are Correspondence Politique—Etats Unis; most interesting are reports of French consuls in Supplement 4 and 5. The series Memories and Documents—Etats Unis 2 (1767–1795) also contain lengthy reports on conditions in the American West of concern to the French government. Among the published collections of French materials the most convenient and helpful is Frederick Jackson Turner, editor, *Correspondence of the French Ministers to the United States, 1791–1797* (Washington: G.P.O., 1904), Annual Report of the American Historical Association, 1903.

On the subject of United States relations with the Barbary states the most complete study is Roy W. Irwin, *The Diplomatic Relations of the United States with the Barbary Pirates, 1776–1816* (Chapel Hill: University of North Carolina Press, 1931). Helpful details on the status of American Mediterranean trade and the extent of British influence are found in volume I of *Naval Documents related to the United States Wars with the Barbary Powers* (Washington: G.P.O., 1939).

Index

CPSIA information can be obtained at www.ICGtesting.com
Printed in the USA
BVOW01s0454080716

454845BV00001B/3/P